Documents in Contempora.

General editor
Kevin Jefferys
Faculty of Arts and Education, University of Plymouth

The impact of immigration

MANCHESTER
UNIVERSITY PRESS

Documents in Contemporary History is a series designed for sixth-formers and undergraduates in higher education. It aims to provide both an overview of specialist research on topics in post-1939 British history and a wide-ranging selection of primary source material.

Documents in Contemporary History

The impact of immigration

A documentary history
of the effects and experiences
of immigrants in Britain since 1945

Edited by Panikos Panayi

Professor of European History, De Monfort University

Manchester University Press
Manchester and New York

distributed exclusively in the USA by St. Martin's Press

Copyright © Panikos Panayi 1999

The right of Panikos Panayi to be identified as the editor of this work has been asserted by him in accordance with the Copyright, Designs and Patents Act 1988.

Published by Manchester University Press
Oxford Road, Manchester M13 9NR, UK
and Room 400, 175 Fifth Avenue, New York, NY 10010, USA
http://www.man.ac.uk/mup

Distributed exclusively in the USA by
St. Martin's Press, Inc., 175 Fifth Avenue, New York,
NY 10010, USA

Distributed exclusively in Canada by
UBC Press, University of British Columbia, 6344 Memorial Road,
Vancouver, BC, Canada V6T 1Z2

British Library Cataloguing-in-Publication Data
A catalogue record for this book is available from the British Library

Library of Congress Cataloging-in-Publication Data applied for

ISBN 0 7190 4684 X *hardback*
     0 7190 4685 8 *paperback*

First published 1999

06 05 04 03 02 01 00 99   10 9 8 7 6 5 4 3 2 1

Typeset in Sabon
by Best-set Typesetter Ltd., Hong Kong
Printed in Great Britain
by Bell & Bain Ltd, Glasgow

Contents

Acknowledgements

For permission to reproduce copyright material, the publishers and editor would like to thank the following: the Controller of Her Majesty's Stationery Ofice (1.4, 1.5, 1.11, 2.1, 2.6, 2.14, 2.20, 4.3, 4.4, 4.8); Museum of London (1.10, 2.18, 3.9, 3.10); *Irish Post* (1.25); *Independent* (1.19); Commission for Racial Equality (2.7, 2.9, 2.23, 2.26, 3.28, 5.24); Birmingham Health Authority (2.10); Indian Workers' Association (2.25); HarperCollins Publishers (2.29); Hodder & Stoughton Ltd (3.3); Telegraph Group Ltd (3.6); Linton Kwesi Johnson and LKJ Music Publishers (3.27); *Northern Echo* (4.9); *Blues and Soul* (5.2); *Guardian* (5.11, 5.12); Transport and General Workers' Union (5.17). The editor would also like to thank the staff at the following libraries: the Resource Centre at the centre for Research in Ethnic Relations at the University of Warwick, Leicester Record Office, the Public Record Office, the British Library at St Pancras and Colindale, De Montfort University Library, Leicester University Library, Birmingham Central Library, the Museum of London, the Black Cultural Archives in Brixton, the Guildhall Library, London, the British Library of Political and Economic Science and Leicester City Libraries. The editor would finally like to gratefully acknowledge the help and encouragement of Kevin Jefferys.

Chronology of events

1945   Polish army and government in exile, together with dependants, a total of some 150,000 people allowed to settle in Britain.

1946–1949 Arrival of 91,151 'displaced persons' as 'European Volunteer Workers'.

1948   British Nationality Act allows entry of Empire and Commonwealth citizens to Britain.

1948   *Empire Windrush* arrives at Tilbury docks from Jamaica with 417 passengers, the symbolic beginning of West Indian immigration into Britain.

1948   Foundation of Oswald Mosley's Union Movement.

1948   Riots against Blacks in Liverpool and Indians in Birmingham.

1958   Riots against West Indians in Nottingham.

1960   Birmingham Immigration Control Association established.

1961   Riot against Pakistanis in Middlesbrough.

1962   Anti-Black riots in Dudley.

Chronology of events

1962	Passage of the Commonwealth Immigrants Act controlling entry into Britain of foreign nationals from the Commonwealth.
1965	Race Relations Act establishing Race Relations Board.
1967	Establishment of National Front.
1968	Enoch Powell speaks publicly about the 'dangers' of Black and Asian immigrants in Britain.
1968	Commonwealth Immigrants Act controlling the entry of Asians and Africans with British passports.
1968	Race Relations Act establishing Community Relations Commission.
1971	Immigration Act standardises previous legislation.
1972	Expulsion of Ugandan Asians and acceptance of 27,000 by Britain.
1974	Attacks upon Irish targets in Birmingham following IRA pub bombs in the city.
1974	Prevention of Terrorism Act allows detention and arrest of Irish people for up to seven days.
1976	Race Relations Act establishing Commission for Racial Equality.
1979	Viv Anderson becomes first black England soccer international.
1980	Riot in St Paul's area of Bristol.
1981	Nationality Act standardises previous legislation.
1981	Inner-city riots throughout Britain, followed by Scarman report into their outbreak.

1985   Riots in Handsworth and Tottenham.

1987   Four black/Asian MPs returned to Parliament at the general election.

1992   Five black/Asian MPs returned at general election.

1993   British National Party wins local council seat on the Isle of Dogs.

1997   Nine black/Asian MPs returned at general election.

1999   Publication of report by the Stephen Lawrence Inquiry.

Introduction

I

Few other social developments in the history of Britain since the end of the Second World War have had the same impact as immigration. The millions of newcomers who have made their way to the islands off the north-western coast of Europe since 1945 have helped to transform them into the more vibrant, multi-ethnic, colourful state that is Britain today. What would Britain look like without the post-war newcomers? Everybody would basically be white. There would be greater dress conformity. England would have less success in sporting competitions. Sections of the inner cities would find themselves in a worse state than the one currently existing, as immigrants have transformed many of them. English diet would remain rather bland.

Since the end of the Second World War millions of immigrants and their offspring have helped to revitalise and transform Britain. They have come from all parts of the world, beginning at the end of the Second World War with Poles, followed by Irish and Italians, and then by New Commonwealth arrivals, most notably from India, Pakistan, Bangladesh, Africa, the West Indies, Hong Kong and Cyprus. Because of the level of their difference, the black and Asian immigrants have had the greatest impact. Since the 1960s, as Britain has implemented increasingly tight immigration controls, the flow of newcomers with dark skins has decreased drastically.

Nevertheless, those immigrants who did make it to Britain have had a profound impact upon the British way of life. The present study will devote much attention to this impact. In addition, it will also look at England through the eyes of the newcomers, from the

1

decision to move taken in their homeland, the hostility which they have faced upon arrival, their experiences of work and the ways in which they have developed ethnic communities.

II

While immigrants into post-war Britain may have had a profound impact on its way of life, immigration has characterised the entire history of the British Isles. If we go back far enough, about 2,000 years, we discover that the English did not constitute the original inhabitants of England, Scotland and Wales. Instead, there resided what have come to be known as Britons, a Celtic group, which had, in any case, previously migrated from farther east.

The English, in the form of 50,000 to 100,000 Angles and Saxons, who entered the south and east of the country from northern Germany and Denmark, did not arrive until the fifth and sixth centuries. By the end of the eighth century this group controlled the whole of England and parts of Scotland and Wales, having conquered and pushed the native Britons more and more to the periphery. After that invasion came the Danes and Norsemen who settled throughout the country. During the eleventh century the Normans invaded Britain, focusing upon southern England, but also colonising the rest of the country.[1]

From the eleventh century until the eighteenth Britain became increasingly mono-ethnic. As all schoolchildren learn, the country faced no further invasions. Small groups of immigrants and refugees trickled in between 1066 and 1815. In the Middle Ages these included Jews, who had first arrived with the Normans and whose numbers do not seem to have exceeded a maximum of 10,000. In any case, they faced expulsion in 1290, meaning that the British Isles remained essentially *Judenrein* until the middle of the seventeenth century.[2]

The only other significant groups in medieval England consisted of merchants from northern Germany, in the form of the represen-

---

[1] Victor Kiernan, 'The British Isles: Celt and Saxon', in Mikuláš Teich and Roy Porter (eds), *The National Question in Europe in Historical Context*, Cambridge, 1993, pp. 1–6; Hugh Kearney, *The British Isles: A History of Four Nations*, new edition, Cambridge, 1995.

[2] Paul Hyams, 'The Jewish Minority in Medieval England, 1066–1290', *Journal of Jewish Social Studies*, vol. 25, 1974.

tatives of the Hanseatic League, and from northern Italy.[3] The former certainly had an impact on English trade for several centuries, while Jews and Lombards controlled money lending. The Irish had begun to make their way to Britain from the twelfth century, many of them working as street vendors and labourers, although others fell into the massive medieval underclass, leading to the passage of a statute in 1243 to expel Irish beggars.[4]

New influxes occurred during the sixteenth century. These included refugees of the Counter-Reformation, who moved to Britain from France, Germany and the Low Countries, but who counted small numbers and had little impact.[5] The sixteenth century also witnessed the arrival of black people in the form of slaves, who, however, faced deportation in 1601 because Good Queen Bess felt that their numbers had become too great.[6]

The seventeenth and eighteenth centuries resulted in further influxes of immigrants on the most significant scale since the Norman invasion. As many as 50,000 French Protestant Huguenot refugees may have moved to Britain at the end of the seventeenth century. The establishment of their own churches represents one of their most visible impacts.[7] Between 10,000 and 15,000 black people, arriving as slaves, lived in Britain in the eighteenth century. They usually worked as various kinds of servant, although some of them moved into manual occupations. They impinged upon the public consciousness, as evidenced by several Hogarth paintings.[8] By the end of the eighteenth century a significant German community also existed in Britain, counting four London churches. The members of this group worked in occupations varying from merchant banking to sugar baking.[9] This period also witnessed an increase in the size of the Irish community, focused especially in poor areas of London, in working-class occupations.[10] Finally, from

---

[3] T. H. Lloyd, *Alien Merchants in England in the High Middle Ages*, Brighton, 1982.

[4] Kevin O'Connor, *The Irish in Britain*, Dublin, 1974, p. 13.

[5] Mark Greengrass, 'Protestant Exiles and their Assimilation in Early Modern England', *Immigrants and Minorities*, vol. 4, 1985.

[6] See, for instance, Peter Fryer, *Staying Power: The History of Black People in Britain*, London, 1984, pp. 4–12.

[7] Robin D. Gwynn, *Huguenot Heritage: The History and the Contribution of the Huguenots to Britain*, London, 1985.

[8] Fryer, *Staying Power*, pp. 33–236.

[9] Panikos Panayi, 'Germans in Eighteenth Century Britain', in Panayi (ed.), *Germans in Britain since 1500*, London, 1996, pp. 29–48.

[10] O'Connor, *Irish in Britain*, pp. 14–15.

the middle of the seventeenth century, after a decision by Cromwell in the 1650s, Jews began to enter the country in significant numbers, laying the foundations for the expansion of the nineteenth and twentieth centuries.[11] Certainly, by 1815, many native urban English people would have been aware of immigrants because of their visible presence around them and because of the flowering of English nationalism and its siamese twin xenophobia.[12]

This consciousness grew during the course of the nineteenth and early twentieth centuries as both the numbers of immigrants and the potency of British xenophobia increased. While the numbers of immigrants and the level of their difference may not have been as significant as those after 1945, British residents of London and most other big British cities would have met, seen or known members of the Irish, Jewish or German communities at various times in the period between 1815 and 1945, as well as perhaps coming into contact with individuals from the smaller minorities.

Certainly, numbers of immigrants change significantly from the middle of the nineteenth century, although numbers need contextualisation within the population explosion which affected Britain and Europe from about 1750, as the British population increased at the same time as the immigrant one. From 1815 to 1945 between 1.5 million and 2 million newcomers made their way to Britain,[13] but the overall size of the country's population increased from just over 20 million in the middle of the nineteenth century to nearly 50 million a hundred years later,[14] excluding 11.4 million people who left between 1815 and 1930.[15]

The newcomers to Britain generally came, unlike many of the post-1945 immigrants, from fairly close geographical locations, most notably Ireland, which supplied about a million people during the nineteenth century. In addition, from about 1870, about 100,000 Russian and Polish Jews moved to Britain. The other significant group of the nineteenth century consisted of Germans, who reached their peak number of 53,324 in 1911. During the Hitler

[11] David S. Katz, *Philo-semitism and the Readmission of the Jews to England, 1603–55*, Oxford, 1982.
[12] Linda Colley, *Britons: Forging the Nation, 1707–1837*, London, 1992.
[13] Panikos Panayi, *Immigration, Ethnicity and Racism in Britain, 1815–1945*, Manchester, 1994, p. 23.
[14] E. J. Hobsbawm, *Industry and Empire: From 1750 to the Present Day*, Harmondsworth, 1969, p. 326.
[15] Dudley Baines, *Emigration from Europe, 1815–1930*, London, 1991, p. 9.

period there followed a further 70,000 refugees from Nazi tyranny, while, during the First World War, about 240,000 Belgians temporarily moved to Britain following the invasion of their country by the German army. As well as these major groupings, other, smaller ones also settled in the country throughout the period 1815–1945, notably Italians, French people, Spaniards, Greeks, Indians, Africans and West Indians, perhaps totalling 300,000 people in all.[16]

The movement of people into Britain took place for a combination of reasons, not dissimilar to those which would cause immigration after 1945. In the first place, the population explosion which affected much of continental Europe represented the underlying push factor,[17] although shorter-term crises, such as the Irish potato famine of the late 1840s,[18] pushed the numbers up over short periods of time. Other groups moved to Britain to escape political persecution, most notably the refugees from Nazism.[19] Enabling factors proved fundamental in the migrations of the nineteenth century. The spread of literacy provided people with information about distant lands which they could now reach with relative safety and speed as a result of the development of the steam engine, which led to the growth of the railways and steamships.[20] Britain had two main attractions. First, its industrialised economy, especially during the nineteenth century, which proved particularly instrumental for pulling in Irish immigrants, who helped in the expansion of the economy.[21] Second, for most of the nineteenth century Britain had no immigration laws, which meant that people could basically enter the country as they wished.[22]

The immigrants who made their way to Britain between 1815 and 1945 certainly became visible because they transformed parts of some of the major cities, owing to their geographical concentration. While some Irish people moved to Britain as seasonal agricultural

---

[16] See Panayi, *Immigration*, pp. 23–4, 50–2.
[17] *Ibid.*, pp. 25–6.
[18] Cormac Ó Grada, *The Great Irish Famine*, London, 1989.
[19] Marion Berghahn, *Continental Britons: German-Jewish Refugees from Nazi Germany*, Oxford, 1988.
[20] Such issues receive attention in M. A. Jones, 'The Role of the United Kingdom in the Transatlantic Emigrant Trade', University of Oxford D. Phil. thesis, 1955.
[21] Robert Miles, *Racism and Migrant Labour*, London, 1982, p. 123.
[22] Panikos Panayi, 'The Evolution of British Immigration Policy', in Albrecht Weber (ed.), *Einwanderungsland Bundesrepublik in der Europäischen Union: Gestaltungsauftrag und Regelungsmöglichkeiten*, Osnabrück, 1997, pp. 123–6.

labourers, the majority of newcomers from all over the globe settled in inner-city areas.[23] For instance, the Irish made up of over 40 per cent of some streets in Liverpool in the nineteenth century.[24] Some groups, such as the Germans, did not focus simply on the inner city, moving out to suburban areas.[25] The age, gender and family structure of immigrants varied from one group to another, so that the large Irish minority was fairly balanced, while the minuscule Chinese community basically consisted of single young males who inevitably entered into relationships with English women.[26]

As to the economic activities and class position of immigrants in the century before 1945, these tended to focus upon the lower end of the scale, although some groups, notably Germans and Jews, had a social structure which ranged from the underclass to the establishment. At the top of the social scale several Jews and Germans had control of some of the largest industrial enterprises and certainly some of the leading banks in Britain, as suggested by names such as Sir Ernest Cassel, Ludwig Mond, Alexander Kleinwort and Nathan Mayer Rothschild. Lower down, many immigrants became involved in retailing and small-scale factory production. By the end of the nineteenth century Germans had made an impact in the sale of bread and meat, while Jews focused heavily on the production of clothing, shoes and caps. Those who owned such establishments tended to employ members of their own ethnic group. But the majority of all immigrant communities, also reflected in the native population, found themselves employed in manual occupations. Some members of all groups fell below the working classes into the sub-proletariat, owing to poverty, caused by unemployment, or old age. Others became involved in criminal activity.[27]

The immigrants who moved to Britain in the century before the Second World War made efforts to maintain their ethnicity against the encroachments of the dominant grouping, consequently establishing organisations which announced their presence to the dominant population. Most important, the newcomers set up their own places of worship, either by opening up new buildings, buying exist-

[23] Graham Davis, *The Irish in Britain, 1815–1914*, Dublin, 1991, pp. 51–82.
[24] Frank Neal, *Sectarian Violence: The Liverpool Experience, 1819–1914*, Manchester, 1988, p. 11.
[25] Panikos Panayi, *German Immigrants in Britain during the Nineteenth Century, 1815–1914*, Oxford, 1995, pp. 89–107.
[26] Panayi, *Immigration*, pp. 58–60.
[27] *Ibid.*, pp. 60–71.

ing churches or praying in rooms set aside for worship in individual houses. Philanthropic and educational activity also sprang from the religious centre of many of the communities so that, to take the case of the Irish, 'the Catholic Church in Liverpool had, by the 1920s, effectively established a micro-welfare state within the city'.[28] Distinct from religion, immigrants also set up cultural organisations, revolving around a variety of secular activities, ranging from card playing, dancing and singing to literature and classical music. Finally, immigrants also established their own political groupings and trade unions.[29]

Unfortunately for the immigrants, their arrival into Britain caused resentment from the British state and populace. This hostility remained ever present but varied in its intensity towards different groups, owing to a variety of factors. Times of severe economic hardship or war led to outbursts of hatred, while the influx of large numbers over a short period of time, notably following the Irish famine of the later 1840s, also caused resentment.[30] The range of negative behaviour ranged from refusal to speak to immigrants to killing them.

The modern British state, which evolved into maturity in the century before the Second World War, underlay the differing manifestations of xenophobia. It also took the lead in practising hostility towards newcomers itself. By 1945 the paraphernalia of the modern nation state in the form of nationality and immigration laws were well developed.[31] More seriously, during the two World Wars, the British state carried out acts of persecution, most notably in the form of internment and deportation.[32] Newspapers and literary stereotypes spread xenophobia,[33] while extremist organisations existed, from the Orange Order in the nineteenth century[34] to the British Union of Fascists during the 1930s.[35] Most seriously of

---

[28] Frank Boyce, 'Irish Catholicism in Liverpool between the Wars', *Labour History Review*, vol. 57, 1992, p. 20.

[29] See Panayi, *Immigration*, pp. 76–101.

[30] Neal, *Sectarian Violence*, pp. 80–175.

[31] Kathleen Paul, *Whitewashing Britain: Race and Citizenship in the Postwar Era*, London, 1997, pp. 9–14; Panayi, 'Evolution of British Immigration Policy', pp. 126–31.

[32] David Cesarani and Tony Kushner (eds), *The Internment of Aliens in Twentieth Century Britain*, London, 1993.

[33] Panayi, *Immigration*, pp. 113–20.

[34] Neal, *Sectarian Violence*.

[35] Richard Thurlow, *Fascism in Britain: A History, 1918–85*, Oxford, 1987, pp. 92–118.

all, hostility often broke out in violence, notably against the Irish in the nineteenth century, Germans during the First World War and Blacks in 1919.[36]

III

Clearly, immigration has occurred during the entire course of British history. Large numbers of people moved into the British Isles during particular periods, while, at other times, the numbers remained low. Whatever the numbers at specific times, immigrants have always lived in the country. Similarly, they have always had some sort of geographical, economic and cultural impact. In addition, they have always faced a level of hostility.

So is there anything new about the period after 1945? In terms of numbers they total 3.2 million people, making up nearly 6 per cent of the population, which is higher than at any time in recent British history. The total excludes the Irish and many members of white groups (2.17).[37] It is unlikely that the foreign population of Britain has ever reached such levels for several millennia.

The origins of post-war newcomers differ from those of previous immigrants, although the European immigrants who made their way to Britain after the Second World War followed in the footsteps of millions of people from the Continent before 1945. The newcomers from the West Indies and South Asia, on the other hand, did not. While the history of black people in Britain may stretch back to Roman times, to suggest that the Jamaicans who moved to Britain during the 1940s and 1950s have a direct connection with the eighteenth-century black population of London is somewhat simplistic. Surely, in terms of numbers, impact and economic activity, to name just three areas, post-war black and Asian immigrants have more in common with nineteenth-century Jews and Irish than they do with a few thousand people who happened to have the same colour skin during the eighteenth century, whose numbers

---

[36] See contributions to Panikos Panayi (ed.), *Racial Violence in Britain during the Nineteenth and Twentieth Centuries*, London, 1996.
[37] These bracketed figures refer to document numbers, which readers should consult.

decreased substantially in the period 1820–1945. There is little doubt that those newcomers who moved into Britain from beyond Europe after 1945 represent a new element in the history of immigration into Britain.[38]

Post-war newcomers also differ from their predecessors in their geographical dispersal. At no time have immigrants in Britain lived over such a wide area as they have since 1945. Only Jewish and Irish newcomers could compare. Certainly, the former lived in urban locations throughout the country by the end of the eighteenth century.[39] After the 1840s the Irish focused heavily upon large industrial areas,[40] but seasonal agricultural labourers from the Emerald Isle wandered throughout England and Scotland.[41] Nevertheless, this still remains different from the situation after 1945, when immigrants have moved into areas previously inhabited only by English people. Two areas in particular stand out. First, the Midlands. Although it welcomed some Irish people in the nineteenth century, towns such as Coventry and Leicester, transformed by post-war immigrants, had hardly seen a foreigner before the Second World War, while Birmingham, which counted nearly 7 per cent of Britain's ethnic minorities in 1981, acted as home to no more than about 10,000 Irish people during the nineteenth century.[42] Similar comments apply to suburban London. Before 1945 areas such as Lambeth, Brent, Ealing and Haringey

---

[38] Numerous works draw direct connections between the twentieth-century black and Asian immigrants and their predecessors from the same areas of the world. These include: Fryer, *Staying Power*, and Jagdish S. Gundara and Ian Duffield (eds), *Essays on the History of Blacks in Britain*, Aldershot, 1992.

[39] Cecil Roth, *The Rise of Provincial Jewry*, London, 1950.

[40] Neal, *Sectarian Violence*, pp. 8–10.

[41] Arthur Redford, *Labour Migration in England, 1800–80*, Manchester, 1964 edition, pp. 145–7.

[42] For Birmingham before 1945 see Zoë Josephs, *Birmingham Jewry*, 2 vols., Birmingham, 1984, 1988. In addition, Alex Peach is writing a De Montfort University Ph.D. thesis on the Irish in the city during the nineteenth century. For Birmingham after 1945 see, for instance: Danièle Joly, *Making a Place for Islam in British Society: Muslims in Birmingham*, Coventry, 1987, and John Rex and R. Moore, *Race, Community and Conflict: A Study of Sparkbrook*, London, 1967. For Coventry see S. W. L. Winchester, 'Immigrant Areas in Coventry in 1971', *New Community*, vol. 2, 1974, pp. 97–104. Leicester is covered by, for instance, Valerie Marrett, *Immigrants Settling in the City*, Leicester, 1989, and Margaret Byron, *Post-war Caribbean Migration to Britain: The Unfinished Cycle*, Aldershot, 1994.

had virtually no experience of immigrants, but the history of these areas since the Second World War is largely the history of immigration into them.[43]

In making comparisons between immigrants before and after 1945 one can also consider other influences which they have had in the two periods. In economic terms newcomers have always had economic power, from medieval Jews[44] and Hanseatic merchants,[45] through to nineteenth-century Jews[46] and Germans[47] and post-war immigrants, who have, for instance, become important in retailing in the case of Asians[48] and building in the case of the Irish.[49]

Post-war immigrants have had a far greater impact on the 'English way of life' than their pre-1945 predecessors, although all changes that have occurred since the end of the Second World War need to be placed within the context of increasing globalisation over the past fifty years. Thus immigrants have little to do with the arrival of hamburgers and chips. But would Italian, Greek, Indian and Chinese food have come to England without immigrants? It seems unlikely. Certainly, British companies have jumped on the bandwagon of ethnic food, while the growth of leisure time and the increase in surplus income at the end of the twentieth century have helped the spread of eating out. Nevertheless, curry, which now seems to have reached the status of the English national dish, would not have become so without the efforts of immigrants. Historically, Italian settlers may have played a role in the consumption of ice cream in Britain from the nineteenth century[50] and Germans may have had something to do with the amount of pork eaten,[51]

---

[43] See Nick Merriman (ed.), *The Peopling of London: Fifteen Thousand Years of Settlement from Overseas*, London, 1993.

[44] Hyams, 'Jewish Minority', p. 273.

[45] T. H. Lloyd, *England and the German Hansa, 1157–1611: A Study of their Trade and Commercial Diplomacy*, Cambridge, 1991.

[46] Israel Finestein, *Jewish Society in Victorian England*, London, 1993.

[47] Panayi, *German Immigrants*, pp. 138–42.

[48] See, for instance, N. K. Basi and M. R. D. Johnson, *Asian and White Businessmen in the Retail Sector: A Comparative Analysis of Development Patterns*, Coventry, 1996.

[49] See David Owen, *Irish-born People in Great Britain: Settlement Patterns and Socio-economic Circumstances*, Coventry, 1995, who lists middle-class professions.

[50] Terri Colpi, *The Italian Factor: The Italian Community in Great Britain*, Edinburgh, 1991, pp. 58–60, 81–2.

[51] See reference to butchers in Panayi, *German Immigrants*.

but the post-war immigrants have had a seismic impact on English diet.[52]

Similarly, arrivals since 1945 have also changed other aspects of popular culture, although such transformations again need consideration against the background of increasing globalisation. Post-war immigrants have brought with them their own dress codes, although in this sense so did late nineteenth-century Jews. However, since 1945 ethnic dress has, to some extent, influenced members of the dominant grouping.[53]

More obviously, again in contrast with the situation before 1945, immigrants and their offspring have become visible in the public arena, in sport, popular music and the media, although in these instances such activities had not developed before the Second World War in the way that they have done since 1945. Nevertheless, Germans played a large role in the spread of classical music[54] during the nineteenth century, while immigrants of all sorts worked as street musicians.[55] Similarly, there were Jewish boxers from the eighteenth century.[56] After 1945 the English football team and the British athletics team have become dependent upon the black contingents, while British boxing seems inconceivable without the children of Afro-Caribbean immigrants. In addition, countless black people born in Britain have had some success as pop singers and musicians, on both sides of the Atlantic, and have developed their own music styles.[57]

In terms of the experiences of immigrants into post-war Britain, these do not differ significantly from what has come before. The

---

[52] This is briefly covered by Arthur Marwick, *British Society since 1945*, Harmondsworth, 1990 edition, pp. 248–9. However, the eating habits of post-war Britons have been largely ignored by historians and social scientists. Guides to eating out give an indication of the number of ethnic restaurants in Britain. See, for instance, *Harden's London Restaurants, 1998*, London, 1997, which, on pp. 188–201, breaks restaurants down according to ethnicity. In a town such as Leicester, with a high Asian percentage in its population, Asian food dominates the restaurant trade. See Document 2.27.

[53] See Tony Sewell, *Black Masculinities and Schooling: How Black Boys survive Modern Schooling*, Stoke on Trent, 1997.

[54] Panayi, *German Immigrants*, pp. 129–30.

[55] *Ibid.*, pp. 127–8; Lucio Sponza, *Italian Immigrants in Nineteenth Century Britain: Realities and Images*, Leicester, 1988, pp. 62–75, 163–94.

[56] See Todd M. Endelman, *The Jews of Georgian England, 1740–1830: Tradition and Change in a Liberal Society*, Philadelphia, 1979, pp. 219–23.

[57] Ernest Cashmore, *Black Sportsmen*, London, 1982; Paul Gilroy, *The Black Atlantic: Modernity and Double Consciousness*, London, 1993, pp. 72–110.

reasons for movement are similar in the sense that personal decisions are influenced by structural economic and political factors
in both the sending and the receiving-societies. The reactions of
the host society changed little after 1945, as newcomers experienced the sort of shunning, rejection and hostility which immigrants
have faced from the British state and populace for hundreds of
years.

IV

Immigration is therefore not a new phenomenon in British history,
but its effects and scale differ from what has come before. The
present volume examines both the impact of immigration since
1945 and the experiences of immigrants themselves. While the
migrants themselves receive most attention, the second generation
is not ignored. After all, part of the impact of immigration most
clearly consists of the changing outward appearance of the British
population in terms of physical appearance, which will remain for
generations, although intermarriage may mean the whitening of the
immigrant population in the long run – assuming, of course, that
present immigration laws, aimed at keeping out people of colour,
continue to operate.

The documents divide into three main categories. In the first
place, the immigrants speak for themselves. Countless oral history
projects have delved into the reasons for migration and the experience of life in Britain. Second, many official documents are quoted,
including Colonial Office files from the 1950s and reports of the
Commission for Racial Equality. Third, newspapers, both mainstream and ethnic, provide information on the life of immigrants
and the reaction of natives towards them. In addition, a series of
miscellaneous documents are included.

V

The documentary section of the book divides into five compact
chapters. Each begins with a few words on the contents that follow,
made up of around twenty-five documents. Each document has
been given a title by me, in keeping with the other books in the
series. Some chapters divide chronologically and others themati-
cally. I have attempted to keep overlap to a minimum, although

some issues, such as immigration control and aspects of ethnicity, could fit into more than one chapter.

The first chapter focuses upon the reasons for immigration, making much use of oral testimony, but also examining the structural factors in both Britain and the countries of origin. Post-war immigration passes through three phases. At the end of hostilities, as Britain faced a labour shortage because of the need to rebuild the war-damaged economy, the government sought to import as many Europeans as possible, in keeping with a desire to maintain a white Britain. The period 1945–51 therefore witnessed the arrival of hundreds of thousands of European refugees from the Continent. In 1945 'Europe choked with refugees', perhaps 11 million[58] forced to move by the consequences of the barbaric 'total' war which had reached its end. Those who migrated to Britain divide into two groups. First, approximately 145,000 Poles, who essentially consist of members of the Polish army and government in exile, who remained in Britain at the end of the war, because Poland fell under Soviet control.[59] Britain also imported 91,151 'displaced persons' in the late 1940s, consisting of individuals who did not wish to return to their homelands because of dissatisfaction with the post-war settlement. They included Balts, Ukrainians and Sudeten Germans who entered Britain to work in a restricted range of industries with a shortage of labour such as the National Health Service, farming, coal mining and textile production.[60] Only about 2,000 of the European Volunteer Workers entering Britain consisted of Jews (despite the presence of hundreds of thousands of displaced Holocaust survivors on the Continent) as the government made conscious efforts to exclude them.[61]

The arrival of refugees from Europe overlapped with the coming of more purely economic immigrants from Europe and the British Empire and Commonwealth, a process which encompassed the period 1945–62. The underlying factor allowing large-scale migration into Britain until the early 1960s consisted of the strength of

---

[58] M. R. Marrus, *The Unwanted: European Refugees in the Age of Total War*, Oxford, 1985, pp. 297–9.

[59] Keith Sword, Norman Davies and Jan Ciechanowski, *The Formation of the Polish Community in Great Britain*, London, 1989. See Document 1.2.

[60] Diana Kay and Robert Miles, *Refugees or Migrant Workers? European Volunteer Workers in Britain, 1946–51*, London, 1992.

[61] See David Cesarani, *Justice Delayed: How Britain became a Refuge for Nazi War Criminals*, London, 1992, pp. 77–80.

the economy, which, between 1953 and 1961, experienced an average annual growth rate of 2.7 per cent.[62]

Most of the early post-war migration to Britain took place unofficially, with a lack of state involvement or direct recruitment. The main European states of origin consisted of Italy[63] and Ireland,[64] which had poor rural economies and a historical tradition of sending people to Britain. The immigrants from farther afield came from the Caribbean, India, Pakistan, West Africa, Hong Kong and Cyprus. Those from the West Indies moved from a variety of islands, including Jamaica, Barbados, Trinidad, Guyana and Nevis. Some direct recruitment of labour took place, most famously by London Transport in Barbados. But the overwhelming majority of the migration remained informal. It was fuelled by the image of Britain as the mother country of West Indians, passed on though the British education system, and by the knowledge of greater economic opportunities in Britain. The movement of West Indians to Britain, in common with numerous other migratory flows, developed into a social movement.[65] Migration from Pakistan took off in the late 1950s, particularly from the hill districts in the west and east of the country, in a new nation state with poor land, limited industrialisation and a consequent surplus of labour. A pattern of chain migration developed whereby those already present in the new country of settlement sent money back to help their relatives pay for their journey. Pakistani migration very much represents an instance of an initial male population of working age preceding wives and children who followed during the course of the 1960s and into the 1970s.[66] The main source of the migration from India lay in the Punjab and Gujarat in the north and west of the country respectively. The partition of the former province in 1947 between the newly created states of India and Pakistan caused massive population movements, a small proportion of which made its way to Britain. Some of the Sikhs who migrated had more economic

[62] Hobsbawm, *Industry and Empire*, p. 262.
[63] R. King, 'Italian Migration to Great Britain', *Geography*, vol. 62, 1977, p. 178; Colpi, *Italian Factor*, pp. 134–5;
[64] Colin Holmes, *John Bull's Island: Immigration and British Society, 1871–1971*, London, 1988, pp. 216–17. See Document 1.9.
[65] Edward Pilkington, *Beyond the Mother Country: West Indians and the Notting Hill White Riots*, London, 1988, pp. 10–21. See Documents 1.4, 1.6.
[66] Muhammad Anwar, *The Myth of Return: Pakistanis in Britain*, London, 1979. See Document 1.8.

motives for their movement. Although they had land in the Punjab, they hoped to accumulate capital and return home with it to improve their economic position.[67]

Hostility to the influx of immigrants from British imperial possessions affected all sections of British society (1.11–12) but the government did not publicly express its opposition until the late 1950s, sparked off by a slight economic downturn and the Nottingham and Notting Hill riots against West Indians in 1958. There duly followed the first piece of post-war British legislation restricting immigration from former imperial territories in the form of the Commonwealth Immigrants Act of 1962, which made entry into Britain subject to the issue of a voucher granted to people in occupations in which Britain needed foreign workers. Although 30,130 vouchers were issued in 1963, the number fell to just 2,290 in 1972, when the scheme ended.[68]

The 1962 legislation represents the end of the second phase of immigration into post-war Britain. The period since that time has essentially consisted of the regular introduction of new pieces of legislation to keep out as many people with dark skins as possible. Following hostility towards the arrival of East African Asians with British passports, the Commonwealth Immigrants Act of 1968 imposed controls upon holders of British passports unless they, or at least one parent or grandparent, had been born, adopted or naturalised in the UK. The measure clearly discriminated in favour of white people living in the Commonwealth. There followed the Immigration Act of 1971, imposing yet further controls upon entry, although despite these measures as many as 155,000 East African Asians entered Britain from 1965 to 1981.[69]

Some small refugee movements occurred during the 1970s,[70] while family reunification also continued.[71] After its election victory of 1979 the Conservative Party introduced further measures which built upon the legislation of the 1960s and early 1970s.[72] British policy proved highly effective in keeping out immigrants and

---

[67] Holmes, *John Bull's Island*, pp. 22–3.
[68] Panayi, 'Evolution', p. 134. See Document 1.13.
[69] *Ibid.* See Documents 1.14, 1.18.
[70] *Ibid.*, pp. 134–5.
[71] See Contributions to Colin Clarke, Ceri Peach and Steve Vertovec (eds), *South Asians Overseas; Migration and Ethnicity*, Cambridge, 1990, and Documents 1.14–16.
[72] Zig Layton-Henry, *The Politics of Immigration*, Oxford, 1992, pp. 180–214.

refugees in the Thatcher years. Between 1980 and 1988, 37,690 people applied for asylum in Britain, of whom 9,057 received asylum or refugee status and 11,742 obtained exceptional leave to remain.[73] Britain experienced a dramatic increase in the number of applications for asylum at the end of the 1980s and the beginning of the 1990s, mostly as a result of political changes in Eastern Europe, as well as in other parts of the world, reaching a peak of 44,800 in 1991. Britain was one of the meanest countries in taking in refugees from the war in Yugoslavia, whose number stood at just 2,000 in August 1992,[74] in contrast to the 220,000 already accepted by Germany at that time.[75]

At the end of the twentieth century Britain has clearly become highly restrictionist in its attitude towards the entry of foreign nationals. Apart from the difficulties faced by refugees trying to enter Britain, economic immigration from beyond Europe has been very difficult since the early 1960s, unless applicants can obtain a work permit proving that they are more suited to take a particular position than any British applicant, a policy which can really apply only to those with skills, usually from the West[76]. It appears that tight control over the entry of immigrants is here to stay for some time to come, therefore raising the possibility of a return to a 1940s mono-ethnic Britain.

The second chapter of the book considers the social and economic position of immigrants and refugees in post-war Britain and divides into thematic sections. The first of these examines issues of geography, where a series of obvious points present themselves. In the first place, immigrants into post-war Britain, following the common Continental pattern, focus upon particular areas of inner cities. Newcomers move into these areas both because of the fact that they tend to work in poorly paid occupations and because of the hostility which they face in their search for accommodation (2.9). By living with other members of their own ethnic group they find themselves in an environment where they can speak their own language and dialect and where they can protect themselves from the animosity of the native British. This clustering has

---

[73] British Refugee Council, *Asylum Seekers in the United Kingdom*, London, 1989.
[74] *Observer*, 16 August 1992. See Document 1.20.
[75] Vladimir Grecic, 'Former Yugoslavia', in Solon Ardittis (ed.), *The Politics of East–West Migration*, London, 1994, p. 127.
[76] Panayi, 'Evolution', p. 136.

helped in the transformation of vast sections of inner cities. In the long run many ethnic minorities have moved out of their initial places of residence to better areas, although ethnic concentration often continues.[77]

Because immigrants initially settled within the inner city, they tended to live in poor housing of a lower quality (with over-crowding and bad sanitation) than that inhabited by the established population (2.5–8). This has applied to most immigrants moving into Britain, again owing to a combination of racism and low wages. In the long run some newcomers manage to move to better-quality housing.

Demographically, many of the post-war immigrants, especially from the Commonwealth, initially consisted mostly of young men, who were followed by large families but, with the passage of time, subsequent generations have increasingly come to resemble the patterns of natives (2.11, 2.13). In the case of the Irish, however, at least 50 per cent of immigrants consisted of women, as they have always outnumbered male emigrants since 1871.[78] The situation with Italians is similar.[79] In the case of Greek Cypriots, males predominated, so that in the period 1955–66 there were 110 males to every 100 females. At that stage only 1.6 per cent of migrants were over sixty-five, while 25.4 were under fifteen.[80] Asian immigrants, on the other hand, were initially mostly males. In 1956 an extraordinary 92 per cent of all Pakistanis and Bangledeshis in the UK were males, while the figure for Indians stood at 79 per cent. Even in 1964 the proportions were 90 per cent and 69 per cent respectively. These early settlers consequently lived in all-male lodging houses, originally white-owned but subsequently purchased by Asians. As the 1960s and 1970s progressed changes took place in the ratio of men to women, which, in the case of Indians, reached 56 per cent to 44 per cent by 1974,

---

[77] Greek Cypriots represent one group which has moved out of its initial concentrations. See Robin Oakley, *Changing Patterns of Distribution of Cypriot Settlement*, Coventry, 1987. See Documents 2.1–4 for ethnic concentration.

[78] Mary Kells, ' "I'm Myself and Nobody Else": Gender and Ethnicity among Young Middle-class Irish Women in London', in Patrick O'Sullivan (ed.), *The Irish World Wide Series: History, Heritage, Identity*, vol. 4, *Irish Women and Irish Migration*, London, 1995, p. 201.

[79] King, 'Italian Migration to Great Britain', p. 178.

[80] Robin Oakley, 'Family, Kinship and Patronage: The Cypriot Migration to Britain', in Verity Saifullah Khan (ed.), *Minority Families in Britain: Support and Stress*, London, 1979, p. 10.

although the figure for Pakistanis still stood at 65 per cent to 35 per cent.[81]

The social structure of immigrants into post-war Britain varies from one ethnic group to another, but they do tend to cluster towards the lower end of the social scale. Nevertheless, enormous variations exist. Newcomers to post-war Britain have always tended to suffer higher levels of unemployment than the native British. In the short run this is largely due to racism, which particularly affected Asians and West Indians. In the longer term, immigrants found themselves adversely affected by the decline of manufacturing industry from the 1970s because they initially concentrated in that type of employment. In addition, the second generation, as it lives in the inner city, with the worst schools and the worst economic conditions, has also suffered higher unemployment rates than white Britons, as racism continues.[82]

Most immigrants found themselves initially working in manual working-class occupations. Although West Indians may have had qualifications which demanded better positions than the ones they actually obtained, the needs of the economy, combined with racism, dictated that they obtained some of the worst jobs.[83] Asians also experienced hostility in their search for employment. Their socio-economic position partly depends upon the group concerned, as some progressed from the overwhelming prejudice which they experienced during the 1950s, forcing them into employment below their training and educational levels. Pakistanis and Bangladeshis have tended to do worse than Indians and refugees from East Africa, largely because of their social origins before arrival.[84]

Most of the European immigrant minorities in post-war Britain have revealed a similar picture to that of Asians, with a significant concentration at the lower end of the social scale but with some social mobility. The overwhelming majority of Polish immigrants 'were for the most part directed to the heaviest, least attractive, least secure or lowest paid sectors of industry, where local labour short-

[81] Vaughan Robinson, *Transients, Settlers and Refugees: Asians in Britain*, Oxford, 1986, pp. 224–5; Dilip Hiro, *Black British: White British*, London, 1971, p. 128.
[82] See John Rex, *The Ghetto and the Underclass: Essays on Race and Social Policy*, Aldershot, 1988, and Documents 2.20–6.
[83] Pilkington, *Beyond the Mother Country*, p. 23; R. B. Davison, *Black British: Immigrants to England*, London, 1966, p. 70.
[84] Anwar, *Myth of Return*, p. 97.

ages were most acute'.[85] Similar comments apply to the Irish,[86] Italians[87] and Greek Cypriots.[88]

In the longer term the social structure of immigrants has changed. By the 1980s, partly as a reaction against unemployment, small businesses had taken off, especially among Asians,[89] although many Greek Cypriots had opened up their own factories and shops from the 1960s. In 1966 19.6 per cent of Cypriots in London were self-employed while the figure for the population as a whole totalled 7.1 per cent.[90] The Irish have developed a broad social structure, with a significant middle class which includes, for example, doctors, dentists, travel agents and, most notably, entrepreneurs working in the construction industry.[91] Although West Indians are one of the most underprivileged minorities the picture for them is not completely negative. One of the main opportunities for social advancement lies in sport, especially football and boxing, where ethnic clustering has occurred. In the former, West Indians made a breakthrough during the 1970s and are now present at all levels in the professional game. Clearly, for people like Ian Wright or Frank Bruno, the earning potential is enormous, but for each Ian Wright (2.29) or Frank Bruno there are probably hundreds or even thousands of black youths who have aspired to be like them but have not succeeded. At the same time, moving away from sport, blacks remain vastly underrepresented in the professions.[92]

Once immigrants settle in a new location they move towards people of their own ethnic group and begin to recreate aspects of their homeland in their new surroundings. Their insecurity within their new environment, caused by the traumatisation of moving and the hostility of the native population, makes this process a virtual

---

[85] Sheila Patterson, 'The Poles: An Exile Community in Britain', in James L. Watson (ed.), *Between Two Cultures: Migrants and Minorities in Britain*, Oxford, 1977, pp. 220–1.

[86] Owen, *Irish-born People*.

[87] Colpi, *Italian Factor*, pp. 144–58.

[88] Floya Anthias, *Ethnicity, Class, Gender and Migration: Greek Cypriots in Britain*, Aldershot, 1992, pp. 53–5.

[89] See Basi and Johnson, *Asian and White Businesses*, and Document 2.27.

[90] E. J. B. Rose *et al.*, *Colour and Citizenship: A Report on British Race Relations*, London, 1969, pp. 154–8.

[91] Holmes, *John Bull's Island*, pp. 229, 231.

[92] See Sharon J. Daye, *Middle Class Blacks in Britain: A Racial Fraction of a Class Group or a Class Fraction of a Racial Group?* London, 1994. For sportsmen see Cashmore, *Black Sportsmen*.

inevitability. However, the immigrants operate within their new environment, which means that whatever institutions they set up, and in whichever type of activity they participate, it has as much to do with their country of settlement as with their land of origin.

Immigrants in post-war Britain have created an ethnicity revolving around religion, politics and culture. The first of these is very important for newcomers. Because of the trauma of immigration, they have a need for spiritual support, which means that they inevitably fall back on their religion. In addition, most of the immigrants into post-war Britain have left rural societies in which religion plays a major part, meaning that any attempt to recreate their previous life must involve the building of churches and temples. Religion has a fundamental role in distinguishing one group from another, especially in the case of the Asian communities, who divide along the lines of Sikhs, Hindus and Muslims, although even this proves insufficient to distinguish them because of their different national and regional origins as well as the different sects within individual religions.

West Indians belonged to a variety of Christian groups when they first arrived in Britain. Many joined English churches, often facing racism even there, while others, over time, established their own places of worship (3.3, 4.5). The vast majority of Greek Cypriots in Britain are Greek Orthodox and most have continued to practise their religion to a greater or lesser degree, helped by the establishment of a significant number of churches, whose number in London alone totalled thirty-two by the early 1990s.[93] The Polish, Italian and Irish immigrants also continued to practise their religion in Britain, and in some cases they found themselves in the same English-speaking congregations.[94] Islam has taken off dramatically since 1945, leading to the construction of hundreds of mosques, together with schools and other institutions.[95] Similarly Hindu

---

[93] Sav Kyriacou and Zena Theodorou, 'Greek-Cypriots', in Merriman, *Peopling of London*, pp. 102–4.

[94] The religion of these three groups is considered by: Mary Hickman, *Religion, Class and Identity: The State, the Catholic Church and the Education of the Irish in Britain*, Aldershot, 1995; Colpi, *Italian Factor*, pp. 230–40; and Patterson, 'The Poles', pp. 230–3. As Hickman points out, the Catholic Church in England was essentially reborn as a result of the nineteenth-century migration of the Irish into the country.

[95] Philip Lewis, *Islamic Britain: Religion, Politics and Identity among British Muslims*, London, 1994; Danièle Joly, *Britannia's Crescent: Making a Place for Muslims in British Society*, Aldershot, 1995. See Document 3.5.

temples (3.6) and Sikh gurdwaras[96] have also taken off. Religion manifests itself not just in places of worship but also in the spread of minority schools and adherence to dress and eating habits.[97]

Immigrants in post-war Britain have also gravitated towards politics. Such developments draw upon their countries of origin and reflect their new surroundings. Political consciousness amongst blacks and Asians in Britain has had a series of aspects since the Second World War. In the first place they have established their own organisations which have focused upon a variety of issues. Among Asians in Britain, one of the most important organisations is the Indian Workers' Association (IWA), which, despite its name, is essentially a Punjabi working-class group.[98] More recently Islam has acted as a major political focus for Asians in Britain, especially after the Rushdie affair and the Gulf War, although obviously for a different religious sect from those attracted by the IWA.[99]

The perennial victimisation of black youth led to inner-city riots throughout England and Wales during the 1980s. The consequences of the racism which blacks faced, forcing them to the bottom of the social scale, meant that they had only one means of making themselves heard, common to all dispossessed sections of any society, in the form of rioting. Although disturbances broke out in Bristol in 1980 and 1986 and in Brixton and Tottenham in 1985, the major nationwide outbreaks of violence occurred in the summer of 1981, when many of the large inner-city areas with black populations experienced disorder. The rioters consisted not simply of Afro-Caribbean youth but also members of other ethnic groups living in the inner city, as well as young whites experiencing the same deprived social and economic conditions.[100]

Nevertheless, not all members of immigrant minorities have resorted to violence as a means of political expression. Most have taken part in the mainstream political processes by simply voting,

---

[96] See Arthur Wesley Helweg, *Sikhs in England: The Development of a Migrant Community*, Delhi, 1979, and Document 3.1.

[97] See Helweg, *Sikhs*, and Documents 5.5, 5.11, 5.12.

[98] John DeWitt, *Indian Workers' Associations in Britain*, London, 1969. See Document 2.24.

[99] Philip Lewis, 'The Bradford Council for Mosques and the Search for Muslim Identity', in Steve Vertovec and Ceri Peach (eds), *Islam in Europe: The Politics of Religion and Community*, London, 1997, pp. 103–28. See Document 3.16.

[100] John Solomos, *Race and Racism in Britain*, second edition, London, 1993, pp. 147–79. See Document 3.17.

although immigrant participation, among those with British nationality who have the vote, remains lower than among native whites. In recent decades, immigrants have also gained seats in local and national government.[101] Some immigrants have established homeland organisations, while others have set up more narrowly focused groups, concerned essentially with their position in England (3.11–15).

Newcomers to post-war Britain have also evolved what can be described as their own culture, combining elements from both their homeland and their new surroundings. In the first place, virtually all groups publish their own newspapers, many of which have a short life span but are replaced by new ones. Some appeal to an individual ethnic group. For instance, about thirty newspapers have come and gone for Greek Cypriots in Britain, the most important of which was *Parikiaki* by the end of the 1980s, containing an English section for second-generation Greek Cypriots whose reading ability in Greek is poor.[102] On the other hand newspapers such as *Eastern Eye* (2.15) and *Voice* cater for more than one ethnic group, appealing to all Asians and all West Indians in Britain respectively.

Immigrants have also established organisations revolving around a wide variety of 'cultural' activities. For instance, early West Indian settlers in Brixton set up associations devoted to cricket, drinking and dancing, as well as informal groups focusing upon unlicensed drinking, gambling and ganja smoking.[103] More recently ethnic broadcasting has developed, so that, for instance, several minority radio stations exist in London devoting attention to different types of music.[104] By the 1990s numerous associations had developed among the Cypriot community in London, which obtained some public funding.[105] London Greek Radio broadcasts from Haringey, receiving advertising revenue predominantly from some of the

---

[101] Layton-Henry, *Politics of Immigration*, pp. 100–23; Shamit Saggar, *Race and Politics in Britain*, London, 1992, pp. 94–171.

[102] Anthias, *Ethnicity, Class, Gender and Migration*, p. 130. See Document 3.7.

[103] Sheila Patterson, *Dark Strangers: A Sociological Study of the Absorption of a recent West Indian Migrant Group in Brixton, South London*, London, 1963, pp. 348–9, 364–7.

[104] Commission for Racial Equality, *Radio for Ethnic and Linguistic Minorities: Prospects for the 1990s*, London, 1990, from which comes Document 3.26.

[105] Sasha Josephides, 'Associations amongst the Greek Cypriot Population in Britain', in John Rex, Danièle Joly and Czarina Wilpert (eds), *Immigrant Associations in Europe*, Aldershot, 1987, pp. 42–61.

numerous Greek Cypriot businesses which exist in London. Finally, immigrants have also developed a high culture encompassing activities such as literature, theatre and serious music (3.27–8).

All immigrants in post-war Britain have experienced some form of hostility, as Chapter 4 illustrates. The chapter takes a chronological approach, illustrating the main incidents and the different forms of hostility which have occurred. The existence of the British nation state provides the prerequisite for all other manifestations of xenophobia. The presence of national boundaries, together with immigration and nationality laws, provides the most concrete and visible manifestation of the presence of in-groups and out-groups.[106]

The institutions of the state display traces of racism. This applies to the juduciary, for instance. Throughout the post-war period a largely white legal profession has existed, particularly in its higher echelons (4.22). Many white judges come into contact with black people only in court. The overwhelmingly white police force has also had problems with black people, as the Stephen Lawrence inquiry made abundantly clear. Apart from everyday intimidation, numerous black people have died at the hands of white policemen (4.4, 4.21).

A racist culture represented one of the deepest manifestations of racism during the early post-war decades. Although it continues to exist, and although it could be argued that all culture is ultimately xenophobic, before the 1980s it had extremely overt manifestations, including images in school textbooks and children's stories (4.2), and the existence of jokes against minorities (4.1). The latter have become increasingly disreputable and rare over the course of the past five decades.

Newspapers have played a major role in perpetuating and spreading racial stereotypes and images. Negative attitudes to immigrants, especially towards newcomers with dark skins, began to manifest themselves during the 1950s. By the 1970s the press, still obsessed with immigration, and the fear that it would 'undermine the British way of life', focused increasingly upon illegal immigrants, despite the small numbers involved (1.19, 4.23). In addition, stereotypes about black muggers and Indian corner shop owners abound in the pages of the press.[107] The newspapers have played a

---

[106] See Paul, *Whitewashing Britain*.
[107] T. van Dijk, *Racism and the Press*, London, 1991; Barry Troyna, *Public Awareness and the Media: A Study of Reporting on Race*, London, 1981.

large role in the passage of xenophobic legislation. The constant references to the threat of has led successive governments to pass increasingly restrictive legislation, which ultimately means that all the mainstream political parties have pursued racist policies since 1945.[108]

The mainstream political parties have also reacted to the threat of the extreme right which has always existed in Britain since 1945. Once such groupings begin to attract votes from the electable parties, the mainstream steals some of the former's clothes. The first significant group consisted of Oswald Mosley's Union Movement, founded in 1948 and focusing upon areas of London which had experienced significant levels of immigration, including Brixton and Notting Hill.[109] Outside London the Birmingham Immigration Control Association came into existence in October 1960. Its activities included protest meetings, the distribution of leaflets, the organisation of petitions and the writing of letters to local newspapers.[110] Extremist organisations continued to exist during the 1960s and in 1967 the National Front (NF) came into existence. At the West Bromwich by-election of 1973 it obtained 16 per cent of the vote and it counted a membership of 14,000. But by the following year its decline had set in, as it obtained less than 4 per cent of the vote in the general election of 1974. Subsequently it split apart, with the British National Party representing its most notable successor. At the same time Margaret Thatcher and her successors attracted many NF voters.[111]

Every immigrant in Britain has had some personal experience of xenophobia. Racial discrimination is endemic and is also hard to detect. During the 1950s, in addition to the problems which they faced in the search for housing and employment, immigrants endured snubs when they wanted to participate in white social activities, a situation which continues to exist, despite the passage of legislation to prevent such discrimination.[112] Black footballers,

---

[108] Panayi, 'Evolution', pp. 132–7. See Document 4.19.

[109] Roger Eatwell, *Fascism: A History*, London, 1996, pp. 261–3; Richard Thurlow, *Fascism in Britain: A History, 1918–85*, Oxford, 1987, pp. 246–7; Pilkington, *Beyond the Mother Country*, pp. 98–100. See Document 4.6.

[110] Robert Miles and Annie Phizacklea, *White Man's Country: Racism in British Politics*, London, 1984, p. 38. See Document 4.10.

[111] Stan Taylor, *The National Front in English Politics*, London, 1982. See Documents 4.14, 4.25.

[112] Pilkington, *Beyond the Mother Country*, pp. 35–9. See Documents 4.3, 4.5, 4.17, 4.23.

meanwhile, faced racism at whatever level they played the game,[113] while immigrant schoolchildren would face hostility not just in the playground but from their teachers and school bureaucrats.[114]

The most potent manifestation of racism in post-war Britain consists of physical violence. Countless examples exist of individuals facing attacks during the 1950s, especially in crimes perpetrated by Teddy boys. Victims included both West Indians and Greek Cypriots.[115] As well as isolated attacks on individuals, the 1940s and 1950s also witnessed larger-scale disturbances against immigrants. In 1948 racist violence occurred in Birmingham, Deptford and Liverpool. The major anti-immigrant riots in post-war Britain broke out in Nottingham and Notting Hill in 1958, between 23 August and 2 September (4.7–8). After these disturbances, similar incidents occurred on a few more occasions, although not on the same scale. Between 19 and 23 August 1961 the few Asian businesses which existed in Middlesbrough came under attack from several thousand natives (4.9). One year later hundreds of whites attacked black people in Dudley.[116]

Since that time, few anti-immigrant riots have occurred in Britain (4.15), replaced by small-scale (4.18) but often fatal (4.20) attacks. In fact, between 1970 and 1985 a total of sixty-three racist murders took place in Britain.[117] In 1986 one in four black residents in the London borough of Newham 'had been victims of some form of racial harassment in the previous twelve months'.[118] Such incidents continued into the 1990s. During the Gulf War in 1991 mosques came under attack up and down the country,[119] and after the conflict attacks upon immigrants and their offspring continued apace

---

[113] See Cashmore, *Black Sportsmen*, pp. 174–99, and Document 4.13.

[114] Lorna Chessum, ' "Sit down. You haven't reached that stage yet": African Caribbean Children in Leicester Schools, 1960–74', *History of Education*, vol. 26, 1997, pp. 409–19. See Document 4.12.

[115] T. R. Fyvel, *The Insecure Offenders: Rebellious Youth in the Welfare State*, Harmondsworth, 1963, p. 34.

[116] The above receive attention from Panikos Panayi, 'Anti-immigrant Violence in Nineteenth and Twentieth Century Britain', in Panayi, *Racial Violence in Britain*, pp. 16–17.

[117] Keith Tompson, *Under Siege: Racial Violence in Britain Today*, Harmondsworth, 1988, p. 171.

[118] Commission for Racial Equality, *Living in Terror: A Report on Racial Violence and Harassment in Housing*, London, 1987, p. 9.

[119] *Guardian*, 23 January 1991.

in Britain. Between 1989 and 1994 the number of such incidents rose from 4,383 to 9,762.[120]

Nevertheless, to suggest that immigrants and their offspring live in the equivalent of a Nazi hell is clearly erroneous. Since 1945 Britain has changed dramatically under the influence of immigrants, which inevitably means that the newcomers have drawn some benefit from such changes. In short Britain has become 'multiracial'. But what does the term mean? It can have at least three meanings, covered in Chapter 5. The first refers to 'culture', to use that term in its broadest possible meaning. In this sense Britain has become multiracial. While British culture is still dominant, it has taken elements from immigrants which have enriched it. This is most evident in food and popular music, which have changed beyond recognition. Britain has also become multiracial because sections of British society have both accepted the newcomers and gone out of their way to help them. The most complicated issue is whether Britain has become multiracial in a political sense, which, in view of the levels of racism which immigrants and their children face, seems problematic. Nevertheless, the state has taken measures to help ethnic minorities, although they have had limited success.

The first section of Chapter 5 focuses upon issues revolving around culture. As we have seen, all newcomers to post-war Britain tried to maintain an ethnicity. This process means not just making conscious bureaucratic efforts to recreate their homeland, but also continuing with everyday activities, most notably food, dress and language. The first of these has spread to transform eating habits beyond recognition owing to the blandness of English cuisine (5.5–8). On the whole dress has not had much impact on the way the native British dress, but the arrival of Asians wearing completely different clothing from white people has certainly changed the appearance of many of the inner-city areas where they have settled. This particularly applies to Asian immigrants, especially women, be they Sikh, Hindu or Muslim (5.10–12), although in the long run some, but certainly not all, of the second generation wear Western clothes.[121] On the other hand European and West Indian immigrants have always worn similar clothes to those of natives.

[120] *Human Rights Watch World Report, 1996*, New York, 1996, p. 215.
[121] Parminder Bhachu, 'Culture, Ethnicity and Class among Punjabi Sikh Women in 1990s Britain', *New Community*, vol. 17, 1991, pp. 408–9

Immigrant language has had a limited impact upon spoken English, with the possible exception of the West Indian dialect.[122] Once again, foreign languages have multiracialised Britain because they play a large role in many inner-city areas (5.13). At the same time immigrant languages have become anglicised because they have borrowed words from English. The linguistic situation of Greek Cypriots, and, more particularly, their offspring, indicates the complexity of immigrant language patterns. Everyday discourse, involving the first generation speaking to each other or to their children, takes place in the Greek Cypriot dialect rather than Standard Modern Greek, which the second generation have difficulty in understanding.[123]

Multiracialism also develops through the initiatives of individuals and non-governmental organisations. Some native Britons have gone out of their way to help new arrivals on their doorstep. In some areas the Church helped the establishment of bodies for the purpose of lessening tension between white people and immigrants (5.19). Furthermore, left-wing organisations such as trade unions did much to help racial integration because, although individual union members at the grass-roots level feared immigrants because of their supposed threat to employment, union leaderships, either through genuine internationalism or through fear of attracting accusations of racism, have spoken up for ethnic minorities throughout the post-war period (5.17–18). In addition, a series of anti-racist organisations have come into existence since the 1960s, with a leadership and membership combining native whites together with immigrants, the most important of which consisted of the Campaign Against Racial Discrimination from 1964 to 1967[124] and the Anti-Nazi League, most active between 1977 and 1979.[125]

The state plays the most important role in the creation of a multiracial society and has introduced a series of measures to improve

---

[122] Phrases such as 'Innit?' and 'Know what I mean?' have West Indian origins.

[123] Evienia Papadaki and Maria Roussou, 'The Greek Speech Community', in Safder Allandina and Viv Edwards (eds), *Multilingualism in the British Isles: The older Mother Tongues and Europe*, London, 1991, pp. 189–201. See also Document 5.14.

[124] Ron Ramdin, *The Making of the Black Working Class in Britain*, Aldershot, 1987, pp. 415–37.

[125] Paul Gilroy, *There ain't no Black in the Union Jack: The Cultural Politics of Race and Nation*, London 1993, pp. 131–5. See Document 5.20.

the position of ethnic minorities. The first Race Relations Act, which came into operation in 1965, outlawed discrimination in public places and incitement to racial hatred verbally or in writing, but did nothing about the core areas of prejudice in housing and employment. The Act also established the Race Relations Board for the purpose of enforcing the legislation, but it could not deal with most of the complaints it received because they lay beyond its scope. There followed the 1968 Race Relations Act, which extended the provisions of the 1965 legislation to cover the obvious areas of housing and employment and also established the Community Relations Commission for the purpose of creating harmonious community relations and of advising and assisting local voluntary community relations councils with this end in mind.[126] The next major piece of legislation, which has remained the longest-lasting, came in 1976 in the form of another Race Relations Act, which established the Commission for Racial Equality, taking over the functions of both the Race Relations Board and the Community Relations Commission. In addition, the new legislation strengthened the provisions of the previous measures, introducing the concept of indirect discrimination, which was, however, not very clearly defined (5.23). No major piece of legislation has superseded the 1976 Act, although the inner-city disturbances of 1981 and the Scarman Report which followed forced the state to take measures in other areas.[127]

Local councils have also made attempts to lessen racial prejudice and promote integration. For instance, from the early 1960s local education authorities made provision to help children of immigrants who could not speak English.[128] In addition, the race relations legislation of the 1960s and 1970s had provided for the establishment of local Community Relations Councils, which, after 1976, became Racial Equality Councils, of which ninety-one existed in 1991. In that year they received £4.5 million, from both the CRE and local councils, to employ racial equality officers.[129]

---

[126] S. Abbott (ed.), *The Prevention of Racial Discrimination in England*, London, 1971.

[127] John Benyon, *Scarman and After: Essays Reflecting on Lord Scarman's Report, the Riots and their Aftermath*, Oxford, 1984.

[128] Department of Education and Science, *The Continuing Needs of Immigrants*, London, 1972, from which comes Document 5.22.

[129] Martin MacEwan, *Tackling Racism in Europe: An Examination of Anti-discrimination Law in Practice*, Oxford, 1995, p. 165.

During the 1980s certain inner-city local authorities began to introduce measures to deal with racial inequality, especially within London, e.g. the Greater London Council, Lambeth, Brent, Hackney and Haringey.[130]

At the end of the twentieth century, because of the influence of immigrants, Britain has changed dramatically in social, culinary, cultural, political, economic and geographical terms. Since their arrival in Britain, the position of immigrants has also altered. Some have experienced social mobility, either for themselves or for their children. Others, however, enduring long-term unemployment, have witnessed a deterioration in their economic position.

In the longer term the impact of immigrants is clearly open to speculation. Some of the changes they have implemented must be permanent. For instance, it is unlikely that there will ever be a return to the eating habits of the 1950s. Some of the companies established may, in the long run, become leading British firms. The physical appearance of people in Britain will continue to change, because of intermarriage, although it seems unlikely that white, black and brown skin will completely disappear. For the black underclass the future may resemble that the position in the United States, where endemic racism confines them to the inner-city ghettoes. However, that represents only one possible scenario.

VI

The impact of post-war immigrants upon historians has remained limited, as they have payed little attention to them, especially those working in the mainstream. For instance, Kenneth Morgan's history of Britain since 1945,[131] part of the *Oxford History of Britain*, devotes just six out of 516 pages to immigration. This is indicative of the negative attitude of many mainstream historians towards ethnic minorities and their study. Until recently few books by historians had appeared on immigrants in post-war Britain, in contrast to social scientists, who started to study them almost immediately after their arrival in the country. We can briefly examine the two disciplines individually.

---

[130] See John Solomos and Wendy Ball (eds), *Race and Local Politics*, Basingstoke, 1990.
[131] Kenneth O. Morgan, *The People's Peace: British History, 1945–89*, Oxford, 1990. Clearly, 'The People' consist of white Anglo-Saxons.

Between the late 1940s and the early 1960s several sociologists and anthropologists published a series of pioneering case studies of minorities in British cities. These included Kenneth Little,[132] Michael Banton,[133] Sheila Patterson,[134] Ruth Glass[135] and Anthony H. Richmond.[136] By the end of the 1960s social scientists had taken immigration, ethnicity and racism to their hearts and since that time it has represented one of the most important areas of research for them. Countless studies have appeared since, focusing upon individual minorities and particular themes.

We can simply point to the most important developments. The establishment of the Institute of Race Relations in 1958 proved instrumental because of the series of books which it issued in association with Oxford University Press. Numerous other publishers have moved into this field, one of the most important in recent years being Avebury. The launching of the journals *New Community* in 1973 and *Ethnic and Racial Studies* in 1978 also furthered the production of research into immigrants in post-war Britain, although this did not represent their only focus. The setting up of the ESRC-funded Centre for Research in Ethnic Relations, first at the University of Bristol, then at Aston and most recently at Warwick from 1984, has also been very important in the growth of the study of ethnic minorities. The centre's various series of research papers, policy papers, monographs, occasional papers, bibliographies and other publications, which may run into thousands of publications, have played a large role in furthering the study of ethnic minorities in Britain. By the end of the twentieth century we have therefore reached a situation in which immigration and ethnicity represent one of the easiest fields in which to publish for social scientists in Britain, a situation reflected internationally. Several leading British academics have made their names in this field, including John Rex, John Solomos and Robert Miles.

Historians, in contrast, have not taken to immigrants so warmly, a situation for which two major explanations present themselves.

[132] Kenneth Little, *Negroes in Britain: A Study of Racial Relations in English Society*, London, 1947.
[133] Michael Banton, *The Coloured Quarter: Negro Immigrants in an English City*, London, 1955.
[134] Patterson, *Dark Strangers*.
[135] Ruth Glass, *Newcomers: The West Indians in London*, London, 1960.
[136] Anthony H. Richmond, *Colour Prejudice in Britain: A Study of West Indian Workers in Liverpool, 1941–51*, London, 1954.

First, the historical profession is dominated by native-born, white, middle-class males who can trace their ancestry in Britain through several generations. The situation in social science, while similar, is not quite as bad. Second, history, unlike social science, plays a central role in group identity. The perceived idea in national histories is that the population has a common ancestry which acts against the movement of immigrant and ethnic history into the mainstream. The *heritage* of a nation state needs to be protected because the acceptance of outsiders as part of a country's ancestry represents an important indication that it has become plural and multiracial.

But the picture for the study of immigrants in Britain by historians is not completely negative, as they have devoted some attention to them, especially in the period before 1945. Numerous books have appeared and are appearing on Blacks, Irish, Jews, Germans and Italians from professional historians and others.[137] But the period since 1945 has received attention only very recently. Colin Holmes played some role in this, although much of his research has focused on the years before 1945.[138] His journal *Immigrants and Minorities* looks at the period before and after the Second World War but does not limit itself to Britain. Most of his former research students have studied immigration and racism, but again their focus covers the nineteenth and twentieth centuries. Others have taken a similar approach.[139]

Only very recently have studies begun to appear by historians on specific themes about the history of Britain since the end of the Second World War, using archival materials. These include Ian Spencer's *British Immigration Policy since 1939* and Kathleen Paul's *Whitewashing Britain*. They appeared within a few months of each other in 1997, covering similar topics. It is to be hoped that similar academic studies and others looking at individual minorities will follow.[140]

---

[137] See Panikos Panayi, 'The Historiography of Immigrants and Ethnic Minorities: Britain compared with the USA', *Ethnic and Racial Studies*, vol. 19, 1996, pp. 825–9.

[138] This is true of *Anti-semitism in British Society, 1876–1939*, London, 1979. Many of his books cover the period both before and after 1945, including: *John Bull's Island; A Tolerant Country? Immigrants, Refugees and Minorities in Britain*, London, 1991, and the collection of essays which he edited entitled *Immigrants and Minorities in British Society*, London, 1978.

[139] See the bibliography in Panayi, 'Historiography'.

[140] This will almost certainly happen. See, for instance, Lorna Chessum, 'From Immigrants to Ethnic Minority: African Caribbeans in Leicester, 1945–81', De Montfort University Ph.D. thesis, 1998.

'Amateur' historians, meanwhile, have made greater efforts to recreate the history of immigrants in post-war Britain, particularly through the use of oral testimony. Many books and pamphlets, some of which are quoted in this study, have appeared from local history groups. The Ethnic Minorities Oral History Project, which published a series of leaflets on individual groups, was extremely important in this context. Certainly there is enormous scope for academic historians to use oral history once they start moving towards the study of immigrants in post-war Britain.

1

Immigration

The history of immigration into post-war Britain has passed through three phases. At the end of hostilities, as Britain faced a labour shortage, the government sought to import as many Europeans as possible, in keeping with a desire to maintain a white Britain. As sources of labour on the Continent and Ireland dried up, immigration began to take place from the Empire and Commonwealth. But by 1962 the government had decided that non-white immigration should cease, and since that time the state has continually lessened the possibilities of black and Asian immigration into Britain. Government policy has played the central role in controlling the entry of newcomers but economic and political factors, as well as individual choices, have been instrumental in the regions from which migration took place and in the individuals who made the move.

1.1   From Belsen to Britain

Despite attempts by the government to exclude Jews at the end of the War, a few did manage to make their way to Britain, including Gena Turgel, saved by her future husband, a British soldier who became engaged to her in Belsen.

On the day of liberation, two British Army sergeants came into the hospital to look for weapons and some SS men whom they suspected were hiding somewhere in the hospital barrack . . .

I said to one of them: 'Do you speak German?'

'Why?' he asked me.

I said: 'I just thought you would. I have a feeling that you understand German.'

I was right and we conversed together. I think he liked my way of speaking. He asked me what I was doing there and I told him I'd been working as a nurse.

I liked him and was impressed when he told me about his work trying to track down the Nazis and to see justice done . . .

Apart from the day when he was ill, he kept coming in every day and made a point of seeing me . . . I grew fond of him, and he grew fond of me.

One day he said he would like me to come to the Officers' Mess for dinner . . .

The tables were laid with crisp white tablecloths and wonderfully decorated with flowers – a sight I hadn't seen for many years. I said to Norman: 'What is all this? Are you expecting special guests?'

He said: 'You are the special guest. This is our engagement party.' And yet he never actually proposed to me! He took it for granted that I would accept.

Then Captain Stephen, his commanding officer, and other colleagues came over and congratulated me. I said to myself: 'They must have had too much to drink.' I didn't take it seriously because, really and truly, my mind wasn't on getting married or on any romantic ties. I just wanted to breathe with my freedom, with the fresh air. I wanted to leave that environment and not have the smell of decay all around me. I was in a trance, a daze . . .

The following day he came over and wanted to give me a kiss. I pushed him away, because in those days a kiss was something very special . . .

He took off a ring he was wearing and put it on my finger. Then he typed a few lines, in English, on a sheet of paper which explained that I was engaged to a British sergeant, that help would be provided for me in his absence and that I should wait for his return to get married. I was the happiest woman in the world.

Gena Turgel, *I Light a Candle*, London, 1995, pp. 124–6.

1.2   A Polish migrant makes his way to Britain

At the end of the Second World War the British state, fearing a labour shortage, made efforts to encourage Europeans to move to its shores. Poles, whose numbers totalled nearly 150,000, made up one of the first groups to arrive, particularly in the form of the Polish army fleeing German and then Soviet forces. Every individual had their own story to tell, although perhaps not many as dramatic as Crezlaw, a Polish soldier, arriving in 1945.

The outbreak of the war affected my family very much. When the Russians came in 1939 we hardly had any food at home. We tried to survive, father tried his best. It was not very safe for me to stay at home because the Russians tried to get me, they wanted to take me to Russia to educate me. I was against this, I didn't want education from the Russians, no way. I was supposed to go to Moscow to be educated but I went to the forest. The Jerries attacked the Russians in June 1941 on 21 June and the Germans caught me, I go from one hands to the other and that's it. They kept me in my home town for about three or four weeks I escaped from there and they got me again. Then they take me to Lithuania, I was there for four months, I was in a big camp. It was very bad, no food, the food was terrible, people were dying of hunger. Then they took me to Germany, I had no way out, I had to eat raw potatoes and grass to survive. I escaped two times from Germany. Four of my friends from my home town were killed and I came out alive. There were many times in my life that I thought I was going to die. I've seen death many times and thought, I can't get out of that.

The first time I was working in a steel mine and I escaped from there and I was in France for one month. For four weeks I was free, I was free but I had nothing to eat. I tried not to get in trouble but the Germans caught me again, beat me up and put me back to camp. They told me they were going to execute me, then shoot me. I said, why not shoot me, shoot me now, they didn't. I waited until I had a chance when they took us to Luxembourg by train, so I jumped out of the train. That was the only way out – to jump out of the train, to survive or die. All my friends died because the Americans bombed the train. They thought they were transporting the German Army but the only Germans were on the top of the coal wagons, they smashed the lot but I jumped out before that.

Then I went to France, back to France. A German soldier came to me and spoke fluent Polish and said to me 'Get out, ' the war wasn't far he said 'Get out or you'll be shot,' they set fire to the village. I ran into the forest but you know when somebody is chasing you have no strength to run, but I did get out and after that I went to a Russian camp. I told them I was Russian, I told them where I came from in Russia, I spoke Russian. I was given plenty of food, cigarettes, plenty to drink. I stayed there about three weeks, after that I saw two Americans and a Polish Officer, they said 'any Polish people step forward'. Only I stepped forward and everybody looked at me because I had said I was Russian. So I went and joined the Polish Army in France. I joined the army and from there, there was a lot of us, it took two big ships to transport us to England.

Ethnic Communities Oral History Project, *Passport to Exile: The Polish Way to London*, London, 1988, pp. 20–1.

1.3 Recruitment of Italian workers

During the first decade after the end of the Second World War the government made efforts to recruit racially acceptable Europeans, including Italians.

During the last few decades the Ministry of Labour and National Service have offered facilities, in certain circumstances, for the bulk recruitment of Italian workers for essential industries and services in Great Britain at the employer's expense.

The arrangements, which have applied mainly to unskilled workers, have worked well, and employers concerned have expressed their general satisfaction with more than 8,000 Italians recruited in this way. Examples of industries which have recruited Italian labour in bulk are: brickmaking, tinplate manufacture, coal mining, railways, foundries, and textiles.

In the light of experience gained, a model contract for the recruitment of men or women has been negotiated and agreed with the Italian authorities, and this is now in use.

Employers in essential industries and services wanting information about the operation of these arrangements are invited to enquire at their nearest Local Office of the Ministry.

Ministry of Labour Gazette, April 1954.

1.4 The West Indian background

In contrast to the booming economy of Britain during the early post-war decades, which acted as the pull factor for immigrants, the push factors consisted of the underdevelopment and unemployment of the homeland, as the example of the West Indies indicates.

1. The Royal Commission of 1938 stated that 'unemployment has taken the place of an unsatisfied demand for labour as the dominating fact throughout the Caribbean area'. It is not, however, easy to put the fact in precise numerical form . . .

2. This Memorandum does not treat of the Bahamas or Bermuda. The territories considered are the island territories of Jamaica, Trinidad, Barbados, the Windward Islands and the Leeward Islands; and the two mainland territories, British Guiana and British Honduras. The mainland territories suffer from underdevelopment and sparseness of population rather than from unemployment, though seasonal unemployment of forest workers and chicleros presents certain problems in British Honduras and the reduction of the labour force at the bauxite mines in British Guiana during the period of the Canadian winter causes seasonal unemployment in that colony too. The island territories, where the density of population tends to be high, have a more pronounced unemployment problem.

3. But the unemployment is not always manifest or complete. As the economies are agricultural and there is much opportunity for part-time occupation in work on estates combined with work on allotments or smallholdings either owned or leased (often on a sharecropping tenure), it is only in the towns that the problem manifests itself as complete want of work. The standard of living is probably more seriously depressed by the prevalence of underemployment. This is widespread in most of the islands and a serious problem in Jamaica, Trinidad and Barbados. In the islands which depend mainly or largely upon sugar under-employment can be expected even in normal years and may become severe in years of drought. Some indication of the measure of the problem is given by the results of the economic survey of a sample of field workers in Jamaica made for the Sugar Industry Commission in 1944 . . . The Sugar Industry Commission reported that in Jamaica about one-fifth of the field force employed by the estates obtained a full measure of employment and not quite two-fifths had work for two-thirds of the working year: the rest were under-employed though a substantial proportion worked on smallholdings when unemployed or intermittently employed. In other islands the findings might be similar.

4. The growth of unemployment reflects the difference between the rate of increase of the population and the rate of expansion of

economic opportunities. The West Indian colonies depend mainly upon agriculture and most of them on a very limited number of export crops. Of these, sugar is by far the most important, and the world market for sugar up to 1939 did not encourage expansion. The prospects for other crops have been damaged not only by market declines but also by diseases and hurricanes. Subsistence agriculture has not been able to absorb the increase of population, partly because arable land of good quality is not everywhere available, partly because the people themselves have been drifting to the towns. Industries other than agriculture, though they have made progress, have not provided employment on the scale required. Except for the petroleum industry in Trinidad, bauxite mining in British Guiana and forestry (along with sawmills) in British Guiana and British Honduras, no industry other than agriculture operates on a scale that calls for workers in large numbers.

5. On the other hand the inflow into the labour market greatly exceeds the wastage. The birth rate remains high while the death rate has fallen and is still falling. The natural increase of population is now in many colonies at a rate that will cause the population to double in twenty-five or thirty years.

PRO HO 213 716, 'Unemployment in the West Indies, Memorandum by the Colonial Office, 8 September 1948'.

1.5   The Empire Windrush

The SS *Empire Windrush*, which arrived at Tilbury docks from Jamaica in June 1948, with 417 passengers, represented the symbolic beginning of West Indian immigration into Britain. However, even before it had landed the Labour government displayed concern about its passengers.

In view of the interest which is being shown in Parliament and in the press in the matter of the 417 Jamaicans who are due to arrive at Tilbury on 21 June on the SS *Empire Windrush*, I think it is desirable that the Cabinet should be aware of the arrangements which the various Departments concerned are trying to make to deal with the situation . . .

The matter has been discussed between the various Departments concerned, and I think it is clear that the problem has got to be tackled, as one outside normal provision such as the Poor Law, and as a combined operation without too much insistence on normal departmental responsibilities. I need not recount all the possibilities which have been considered and rejected as impracticable on one ground or another. The most hopeful solution so far suggested is that the men should be provided with transport from Tilbury to some central point which can be used as a 'clearing house' or 'transit camp'. For this purpose I have asked the Secretary of State for War whether he can make available the Deep Shelter at South Clapham. If this can be done, the immediate problem of accommodation will be solved, though arrangements will have to be made for meals. It is not ideal, but ordinary surface accommodation for so large a number is apparently unobtainable; and there is considerable convenience in having the men (other than the odd seventy at the Colonial Office hostel) all together.

Arrangements are being made for the boat to be met by representatives of the Colonial Office and the Ministry of Labour, and the Ministry of Labour have undertaken to do everything in their power to help the men find employment in England as quickly as possible. It is understood that some at any rate of the arrivals are anxious to join the Armed Forces. About two-thirds of the total are in fact ex-servicemen.

If the Clapham Deep Shelter can be used as a clearing-house it may be possible, if all goes well, to arrange for the dispersal of the men and their placing in industry in a period of three or four weeks.

Many of them will arrive with only a limited amount of funds, having spent most of their savings on buying their passages to England. It may therefore be necessary to grant them public assistance until they find employment, but there is machinery for dealing with this particular problem through the Assistance Board. They may also need assistance towards railway fares to their ultimate destination.

The whole matter is being vigorously dealt with by the Departments concerned under the Chairmanship of the Ministry of Health, and I believe that if the Clapham Shelter can be made available the situation can be dealt with without getting out of control.

PRO CO 876 88, 'SS *Empire Windrush* – Jamaican Unemployed: Memorandum by the Secretary of State for the Colonies, Arthur Creech Jones, 15 June 1948'.

1.6   The image of England

During the early post-war decades many West Indians who made their way to Britain had a positive picture of the country, which they had obtained largely from the education system as they grew up. This impression played a large part in the decision of many African-Caribbeans to migrate, including Roy, who moved from Barbados in 1956.

I knew that the money was slightly better to start with in Britain, but the main thing that attracted me was to see Britain. So much was taught down our throats about the Mother Country and so forth and we really believed that we're going home to a Mother Country, a place that's going to be loving and nice. And I, despite the fact that I had travelled before, was very, very keen to come to England more than any place else. That was my first motivation, my first attraction . . .

I had just the ideas which were instilled into us [about England]. We were told that the place and everybody in it was nice, virtually angels. I mean, that's the story that was told to us down here from the time we were training school from *Britannia*, raise the flag on Jubilee day and drink your lemonade, you know, we think of England. The Union Jack and the National Anthem. And we thought this is a good chance to go to England, everybody up there is going to be nice and lovely, we were virtually told that up there everybody was a Christian. That's true and we believed it.

The mass emigration started in 1956. The first lot was in '55 and I was in the second lot, '56. But prior to then, you was getting nothing, whether people was up there and didn't want to say what they were going through, or there wasn't sufficient people to spread enough about it, or people, even if they hear things, they probably won't believe it, they probably don't tell it to anybody else. I can assure you that up to when I left [for] England in 1956 I had nothing but a hundred per cent good picture of England and everybody else that is in England. I felt I was going to a place which would be second to Heaven, and that is true.

Mary Chamberlain, *Narratives of Exile and Return*, London, 1997, pp. 213–14.

1.7   Direct recruitment of West Indians: British Rail

Many of the West Indian immigrants who made their to Britain arrived as a result of direct recruitment from British firms.

In 1960 I was in charge of the Barbados police canteen. British Rail were recruiting in the West Indies at the time, and my superintendent said it would be a good experience to spend two years overseas before returning to train as an officer. So I went through the recruitment stages at the Barbados Labour Office. You had to take a test, write an essay on why you wanted to go to England and what you intended to do. Then there was a medical, and they checked that you didn't have a criminal record. At the end I was given a contract as a guard on the trains. They gave you a loan. You had to repay your fare over a period of years.

Black Birmingham, Birmingham, 1987, p. 14.

1.8   Direct recruitment of West Indians: London Transport

London Transport implemented one of the largest direct recruitment schemes in the West Indies, focusing especially upon Barbados.

Recruitment of 120 men and twenty women for work with the London Transport Service begins this morning at the Enmore Health Centre and at Queen's Park when Mr Charles Gomm, Recruitment Officer of the London Transport Executive and Dr James Fyfe, Medical Officer will be on hand to test and interview applicants for work on the London buses and underground railway.

Mr Gomm said yesterday at a Press Conference that employment with the London Transport Service is a good steady job with good wages, free travelling on the buses, free uniform, holidays with pay, very excellent canteens and good sports and social facilities. There is also a pension scheme for men he said.

Arrangements for the recruitment of such labour were made in the initial stages by Minister of Trade, Industry and Labour, Hon. R. G. Mapp, in conjunction with Mr Anthony Bull, a member of the London Transport Executive and much assistance has been given by the labour ministry and Mr R. N. Jack, Acting Labour Commissioner.

There was full employment in England, said Mr Gomm, and in many industries, staff was required, public transport being no exception. The London Transport Service wanted conductors and drivers to work on the underground railway system.

There were jobs, he said, in which employees could really serve their fellow men, which was a good thing at anytime. Nearly 1,000,000 people travelled every day on London Transport buses and trains, more than anywhere else in the world. It therefore followed that if they were short of staff to operate those buses and there was a difficulty, the first to feel the effect would be the public and that is why they were down here to recruit workers. London Transport, he said, needed staff if they were to do their job properly . . .

Replying to a question as to colour, Mr Gromm said there was no colour bar. The minimum height for a station man was 5 ft 4 ins, and the maximum height for a conductor was 6 ft. Applicants would be given a written test, an application form to fill in and an interview. The primary requirements were a good knowledge of figuring and an ability to cope with all types of passengers without getting flustered.

For the railmen, prime requisite was good colour vision, and for all sections, good physical condition was necessary.

Selectees will be required to sign an agreement to remain with the London Transport Service for minimum of twelve months, and will be on the payroll of the Service from their arrival in England. They will undergo a two weeks training session starting one day after arrival. They will be accommodated at hostels within easy reach of work and they will have to pay approximately £3 10s for board and lodging.

If they so desire, they can attend evening classes. The services of the National health Service will be at their disposal and periodical health checks will be made by the medical officers of the London Transport Service.

Barbados Advocate, 7 February 1956.

1.9 Emigration from Ireland

Migration from Ireland to England is a centuries-old tradition which continued into the post-war years for the same basic reason, a richer England attracting people from a poorer Ireland. Nevertheless, a particular set of circumstances usually played a role in each decision to move. Ainna Fawcett-Henesy recalls her own particular move away from Limerick.

I knew I had to get away from home as my parents were rigid and strict. If you kissed a boy you were 'cheap'. Really, I didn't have a social life in Ireland. I wasn't allowed out to my first céilí until I was eighteen. I was told to be home at half past ten, and when I arrived at the door at eleven, I got walloped. Being walloped was not an unusual occurrence in our household. If you were home late, you were out to get yourself pregnant . . .

I just knew I had to leave home to survive. There was no question of me going to university when I left school. I can remember my father saying, 'You'll get married and have children, right?' Though when I said I wanted to be a nurse, he pulled out every stop to encourage me.

I had an interview for the Regional Hospital in Limerick. There were people my father knew on the board. I had my hair done in a real sixties look, turned out at the ends. I wore this bright pink suit with a navy blouse. I thought I looked terrific. When I arrived in, they asked me why I wanted to be a nurse. I replied, 'Do you know, I'm not sure!' I remember deciding that I was going to tell the truth and not give them the usual 'Oh, it's because I care about people.' I wasn't selected and there was furore at home. 'Who'd be giving you a job looking like that? Sure you look like a street-girl.' My justification for not being appointed was because there were 144 applicants for four vacancies. In later years I thanked God I wasn't offered that job, because I would have had to live at home, which would have been dreadful.

My father really suffered. He was embarrassed and angry that his daughter had not been selected. Then it was decided that I would train in England, where an uncle of mine was on the board of governors at a Warwickshire hospital; he could 'keep an eye on me'. My father made an advance trip to the UK to prepare the way for me! He drove us all up to Dublin. I had a new dressing gown and suitcase. It was a parting of the ways. I was very frightened.

Rita Wall, *Leading Lives: Irish Women in Britain*, Dublin, 1991, pp. 77–9.

1.10   Arrival in England

Upon first arriving in England many immigrants had problems with orientation, often desperately trying to find a single contact, as Mr Chaudry from Pakistan remembered. Asked if he knew anyone in London, he replied as follows.

Er, yes. I know there was Mr M. X. who was a radio mechanic there and I have his address and I have a couple address in Glasgow. But I have only three pound in my pocket went from airport to Victoria and ask for Glasgow ticket. It was about two pound fifty. And then I haven't got that two pound fifty to reach Glasgow, otherwise I have few friends in Glasgow who were doing some rag trade there. So if I end up in Glasgow then I was working in a, er, either in some distillery or some rag trade . . . This was an accident where I enter in it but I came Victoria to Euston to Onslow and then end up at address Hayes in the middle of the night about, that was the last Tube. And there was an English man who helped me to enter in the house and suddenly we're entering the back door. Nobody was opening the door, so we went through the kitchen window and, er, he said, Are you sure this is your friend's house? I say, yes. And suddenly they got up and that fellow ran away and left me there. An I said who I am and they say, All right. There was M. X., who was working in company name Aviation. He knows me through Mr M. X. that Doctor M. X. is coming here. So he say, come on, and I slept on his bed and start snoring and he start reading because he was tutored in Southall Technical College. So I snored about six or seven hours and then I left, saw a note there that where is my breakfast, what shall I eat and where. So I got up in the morning and have my breakfast there and then in the following day I met M. X., who was in Abbot's Road, and there was another four or five Pakistani boys and Indian. So we became a part of a family and from there we change another house in Beaconsfield Road. And then there was another person came and he said that he has bought a new house which is address just along the road. So I was there and spend nearly two years. Then my children came in 1963 and we moved to Ranella Road.

Museum of London, Oral History Archive, 93/117, Interview with Mr Chaudry.

1.11 Government attitudes during the 1950s

Although the Conservative and Labour governments did not display overt hostility towards the entry of Commonwealth immigrants during the course of the 1940s and 1950s, they, and the civil servants who served them, never felt comfortable about the numbers entering and had considered restrictions throughout these two decades. The Conservative Home Secretary, Sir David Maxwell Fyfe, drew up the following memorandum for a Cabinet meeting on 30 January 1954.

At their meeting on 18 December 1952 the Cabinet invited me to arrange for officials of the Department concerned to examine the possibilities of preventing any further increases in the number of coloured people seeking employment in this country (C.C(52) 106th Conclusions, Minute 7). I have recently received the report of the inter-departmental Committee which I set up to enquire into this matter and which has reviewed the general position arising from the continued immigration into Great Britain of coloured people from the colonies.

2. It would obviously be impossible to discriminate openly against coloured people as such in administration or legislation in the field of employment. After a thorough examination of the possibilities the Committee have come to the conclusion that it is not practicable to take steps to prevent coloured people obtaining employment once they are in this country. Any action to that end would have to be directed to preventing them or discouraging them from entering the United Kingdom.

3. In accordance with Ministerial directions, such administrative action as is possible to discourage immigration of coloured people into this country from the colonies has been taken over the last few years. For instance, special action has been taken in colonial territories to make stowing away on ships more difficult by tightening dock control. The governments of West African territories have taken special steps to hinder the issue of passports and travel documents to men not known to follow regular employment and whose financial position is not sound. In those colonial territories from which most of the coloured immigrants come publicity has been given to the fact that accommodation over here is hard to find and unskilled workers often have difficulty in getting employment. In this country immigration officers have been given instructions to

require strict proof of British nationality and to refuse leave to stowaways and others who cannot produce written evidence that they are British subjects.

4. The general effect of these measures has been to reduce by more than half the number of coloured stoaways who succeeded in entering the United Kingdom, but stowaways represent only a small part of the problem. It is possible that the measures have had a slight effect on the numbers leaving colonial territories as fare-paying passengers from the West Indies. The governments of the West Indian territories have been unwilling to put restrictions on the issue of passports to British subjects who appear to be entitled to them and it would seem that in any case such action would require legislation which is not politically practicable. It is not to be expected that administrative measures alone will do much to prevent an influx to the United Kingdom, with its better employment prospects and social services, of coloured people from colonial territories with employment problems.

5. The conclusion is, therefore, that there is no effective means of stopping this influx without legislation which would give power to control immigration of British subjects to this country by giving immigration officers authority to refuse leave to land, as in the case of aliens, and would confer power to deport to their place of origin British subjects from overseas who failed to abide by the conditions attached to the grant of leave to land. There could be no question of seeking such power to deal only with coloured people; it would have to be a power which could be exercised in relation to any British subject from overseas. Not only would such legislation be a complete break with the traditional British principle that any British subject has a right to enter freely and remain in the United Kingdom but the administration of the control would put a greatly increased burden on the immigration service, and also on the Ministry of Labour if, as would probably be thought desirable, some system of regulation of the employment of British subjects from overseas was adopted as part of the arrangements. The need to grant leave to land to British subjects arriving at ports in this country would lead to much greater delay in clearing travellers through the controls and would undoubtedly give rise to much resentment.

'Employment of Coloured People': Cabinet memorandum drawn up by Sir David Maxwell Fyfe, 30 January 1954, quoted in David

Goldsworthy (ed.), *The Conservative Government and the End of Empire, 1951–1957*, Part III, *Economic and Social Policies*, London, 1994, pp. 389–90.

1.12   The campaign for the Commonwealth Immigrants Act, 1962

Although the first piece of legislation to prevent the entry of immigrants in the Commonwealth was not passed until 1962, the campaign for it had begun as soon as former colonials began entering Britain. Cyril Osborne, Conservative MP for Louth, did as much as anyone else to bring national attention to the issue, both in the country at large, and, as here, in the House of Commons.

The real crux of the problem is this. Has the United Kingdom, as the mother country, any duty to the rest of the Commonwealth which other members of the Commonwealth say they do not owe to one another?

I want to deal with this problem not so much from the moral issue as from the practical economic, social and industrial point of view, and ask the House to consider whether the United Kingdom can continue to accept indefinitely unrestricted immigration irrespective of its quality and quantity . . .

Why is it that, apart from the social and difficult racial problems that arise, I think that there must be some control of immigration, starting with a limitation on the least desirable types? I would remind the House of our basic economic situation. There are more than 50 million people in these islands, and we grow enough food for only 30 million. On the basis of our own food production there are already 20 million too many in these islands. We have no raw materials except coal. Two days ago we discussed the very difficult situation of the coal industry. We have to import 40 per cent of our foodstuffs and 100 per cent of our raw materials to keep us fed and employed. These have to be paid for by our exports or we face serious hunger and mass unemployment. That is why it is so important that we should limit the number of immigrants . . .

Hansard, *Parliamentary Debates*, fifth series, vol. 596, 5 December 1958, cc. 1552–6.

1.13   Entry voucher under the Commonwealth
Immigrants Act, 1962

Although the Commonwealth Immigrants Act of 1962 aimed
at curtailing immigration from the Empire and New Commonwealth, individuals from those parts of the globe could
still enter the country, provided that they obtained a voucher
to prove they would work in areas with a labour shortage.

Ministry of Labour   Ref. No.   *0150706*
VOUCHER
Issued for the purposes of Section 2 of the
COMMONWEALTH IMMIGRANTS ACT, 1962

Voucher   *No. 012733*   Date of Expiry   *2nd March, 1963*
Full Name   Gurdial Singh
                 V. & P. O. Paddi Sura Singh
Address   *Teh. Carshanker, Distt. Hoshiar Pur (PB)*
Date of Birth   *12.5.26*   Sex *M*   Country of Birth   *India*
Occupation   *Ex-Govt. Employee*
Passport No.   ——   Country of issue of passport   ——

Notes

1. This voucher must be produced together with a valid passport to the Immigration Officer at the port of arrival in the United Kingdom. Failure to produce it may result in refusal of admission.
2. This voucher may be represented only by the person described therein.
3. This voucher cannot be used for entry to the United Kingdom after the date of expiry shown above, unless an extension has been granted. It does not entitle the holder to take work in Northern Ireland.

Signed on behalf of the Minister of Labour
Date   *3rd September, 1962*

Original document in the possession of Professor Gurharpal Singh,
University of Hull.

1.14   Commonwealth Immigrants Act, 1968

The Commonwealth Immigrants of 1962 still allowed people
with dark skins to settle in the country freely as long as they
held British citizenship. The Commonwealth Immigrants Act
of 1968 solved this problem by making family connections an

essential prerequisite of settlement in Britain, essentially excluding those dark people who had never lived in the UK before.

An Act to amend sections 1 and 2 of the Commonwealth Immigrants Act 1962, and Schedule 1 to that Act, and to make further provision as to Commonwealth citizens landing in the United Kingdom, the Channel Islands or the Isle of Man; and for purposes connected with the matters aforesaid.

Be it enacted by the Queen's most Excellent Majesty, by and with the advice and consent of the Lords Spiritual and Temporal, and Commons, in this present Parliament assembled, and by the authority of the same, as follows:

1. In section 1 of the principal Act (application of Part I), in subsection (2)(b) after the words 'citizen of the United Kingdom and Colonies' there shall be inserted the words 'and fulfils the condition specified in subsection (2A) of this section', and after subsection (2) there shall be inserted the following subsection:

'(2A) The condition referred to in subsection (2)(b) of this section, in relation to a person, is that he, or at least one of his parents or grandparents, –

(a) was born in the United Kingdom, or
(b) is or was a person naturalised in the United Kingdom, or
(c) became a citizen of the United Kingdom and Colonies by virtue of being adopted in the United Kingdom, or
(d) became such a citizen by being registered under Part II of the British Nationality Act 1948 or under the British Nationality Act 1964, either in the United Kingdom or in a country which, on the date on which he was so registered, was one of the countries mentioned in section 1(3) of the said Act 1948 as it had effect on that date.'

Commonwealth Immigrants Act 1968.

1.15 Family reunification

The majority of Indians and Pakistanis who initially moved to Britain consisted of single males who hoped to save up enough money to enable them to return home. While some achieved their aim, others chose the alternative of remaining and sending for their families, a process which took off during the 1960s and early 1970s. However, before they could enter the country, family members had to negotiate a series of bureaucratic hurdles, as the son of one Pakistani immigrant, born in 1959, recalls.

In 1975, I joined the Government Degree College Dudyal for further education. Our relatives often told me stories about Britain and the people of this country which interested me. So I wrote to my father saying that I would like to come to Britain. He sent me a sponsor letter and I applied for the visa to the British Embassy in Islamabad.

After one year, they wrote us a letter for an interview. We arrived after a long journey in very hot weather and we were interviewed. In the interview, they asked me so many questions that I was puzzled, but they said our documents were not enough. Their excuse was that my father didn't send us the photostat copies of his old Pakistani passport, although we had the photostat copies of my father's British passport. Then we went back home after being away for three days and spending a lot of money. I wrote a letter to my father, asking for photostat copies of his old Pakistani passport. He sent the copies direct to the British Embassy in Islamabad and they wrote to us a letter again giving us another interview and asking to bring any close male relative. We took my grandfather (my mother's father) with us. He was an old man and he had difficulty travelling a long distance. We arrived on the second day away from home. First of all, they kept us waiting from nine o'clock to three o'clock without having dinner or even a cup of tea. At last, at three o'clock, they called us and looked at everybody, then gave us another appointment without telling us the reason. The new appointment was for four months later. When we asked the reason for not having an interview, they said my grandmother was too old. Then we went back home after three days' absence and spending a lot of money for nothing. This time I was really disappointed and my interest was growing day by day.

I wrote a letter to my father again, then he wrote a letter to the British Embassy in Islamabad, complaining about [our] not having the interview. This time we didn't take my grandfather with us. Again they kept us waiting from nine o'clock to two o'clock. This time, was 20 January 1977. It was not hot and was a bit easier to wait. We were interviewed for one and a half hours and then they said, 'Come back tomorrow.' So we went back the next day and got the visa. Then we went back home after four days but I was very happy.

Saltley Local History Project, *In Search of a Future* . . . , Birmingham, n.d., pp. 10–11.

1.16   A Bangladeshi wife moves to Britain

In some cases the wives of South Asian immigrants moved to Britain reluctantly.

I was sixteen at the time of marriage. There was much that I didn't understand about marriage and having a family. But in those days it was the usual age to marry. My husband was already living in England before we wed. For quite a few years after marriage in Bangladesh I remained with my parents and parents-in-law. After every two or three years my husband would visit and stay with us for several months. In the meantime I had two children. It never crossed my mind that I would come to England some day. I didn't want to come, in any case. I still remember how it came about. My husband suddenly arrived in Bangladesh and announced: 'This time I shall take you with me to England.' It didn't take long to get our passports and visas. In those days it was not very difficult to get a visa for Britain. Nor were there all the severe restrictions that they've imposed these days.

I am uncertain of the exact date or year when I arrived in England . . . As near as I can recall, it was 1969. I think I was the first Bengali woman in Sheffield.

Safuran Ara and Debjani Chatterjee (eds), *Home to Home: Reminiscences of Bangladeshi Women in Sheffield*, Sheffield, 1995, pp. 11–12.

1.17   The expulsion of Ugandan Asians

One of the last significant influxes into Britain consisted of approximately 28,000 Ugandan Asians who entered the country in the early 1970s as a result of intolerance in Uganda

51

and the fact that they held British passports. The movement reached a peak in the late summer and autumn of 1972.

President Idi Amin announced tonight that Uganda will ask Britain to take over responsibility for all the Asians holding British passports. In a speech to troops he said there was 'no room in Uganda' for British Asians, whom he described as economic saboteurs and corrupters . . .

General Amin told the troops at Toroto, eastern Uganda: 'I am going to ask Britain to take responsibility for all Asians in Uganda who are holding British passports because they are sabotaging the economy of the country.

I want the economy to be in the hands of Ugandan citizens, especially black Ugandans. I want you troops to help me protect the country from saboteurs.'

The Times, 5 August 1972.

1.18   The last sight of Uganda

Clearly, leaving Uganda for the last time proved a painful process, as one refugee recalled.

At the airport, there was the expected long queue and the endless arguments about whether the weight of one's baggage was excessive. Once into the lounge, the old collapsed into the cushioned chairs, the babies went to sleep, and the young took to some serious drinking. While emptying my second glass of Uganda *Waragi* (a drink with a banana base), I felt a hand firmly grip my left shoulder. It was Ahmed, an old high-school friend; his brother was a major in the army. The last I had seen of him was in early September when we had bitterly argued over the political implications of Amin's decree and the class basis of his support. He ordered two drinks. Without saying a word, we gulped it down. I tried to reciprocate the gesture. He held my hand and ordered a second round and then a third. The loudspeakers announced it was time to embark. I got up and arranged my hand luggage. Ahmed extended his hand.

'Goodbye, comrade.'
'Goodbye, brother.'

Once on the East African Airways plane I took my seat and tried to sleep; but sleep I could not.

'A drink?' the ever smiling and polite hostess suggested.

'No thank you.' I had drugged myself with enough drink already. I tried to look out the window. It was too dark. Just as well. But I could still see clearly in my mind my home, or rather, the different houses we had lived in while my father moved up from a petty clerk to a well-to-do auctioneer, in times when commerce had been lucrative, when an hour of a trader's labour was worth days of a labourer's work. I could see the mosque around which we played as children, the primary school which we used to walk to early in the morning, carrying our lunch packages of chapati and curried potatoes; the years in a secondary school when, as a Boy Scout, I went climbing the mountains, trekking through the swamps and savannas of the countryside, swimming in ponds and lakes and learning to climb trees the way a monkey does.

Mahmood Mamdani, *From Citizen to Refugee: Uganda Asians come to Britain*, London, 1973, pp. 67–8.

1.19   Britain as an impenetrable fortress

At the end of the twentieth century Britain has become one of the most difficult countries in the world for refugees to enter. Immigration and asylum laws play a large role in this, but receive support from the press. Under the headline 'Gypsies invade Dover, hoping for a handout' the *Independent* reported the following story.

Scores of gypsies from the Czech Republic and Slovakia . . . have been put into bed-and-breakfast and guest houses on the Kent coast after arriving in Dover at the weekend in the hope of being granted asylum here.

The influx of would-be immigrants, who are claiming racial persecution at home, took local authorities by surprise. They are being put up in bed-and-breakfast hostels in Dover and in a family centre in the town and at a nursing home in Margate. On Friday 113 gypsies arrived by ferry after travelling by coach through Europe; another thirty-two landed on Saturday and twenty-two more yesterday.

Gwynn Prosser, Labour MP for Dover, will today meet Mike O'Brien, the immigration minister, to request assistance. A warning by Roger Gale, Conservative MP for Thanet North, that 3,000 more gypsies were on their way, was condemned as scaremongering by Mr O'Brien yesterday. However, Mr O'Brien acknowledged that further arrivals were inevitable until word filtered back to Slovakia and the Czech Republic that Britain was not a soft option. Some gypsies report having seen a television programme at home which said that the British welfare system would support them.

The influx of gypsies began several months ago, but until Friday was just a trickle, comprising about sixty families in total.

Of the weekend's arrivals, thirty-six people were immediately deported and twenty-eight left voluntarily. Twenty-two others, mainly heads of families, were detained by immigration authorities. 'Our resources are being drained quite rapidly,' said Terry Birkett, leader of Dover District Council. 'Kent cannot bear the full burden of these people.'

Mr O'Brien said that each of the cases was being considered individually. He added that asylum had not been granted to any of the gypsies who had arrived in recent months. 'We are determined to protect the integrity of the system from abuse, so that we can continue to provide for genuine refugees.'

Independent, 20 October 1997.

1.20   Escape from Sarajevo

Despite the restrictions upon entry during the 1990s some refugees still managed to enter Britain to begin a new life, escaping from intolerable conditions in their homeland and making a difficult journey, as 'S.H.' recalls.

In June 1988 I finished secondary school as a straight A student. In October of that year I enrolled at the Medical School of Sarajevo University. I completed my pre-clinical training. It was a promising start, and I felt great. Then in April 1992 war broke out in Sarajevo. For the first few weeks we attended lectures regularly, but as the war claimed its first victims, classes were cancelled. On 30 April I took the last train out of Sarajevo. I went to Jajce, where I joined my parents. We all thought the war would soon stop and that we would get back to our normal lives. But the war spread like wildfire, and at the end of May we found ourselves surrounded by the Serb army. The only way out of the besieged town was past the gunfire between the two front lines. We managed to escape by running. The elderly and children were killed because they could not run fast enough. My father was badly wounded when he tried to protect me. (Our escape was a nightmare; I want to forget it.) After fifty-two hours of marching through no man's land, across Mount Vlasić, we reached the town of Travnik, where we received first aid and were given something to eat. I was allowed to leave Bosnia, but my parents had to stay. I went to Zagreb, Croatia, where I met a family friend. She took me to Graz, where she lives. Since my sister was already in England (she went there as an *au pair* in February 1992), I wanted to join her. I arrived in London on 21 July 1992 and applied for political asylum in November of the same year. In September 1992 I started to attend an English language school to study for the First Certificate in English, and in October 1993 I enrolled at the Charing Cross and Westminster Medical School as a full-time student. I am determined to finish my studies.

Zdenko Lešić (ed.), *Children of Atlantis: Voices from the Former Yugoslavia*, Budapest, 1994, p. 67.

1.21   Arrival in London

> Once they arrive in Britain, refugees face basic practical problems of money, food and accommodation. The plight of Anab Ali Mohammmed, who fled from Somalia to Britain in 1986 with five children, was especially difficult.

In Somalia I was working for the Somali Academy of Sciences and Arts and I was a clerk there and my husband was a police officer. I came here on the 1st of January 1986 with five children, four of my own and one other.

In Somalia we met many problems from the Somali government – not me really but my husband. The main problem is that the government decided to destroy the tribe that's called the Isaak tribe who wanted to live in the north of Somalia. The government tried to sack the people from the departments and throw people in prison and some of them they killed without reason. By that time me and my husband decided to escape. The problem was that my children were all young because it was four years ago – the eldest one was six, the youngest four months, Abdi was eighteenth months.

My husband went to Ethiopia, escaped from the border by foot. I got to the airport in secret. Some of my relatives helped me because in Africa if you give some money to some of the police in the airports they try to help you. I escaped at midnight to London I didn't know anyone.

I had $1,000 cash and my plan was to ask the British Government for political asylum but I didn't know what to do first. When I came to Heathrow I went from the airport to try to find a taxi to go to a hotel and I met a Somali man and he asked me,

'Where do you want to go?' and I said,

'I want to go to a hotel', and he said,

'Do you know any Somalis in London?' and I said,

'I don't know anybody'. He said,

'How much money do you have?' I told him and he said,

'It's little money, in one week, if you go to a hotel, the hotel will take 200 a night. How can you manage?'

It was difficult for me to know what to do. The man tried to help me. He called me a taxi to bring me to the Seamen's Mission on the Commercial Road, he goes inside and said, 'I have a woman with five children here and she doesn't know where to go. Can any of you help to give her somewhere to sleep tonight?' The people didn't take this decision quickly, because it's a large family, so one of the Somalis, a seventy-five-year-old man, said, 'Yes, I can give these people my flat tonight, but tomorrow where are they going?'

At that time the Somali people who lived in Tower Hamlets didn't know anything about immigration problems or political asylum because I think I was the first or second person in Tower Hamlets to come for political asylum. After one month I'd finished all my money. I buy some clothes for the children, because it is winter, so when I have left they bring me to the homeless section of Tower Hamlets and they sent me to a bed and breakfast hotel in Edgware Road where I lived for seven months. It was very difficult for me because there's no other Somalis living there. I only knew a little bit English so it was very difficult because when I lived in Somalia I lived in a large house but when I got to bed and breakfast there were two rooms – one is on the fourth floor and the other one is downstairs. There were other foreigners there who complained about the children. Then they gave me this flat.

The two youngest children were going to the children's hospital at the time, so the doctor tried to help me and called me a social worker. She came and saw where I lived and wrote a letter to Tower Hamlets and then Tower Hamlets gave me this flat. I came here and I started my life again. It's nice but I had no central heating for the first three years, so it was very cold. In 1987 we lived in the living room, as it was a bad winter. Anyway, I pass all the bad things now. My flat has full central heating and double glazing now and the children are growing up.

Somali Relief Association, *The Somalis: An Invisible Community in Crisis*, London, 1992.

1.22   Britain abuses the human rights of refugees

> Those few people who actually did manage to make it into Britain in the 1990s often found their human rights abused.

In November 1994 the British government stated that over 650 people seeking asylum in the UK were being held in various prisons, detention centres and police cells around the country. The government estimated that the cost of holding these people was £800 per detainee per week . . .

The British government's treatment of refugees and asylum seekers, and its human rights record in relation to immigrants, seriously undermine any claims it may have to be a liberal, tolerant and compassionate state. Formidable legal barriers have been put up in recent years to prevent people who are escaping persecution from arriving in the UK. Each year the authorities subject thousands of people (asylum seekers and visitors) to administrative detentions, over which there is no judicial oversight. Hundreds of people are held in detention in conditions which allow them no dignity and are sometimes cruel and degrading. Many are subject to expulsion without an adequate opportunity to appeal or, if they are deported on grounds of 'national security', without an opportunity for a fair and public hearing. Deportations are sometimes carried out with excessive force.

Families are kept apart by the operation of immigration law and rules. The onus of proof is always on the applicants to satisfy an immigration official about the validity of their claim to enter the UK – and officials interpret the law very differently when processing the claims of people of different countries, cultures and races. Children who fail to satisfy an official that they are 'related as claimed' to parents in the UK, and spouses who fail to satisfy an official that they did not marry 'primarily' for immigration reasons, are refused permission to travel to the UK. Families are split up, sometimes permanently.

National Council for Civil Liberties, *The Last Resort: Violations of the Human Rights of Migrants, Refugees and Asylum Seekers*, London, 1995, pp. 7–8.

1.23   The case of two Zairian women

Those people whose human rights the British state ignores have already faced traumatic experiences in their country of origin. Two Zairian women, who had been raped by state officials at home, then spent years trying to secure political asylum in Britain.

The first, Marie [pseudonym], was found wandering around London airport in 1993, alone and confused. A few days earlier she had been gang-raped by five or six soldiers in her home in Kinshasa, capital of Zaire. Her husband, a member of an opposition group, had 'disappeared'.

Marie's application for asylum in the UK was refused. On appeal, the adjudicator dismissed her appeal but recommended that, given her suffering, she be allowed to stay on compassionate grounds. This was ignored. In March 1995 the government made arrangements to deport her to Zaire. She went into hiding and at the end of the year was granted one year's leave to remain.

At last she received welfare payments to buy food and shelter. Another Zairian woman, Bénédicte, was denied this basic right. She arrived in the UK in February 1996, days after a legal ruling that only those who apply for asylum immediately at the port of entry are eligible to receive welfare payments while the claim is assessed. The process can take more than nineteenth months.

Bénédicte had been arrested in Zaire at a memorial for her husband, who had been shot dead during an anti-government rally. In prison she was repeatedly raped by her guards. An older guard finally took pity on her and smuggled her out in a sack.

She arrived in London by train, and then made her way to the Home Office, some miles away, where she applied for asylum. She was subsequently denied welfare payments on the grounds that she had not applied for asylum immediately on arrival.

A legal challenge was made to the Court of Appeal about the denial of welfare payments, which ruled in her favour . . .

The legal victory was short-lived. In July 1996, the British parliament passed legislation denying welfare payments to all those who failed to apply for asylum immediately on arrival and to people appealing against rejection of their asylum claim. However, in October a new High Court ruling required local government authorities to provide some assistance to asylum-seekers. In December, for the first time in fifty years, the Red Cross distributed food parcels in London, the capital. The recipients were destitute asylum-seekers.

Amnesty International, *Refugees: Human Rights have no Borders*, London, 1997, p. 62.

1.24 Do you really want to leave Ireland?

> For those who can still move to Britain at the end of the twentieth century the decision to migrate requires much thought and pain, as one organisation pointed out to Irish young people.

Whatever your reason for leaving Ireland, emigration means that you leave your home and family in search of work, new opportunities and/or a life elsewhere.

It means that you leave behind your friends and colleagues and start afresh in a strange, unfamiliar and foreign place with unfamiliar people in a different culture.

It also means that you may never again live permanently in Ireland; going back there just for holidays and family visits. You owe it to yourself to make a informed and responsible decision about emigration.

Be honest and weigh up your present life in Ireland with that which another country may offer. Remember you will lose daily contact with family and friends and a secure roof over your head.

To make the change you will need to be independent, be able to make decisions, budget your money, pay your bills and be able to survive without the support of your family and friends. It might be that you will be taking on responsibility for the first time – remember you will be responsible to yourself for yourself.

Emigration is not like going on a few weeks' holiday; it is not the same as travelling about; it is not the same as a cultural exchange. For some it is an opportunity to broaden horizons, for others a forced course of action because of unemployment or lack of opportunity at home and may mean a permanent stay in another country.

Action Group for Irish Youth, *A Guide to London for Young Irish People*, London, n.d.

1.25   The Irish government calls its people back

A significant percentage of all immigrants who have made their way to Britain have returned to their land of origin of their own free will. The Irish government has made efforts to entice many of its skilled and professional people who moved to England.

The Irish Government's recruitment drive for hundreds of skilled workers continues throughout Britain for the next two weeks.

The Republic's fast-growing industries have vacancies for up to 500 mechanical/production engineers, electrical/electronic engineers, electronic technicians, chemical technologists, systems analysts, mechanical/electrical draughtsmen, toolmakers and fitters.

Relocation grants of up to £2,000 are being provided – as are other financial inducements plus assistance in securing houses.

Interviewing began on Monday at the London Tara Hotel. This Wednesday and Thursday interviews take place in Coventry – followed by Birmingham, Leeds, Manchester, Liverpool, Glasgow and Edinburgh.

The campaign supplements recruitment by individual firms and a spokesman for the Industrial Development Authority has said that, in addition to filling current vacancies, they want to keep a register of technically qualified people interested in moving back to Ireland when suitable jobs become available.

Most technical people in Ireland are now more highly paid than their counterparts in Britain. The relocation grants and aid with housing are seen as additional inducements.

It's the biggest recruitment campaign ever carried out in Britain by Irish sources. The country's own educational institutions and training establishments aren't able to meet the demands of the industrialisation which is now taking place in many areas. In recent years some 800 overseas firms have established factories in the Republic.

'The fact is that we now have the highest rate of growth in manufacturing output and also the highest rate of export growth in Western Europe,' a spokesman for the IDA said.

The likelihood is that for a number of years to come the Republic will have to recruit abroad, and particularly among the Irish in Britain, for a large proportion of its technically qualified people.

Irish Post, 9 June 1979.

1.26   The desire to return

Even immigrants who have not returned to their place of birth often have a strong desire to do so, as Irene Maddon, a Jamaican living in Sheffield, asserted.

I want to go back. It's my home. My house is there, my sister and brother-in-law is looking after it. My sisters are there, I am the only one that left and come here.

I always says, 'I may be slow but I'm coming back.' I've been home four times, you know, the last time is August '86. I take the boys that were born here, take them there to show them my country. And when they land in the land of Jamaica, they were shocked. They says, 'Mum, why did you leave this country and go to England?'

I says, 'I like to know different place. You can't sit all the time in your own town. You have to travel and know different people.'

They always say to me, 'Mum, you come here all work, work, work. You never stop. You don't do that in Jamaica.'

I says, 'No, love, you do what you feel like to do. If you don't feel like work today you just sit at home and do home work. If you feel you want to go out and do something for money, well, you do that.'

I've got a lot of experience in this country. Don't get me wrong, I'm not an ungrateful woman. I like it here in some ways but when it comes to the colour bar I hate that. I think all of us are one people. We're all God's children.

From the start I never had the intention to stop here forever. 'Home, sweet home.' No matter if I'm getting a thousand pounds a day, at the back of my mind is still my country. I may be happy outward but I'm not happy inward. I'm going back home if it pleases the Lord.

Christine Gregory (ed.), *Taste the Roughness: Kelvin Caribbean Lunch Club Memories*, Sheffield, 1991, pp. 103–4.

1.27   Contentment in England

Despite the problems faced by immigrants, some have no regrets about their decision to move and have no desire to return. Such individuals include Syed Rasul who moved to Birmingham from Sylhet (now Pakistan) in 1944.

I am very glad I came to England, because . . . although it's different from how it used to be, still . . . better than my country. I think that for every one thousand people who don't like us, there are a million who do. I love this country, and I would like my children to stay here. The young generation is too different. I still think of my own country – my mother and father – because I was born in a different life, lived in a different life and my children don't know any of that. I still think of all my family, my mother's family, father's family, everybody . . . my family is so big . . . My brother lives over here – I say to my son, 'You must go to your uncle's house.' He says, 'Who is my uncle?' I say, 'Don't be silly.' But he doesn't want to know . . . these days it's all different. He says, 'Daddy, you are my family, I am your family, that's all.' I say, 'Alright, if that's what you want.'

Caroline Adams (ed.), *Across Seven Seas and Thirteen Rivers: Life Stories of Pioneer Sylhetti Settlers in Britain*, London, 1987, p. 186.

2

Geography, demography and economics

The geographical, demographic and economic patterns of post-war immigrants to Britain have tended to differ from those of the native population, although the degree of difference has varied from one group to another. In geographical terms, most newcomers tended to settle in the inner city, as a result of discrimination, economic position and desire to concentrate near their countrymen, although, in the long run, many groups have moved into the suburbs. Demographically, many of the post-war immigrants to Britain, especially from the Commonwealth, initially consisted mostly of men, who were followed by large families but, with the passage of time, subsequent generations have come to approximate more and more to the patterns of natives. Economically, most post-war immigrants and their offspring have worked in occupations towards the bottom of the employment ladder, although many have experienced social mobility.

2.1   The early emergence of urban concentrations

From the early days of their arrival in Britain, post-war immigrants tended to settle in cities, as the example of Jamaicans illustrates.

The migrants tend to be distributed among the largest cities, with London retaining the lion's share, approximately 15,000, and the following cities:

Birmingham (including Coventry,   approx.   2,000
   Wolverhampton, Dudley)

Manchester (Greater)	approx.	1,000
Liverpool	"	1,250
Leeds	"	250
Sheffield	"	250
Nottingham	"	400
Newcastle	"	250
Glasgow and Edinburgh	"	250

All these figures are, of course, based on estimates and are reasonably approximate.

It is difficult to explain the shape of the distribution, but it has been observed that approximately 80 per cent of any large group on landing entrain for London (out of 850 West Indian arrivals in the first nine months of 1953, 650 went to London addresses) and it is known that individuals constantly seek advice to move to the provinces in search of work. Most of the post-war settlement has been in areas where there were already coloured communities existing before the war. This tendency has encouraged a great deal of overcrowding in bad housing and social conditions which have thus become associated in the public mind with the migration of coloured people. London has always possessed a large Colonial population, which might have attracted other coloured migrants, who would have found the environment more cosmopolitan, and accustomed to their presence. It would have been less difficult to find accommodation, obtain employment and enjoy social intercourse in a host community that had accepted the presence of the former coloured group. Further, the new migrants will have found security and friendship and valuable advice from the older settlers.

PRO CO 1028 36, 'Interim Report on Condition of Jamaicans in the United Kingdom, 1954'.

2.2 The development of ethnic minorities in cities

The concentration of immigrants in cities continued throughout the post-war period. Places and percentages are listed in the accompanying table.

Black and minority groups by district, 1991

District	Thousands	% of black and ethnic minority	% of total minority population	Largest minority (%)
Birmingham	206.8	21.5	6.87	Pakistani (6.9)
Brent	109.1	44.9	3.63	Indian (17.2)
Newham	89.9	42.4	2.99	Indian (13.0)
Ealing	89.1	32.4	2.96	Indian (16.1)
Leicester	77.1	28.5	2.56	Indian (22.3)
Lambeth	73.8	30.1	2.45	Afro-Caribbean (15.3)
Bradford	71.5	15.6	2.38	Pakistani (9.9)
Hackney	61.0	33.7	2.03	Afro-Caribbean (15.3)
Haringey	58.7	29.0	1.95	Afro-Caribbean (11.6)
Tower Hamlets	57.1	35.4	1.90	Bangladeshi (22.9)
Croydon	55.7	17.6	1.83	Afro-Caribbean (6.0)
Waltham Forest	54.3	25.6	1.81	Afro-Caribbean (8.5)
Barnet	53.7	18.3	1.79	Indian (7.3)
Southwark	53.4	24.4	1.78	Afro-Caribbean (10.6)
Harrow	52.6	26.3	1.75	Indian (16.1)
Manchester	51.2	12.6	1.70	Pakistani (3.8)
Wandsworth	50.9	20.2	1.69	Afro-Caribbean (7.7)
Lewisham	50.8	22.0	1.69	Afro-Caribbean (12.5)
Hounslow	49.9	24.4	1.66	Indian (14.3)
Redbridge	48.4	21.4	1.61	Indian (10.2)

Source Richard Skellington, *'Race' in Britain Today*, Second Edition, London, 1996, p. 58.

2.3   Italian Bedford

The newcomers of the post-war period often moved into areas with no previous experience of immigration, transforming English ones into immigrant enclaves, as the example of Bedford illustrates.

British, Bedford still is – but only 90 per cent so (and a 90 per cent that includes several thousands of coloured Commonwealth subjects). Nearly 7,000 of its townsmen share twenty-seven languages among them, and one of those – Italian – is a constant, musical noise in the streets. In the Roman Catholic Church, priests hear confessions in Italian. Inside Barclays Bank on the High Street, the first notice that catches one's eye reads: *Avviso ai nostri clienti Italiani.*

In the side streets, tiny greengrocers with names such as *La Bottega Italiani, Milita & Ciampa*, and *Ferretti's* practically spill great bags of pasta and jugs of Chianti on the pavement, and not to speak Italian there is to be an ignorant 'foreigner'. In the Little Italy section near Midland Road Station, an Italian Vice-consulate hangs out its sign. In Shakespeare Road, plump women in black dresses and black headscarves stand cross-armed before their doors and shout *Buon giorno* and *Come sta?* to passers by. And there are nearly 6,000 who could pass by, understand, and reply.

The roots of Napoli, Bedfordshire, were put down in 1951 in the broad belt of the Oxford Clay south of the town, where the bulk of Britain's bricks are made. Happily faced with the insatiable demands of the post-war building boom and unhappily faced with a desperate shortage of English labourers willing, in a time of affluence, to do the tough, dirty work of the brickfields, Bedford's major brickworks, in co-operation with the British and Italian Governments (but without Bedford Council's approval, a point which rankles with some) launched their 'bulk recruitment schemes', to lure underpaid, underemployed (often totally unemployed) Campanians and Calabrians from their homes 1,000 miles north from Italy's toe with promises and realities golden to them: steady, well paid, secure jobs.

John Barr, 'Napoli, Bedfordshire', *New Society*, 2 April 1964, p. 7.

2.4   The transformation of Brixton

West Indians transformed Brixton in the same way that Italians affected Bedford.

Brixton is the central area and the central parliamentary constituency of the Borough of Lambeth, South London, and the main settlement area of Lambeth's 10,000 or more West Indians ...

The transformation of Brixton into one of London's largest West Indian settlements has come about with dramatic speed. Unlike London's East End and dock districts, this was never an area of immigrant settlement ...

Before 1948 coloured people were so rare in Brixton that they are remembered as individuals and personalities, not lumped together as an out-group. By 1951 the census recorded 414 West Indian-born residents and by 1955 the settlement was credibly estimated at 5,000. Over the next few years the total was stabilised at about 7,500, but jumped again in 1960–62, probably in anticipation of the immigration controls which were introduced in mid-1962. After the census enumeration in early 1961 the total of 10,000 West Indians was probably swelled by a thousand or so before the controls came into force, but this again may have been more or less counterbalanced by the loss of older residents returning home or moving out of the borough ...

Most West Indians in Brixton have evolved their own short-term solutions to the housing shortage by living in single-room units, usually in one of the several hundred houses now owned by West Indian landlords.

Over the last decade or so three zones or stages of settlement and socio-economic differentiation have evolved within the West Indian settlement. First in sequence were the two crowded reception areas, Somerleyton–Geneva Roads and Angell Town. These are now mainly tenanted by new arrivals, the impoverished, the unsuccessful, the solitary, the restless and the minority of anti-social or criminal types; and this is where most basement clubs, gambling joints, noisy weekend parties and punch-ups are found. Those West Indians who become settled and financially secure usually move from these areas to the second zone: streets with longer leaseholds, a better social standing and a lower concentration of West Indian immigrants, a mile or so from the central focus of Brixton Market. In the third zone or stage comes a small group of professionals, white-collar workers, old-timers and settled artisans, living with their families in suburban houses or private or council flats in predominantly white areas ...

Cultural or recreational activities are for the great majority of Brixton West Indians confined to jazz or pop music, dancing, gambling, visits to pubs or basement drinking clubs, the occasional wedding or christening party, and watching or playing cricket or, more rarely, soccer.

Sheila Patterson (ed.), *Immigrants in London: Report of a Study Group set up by the London Council of Social Science*, London, 1963, pp. 7–12.

2.5 Difficult housing conditions

Upon their first arrival in Britain many immigrants found that the discrimination they met with, as well as the low pay they earned, meant that they found themselves living in poor, over-crowded conditions. Avtar Singh Jouhl recalled his own experience.

We came to Smethwick, my brother's house, it was in Oxford Road, Smethwick. There were many people, I thought maybe waiting for me to come, but when everybody went away there was still fifteen or sixteen people, Indians, staying at the house. In the front room, two double beds, in the bedroom upstairs, each bedroom two double beds and in the small room, one three-quarter bed and those beds with like the metal springs and big wooden headboards. No carpets in the house, it was lino in all the rooms. The food was kept under the beds and in the kitchen there was electric cooker and this – not like the present-type steel sinks, it was this china-type big sink. No hot water system, the toilet was outside, there was a tin bathtub. It was a surprise to me to see the house, a villa-type house, small one, much smaller than my own house in Jandiala, much smaller than that.

Doreen Price and Ravi Thiara (eds), *The Land of Money? Personal Accounts by Post-war Black Migrants to Birmingham*, Birmingham, 1992, p. 13.

2.6   State concern about overcrowding

From the 1950s the British state, at both the local and national level, developed concern about immigrant overcrowding.

The Council are very much concerned with cases of overseas immigrants to this country living in grossly overcrowded conditions.

In two cases recently brought to their notice the circumstances were as follows:

Case A – Man, wife, son aged four years, daughter aged twenty-two months and baby aged four months living in one furnished basement room; rent £2 10s 0d a week.

Case B – Man, wife and four children (three boys – thirteen, twelve and nine years of age and baby three weeks old) living in one furnished ground floor room; rent £3 a week.

It would appear in both the above cases that, had the landlord made the enquiries which the Housing Act says he should make before letting the accommodation, he would have ascertained that the rooms would be overcrowded. It has been found in a number of cases, however, that prospective tenants give false information as to the size of their families and, after taking possession, bring into the rooms more people or children than they said were to occupy them. In both cases the tenants have made themselves liable to prosecution but it is open to question whether any useful purpose would be served by such a course of action. The Council, however, have given instructions for overcrowding notices to be served.

In the event of certificates of overcrowding being issued by the Medical Officer of Health and forwarded to the London County Council to assist the families' application for rehousing, it would have the effect that such families might be given priority over many other cases which have been on the housing waiting list for some considerable time and it is felt that such a procedure would be grossly unfair to residents of long standing.

The Council feel that the whole position with regard to the housing of these overseas immigrants is most unsatisfactory and that the problem is a national one with which local authorities cannot be expected to cope. It is considered that some steps should be taken at national level to ensure that these immigrants have satisfactory living accommodation in this country before they arrive.

PRO CO 1028 37, 'Letter from Hammersmith Town Clerk to Ministry of Housing and Local Government and to the Ministry of Health, 2 January 1956'.

2.7 The persistence of poor housing conditions

Despite the passage of time, the poor state of ethnic minority housing showed limited improvement, as the Commission for Racial Equality made clear, by pointing to specific issues.

(a) *Concentration of ethnic minorities in areas of poor housing.* Seventy per cent of the ethnic minority population are concentrated in 10 per cent of census enumeration districts and these districts contain disproportionately high numbers of households living at the statutory overcrowding level and lacking basic amenities.

(b) *Allocation to less desirable accommodation in local authority housing.* A study of council housing in Inner London Boroughs carried out by the Runnymede Trust shows that 52 per cent of ethnic minority tenants (defined as tenants with both parents born in the New Commonwealth) live in high density pre-war council estates compared with 22 per cent of the general council tenant population. Seventy-seven per cent of minority tenants live in high density estates compared with 56 per cent of the total population, and the proportion of minority tenants living on estates built since 1961 is only half that of tenants as a whole. Recent lettings by the GLC and Islington confirm that ethnic minorities are disproportionately represented among those allocated less desirable accommodation.

(c) *Shared dwellings and density of population.* The 1971 Census Household Composition Tables showed that 21 per cent of households whose chief economic supporter was born in the New Commonwealth lived in shared dwellings compared with 4 per cent of all households. The average number of persons per room in the total population was 0.59, the figure for New Commonwealth was nearly double, 0.93. The PEP Survey of Racial Disadvantage has shown that 30 per cent of West Indian households and 22 per cent of Asian households live in shared dwellings compared with 3.8 per cent of the general population. Using a person per bedroom measure of density of occupation, the median number of persons per bedroom for whites is 1.25, for West Indians 1.66 and for Asians 1.83.

(d) *Housing amenities.* Whereas less than one household in a hundred in the total population does not enjoy exclusive use of both cooking stove and sink, 8 per cent of New Commonwealth households are in these circumstances. Eighteen per cent of the general population have to share the use of bath, hot water and inside WC, whereas 33 per cent of West Indian, 35 per cent of Indian and 57 per cent of Pakistani/Bangladeshi households share these amenities.

Commission for Racial Equality, *Housing Need among Ethnic Minorities*, London, 1977.

2.8   The consequences of poor housing conditions

Poor housing conditions had detrimental effects on the sanitary conditions experienced by immigrants, as the case of Slough indicates.

It should be obvious, even to the lay person, that overcrowded living conditions present dangerous opportunities for the rapid spread of communicable diseases if and when they occur. To stop at the foregoing statement would be an oversimplification of the matter, however, since two factors are concerned when we speak of 'dangerous opportunities' in connection with communicable diseases. The first is the matter of residential proximity of social contact between the ill person and others. Little can be done at present to radically change the overcrowded living conditions of coloured immigrants in Slough and so there would seem to be a considerable possibility of epidemical problems in connection with certain illnesses. Lest prejudiced minds jump to prejudiced conclusions, we would point out that coloured immigrant concentrations are not the only possible causes of such health hazards. Crowded factories and public transport are two examples of others.

The second factor relates to cleanliness and sanitation measures. We are prepared to admit that some – a definite minority, in our opinion – coloured immigrant dwellings are not regularly maintained inside to a desirable level of cleanliness, in the face of difficult and crowded conditions. The interiors of virtually all the many dwellings visited during the study were visibly clean and neat.

We have favourably mentioned the interior living space of immigrant dwellings, but the apparent problem is one of group sanitation. Dustbin collections intended to serve the needs of a block of ten semi-detached houses become less efficient, if not adequate, when two or three of those houses are occupied by from nine to sixteen (or more) persons each. A house with one small bathroom is satisfactory for perhaps five adults, but cannot really be considered adequate for two or three times that number. Cooking facilities suitable for one family may not be kept up to a necessary standard of cleanliness under the pressure of regular use by three or four families. Our observations disclosed that it is quite possible for a building exterior to be drab and untidy, for entrance halls to be dingy, but for the individual living rooms to be acceptably clean throughout. The cleanliness of actual living space was, in fact, the rule rather than the exception. We cannot, therefore, accept as valid the occasional and generalised condemnation of coloured immigrants based on the theme of 'they live, by choice, in squalid filth'. Immigrants do not enjoy their housing situation, but they seem to accept the realities of a compressed population structure and frequently display considerable ingenuity in dealing with the problems arising from a shortage of living space.

Slough Council for Social Services, *Colour and Community*, London, 1964, p. 49.

2.9   Prejudiced estate agents

Throughout the post-war period immigrants have faced hostility in their attempt to find housing, whether they rent from the private or the public sector, or attempt to purchase their own property. Estate agents have practised racism in a variety of ways, as an employee of one south London firm recalled.

Miss Stratton said that Mr Hughes had instructed her to put details of coloured applicants on pink cards and of white applicants on white cards. She denied Mr Hughes's claim that it was an applicant's accent rather than colour that determined the type of card on which his details and requirements were recorded. She said that a black applicant with perfect English would still be registered on a pink card.

Miss Stratton also stated that the coloured card system was designed for use in association with discriminatory instructions from vendors. She explained that, when Mr Hughes had been to view a property where the vendor had given discriminatory instructions, he would tell her this so that she could note the comment 'No pink cards' on the property cards when she typed them. In such cases, she said, she also had to pass the discriminatory instructions on to the Stondon Park office. Miss Stratton also said that vendors sometimes asked about an applicant's race or colour when staff telephoned them to make an appointment for an applicant.

Miss Stratton stated that, if a vendor had expressed a racialist preference regarding prospective purchasers, details of that property were not given to applicants listed on pink cards. She said that this was generally accepted practice in the Brockley Road office and it was done in order to avoid losing the custom of the vendors concerned. She said that if she found that, by mistake, she had given details of a property which was subject to discriminatory instructions to a coloured applicant, she would either send the applicant to view anyway and hope for the best, or make an excuse as to why the applicant could not view the property.

Miss Stratton thought there had been about four properties with discriminatory instructions during the five or six months she had

worked at the firm and that one of the vendors had been a Mrs
Florey, who may have lived in Millmark Grove. The comment 'No
coloured applicants', she said, had been written on one property
card and was later crossed out. She recalled that Mr Hughes had
been cross when he found it because it had been so obvious. She
mentioned that the comment had been put on the card by a nego-
tiator employed before she joined the firm. She said that occasion-
ally it might be pointed out to a vendor that in view of the area in
which the property was situated, they might find it easier to achieve
a sale if they were prepared to consider a coloured buyer.

Commission for Racial Equality, *Cottrell & Rothon Estate Agent: Report
of a Formal Investigation*, London, 1980, pp. 6–7.

2.10   The health of ethnic minorities

> Owing to a combination of reasons, including poor social con-
> ditions, members of ethnic minorities have experienced signifi-
> cant health problems.

The mental and physical health problems of black and ethnic
minorities [are] affected by bad housing, high unemployment and
poor access to good preventative health care. The variations can be
linked to a variety of factors, but these communities also face the
dual problem of racism and social exclusion.

The major health issues affecting the black and minority ethnic
communities tend to be similar to those that affect the white population. However, some of these conditions disproportionately
affect these communities . . .

Child Health

Perinatal mortality is higher than the British norm in African
Caribbean and Asian babies, where the perinatal mortality rate
is almost 70 per cent above that for babies born of UK born
mothers.

There is an increased incidence of congenital malformations
amongst Pakistani babies.

Children of Asian origin are more likely to have untreated dental
decay.

Poor socio-economic conditions place some black and minority ethnic groups, particularly children, at risk of accidents in the home.

The incidence of sickle cell, thalassaemia and other haemoglobinopathies amongst the African Caribbean communities is greater than in the majority population.

Young People

Diagnostic rates for schizophrenia are very high for African Caribbeans. British born African Caribbeans are diagnosed two to seven times more often than the white population.

African Caribbeans have higher rates of admission to psychiatric hospitals and are disproportionately over-represented among compulsory admissions and in specialist facilities for secure detention.

Suicide rates are high in young Asian women and in African Caribbean men.

Heterosexual intercourse has been the predominant method of transmission of HIV infection in some black populations.

Middle Age

Coronary heart disease is a major cause of premature death amongst Asian people. Between 1979–1983, mortality from CHD among people born in the Indian subcontinent was higher than the national average by 36 per cent and 46 per cent respectively.

Smoking rates are generally low amongst the Asian communities, but is significantly higher amongst Bangladeshi men.

The incidence of diabetes is four to five times greater in Asian men and women than in non-Asians. The associated mortality rate is three times the national level.

The prevalence of diabetes in African Caribbeans is double the UK rate. The associated mortality is three to four times the national level.

Elderly

Stroke and hypertension are common among people from the Caribbean and African Commonwealth. Evidence shows that mortality from stroke among African Caribbean men and women was higher than amongst the majority population by 76 per cent and 110 per cent respectively in 1983.

Screening services for high blood pressure and for cancer are accessed less frequently by black and minority ethnic people.

Access to Health and Social Care

GP consultations are higher among black and minority ethnic

people, but especially in Asians, who also tend to rely heavily on their GP for medication.

There is a lack of awareness amongst black and minority ethnic communities of other primary and community care services, such as chiropody and counselling services.

Birmingham Health Authority, 'Action Plan for Black and Ethnic Minority Health, September 1996–April 1998', 6 November 1996.

2.11   The uneven age structure of immigrants

Although the age structure of immigrants has evened out in the long run, upon their first arrival they tended to be concentrated in the most economically productive age groups. The table compares age structures in the early and mid-1960s.

A comparison of percentage age structures, 1961 and 1966

Age (years)	1961		1966	
	All coloured groups	Total population	All coloured groups	Total population
Under 15	29	23	34	23
15–24	16	14	13	14
25–44	45	26	42	25
45+	10	37	11	38

Source E. J. B. Rose and Associates, *Colour and Citizenship: A Report on British Race Relations*, London, 1969, p. 111.

2.12   The problems of old age

While most immigrants and refugees may have arrived in their youth, their ageing creates new problems. Some of these difficulties are common to all old people but others are not, as the experiences of Poles illustrates.

It must not be thought that all or even a high proportion of Poles in this country are in need or have failed to make their way successfully, but old age inevitably brings to them specific problems. In 1961, over 15 per cent of the Poles were over sixty years of age; the proportion now is likely to be 30 per cent to 40 per cent . . .

Old age brings many tribulations, and for these Poles they are augmented by the sadness of facing the twilight of life many miles from home, often alone, and often poor to the point of being little above subsistence level. Many have memories of relatives lost in the mass murder at Katyn, and who vanished from Starobielsk, Ostashkov and many other places . . .

Mental illness is exceptionally high among refugees. The Polish Ex-Combatants Association, which runs a department for employment and assistance, has under its care, in London alone, over 100 mentally disabled. Others are looked after in homes and hostels run by the Relief Society of Poles, and within the capability of their slender resources, these and other organisations do magnificent work. The same care is extended to the old, and several homes and settlements have been set up to care for the aged and the infirm. But again funds do not permit a comprehensive scheme, and many are still in a distressed condition.

Polish funds have also to be diverted to families still living in Poland, so that although the Poles do all that they can for their countrymen, they cannot always give as much as they would like. They have all had to restart their lives from scratch in this country, and inherited money is non-existent.

Then there is the question of the ageing Polish Ex-Servicemen in need, since the Polish Forces were disbanded without pension. It was only since 1962 that as a result of a personal intercession of Field Marshal Lord Alexander, Lord Ismay and Lord Astor that the Ministry of Defence has been according a Grant Aid of £70,000 for the Relief of Distressed Polish Ex-Servicemen, distributed by an Advisory Committee composed of Polish and British Members. An allowance of 15s per week is made in approved cases, and special grants are given in emergencies. But these regular allowances are not available to widows, although the loss of a husband often leaves the widow in a worse position than before.

Polish Ex-combatants' Association, Great Britain, *The Poles in Great Britain*, London, 1971, pp. 6–7.

2.13   The uneven sex structure of immigrants

The early post-war immigrants contained an uneven age structure in which men tended to dominate, especially among Asian
groups, but not so much in the case of Cypriots, while the Irish
migrants contained more women than men. The proportions
are shown in the table.

Males per 1,000 females in England and Wales, 1961 and 1966

Area of origin	At 1961	Arrivals 1961–66	At 1966
India	1,568	1,373	1,479
Pakistan	5,380	3,541	4,231
Jamaica	1,258	773	1,066
Other Caribbean	1,264	809	1,026
British West Africa	1,949	1,452	1,614
All coloured	1,548	1,279	1,384
Cyprus	1,273	1,016	1,191
Ireland	925	234	912
Total population	937		940

Source E. J. B. Rose and Associates, *Colour and Citizenship: A Report
on British Race Relations*, London, 1969, p. 105.

2.14   White women and black men

Upon arriving in Britain during the 1950s many Africans and
West Indians entered into relationships with native English
women, as the example of Stepney, in the East End of London,
illustrates.

The women have a great influence in shaping the coloured man's
future in this country. It should, however, be noted that the larger
number of women that go in for promiscuous living are not necessarily natives of Stepney, but a floating lot of women who spend
their time between towns like Cardiff, Liverpool, Newcastle,
Manchester, etc. Their whole intention is to live on the coloured
man. They are usually of very little education, and indeed, some
are illiterate, but by no means unintelligent.

They will push them on to do the most amazing things for the sake of gain. They will arrange black-marketing for them, and will instruct them in how to make money in all sorts of shady ways, and as to how they can actually steal from docks, etc.

I know of one woman who had no scruples at all, and had the cheek to relate to a friend of hers, whilst I was standing near them, how she managed to 'pinch' some money from a Dutch seaman who had come on shore for a day. With this money she had furnished a basement and started a gambling den. She had also got bottles of drink and cigarettes which she made money on because she could serve them at an extra cost after pub closing times. At closing [time] she went round asking men if they would go down to the basement for some fun as they would get drinks and so forth. She charged an initial entrance fee or gate money of 5s. She went on to explain as to how on pay nights when there was plenty of money about she got the men to deposit money with her for a full week's gambling, so that if at any time in the week a man was 'broke' he could still try his luck . . .

Women make their contacts with the men in cafés, and then invite themselves to drinks in the evening, and if the man has a room of his own and takes the woman back with him he is as good as married, because once the woman is sure of a place to live she will stick to him like a limpet. One of my friends was very concerned that I did not have a woman, and suggested that when I got a room of my own I only had to pick any woman up and take her home. She would then be my wife, but be careful to pick one that you are likely to like for some time, because if not you will soon be very sorry, because once you get them they will not leave until they have taken all you have, and no amount of beating will get rid of them.

I must remark here that I knew of one very sensible girl. She seemed a decent girl too – she lived with a West African and kept house for him, but she was also employed and contributed to the family budget. I asked why she did not get married to the man, and she said that he did not trust white women. I suggested that as she was working, why not leave him and look after herself? She said she could not leave him as he was one of the kindest men she had ever met, and looked after her far better than any white person ever could. It was apparent here that this girl was happy with her choice. And in actual fact she had such a standard amongst the others that if she came into a place, the others seemed to look up to her as the lady of society.

PRO CO 876 247, 'Report of an Investigation into Conditions of the Coloured People in Stepney, E1, by Derek Bamuta'.

2.15 Asian boy seeks Asian girl

Many Asian marriages have occurred through the efforts of relatives and friends. More recently some people seeking partners have advertised through the columns of Asian newspapers in Britain.

I seek a warm hearted Muslim lady (23–35) who will take me for what I am and not what I have – a slight disability! Do you want to be loved, cherished, and be respected and treated as an equal? Are you caring, honest, intelligent, broad minded, with a warm personality? If I'm describing you then please write to me as I may be able to offer you the life you seek!! I am a 33 year old British born Sunni Muslim male, well educated (MSc) professional, home/car owner possessing a kind, responsible, loving nature. I respect Islamic values and am a N/S, N/D, N/clubber and enjoy reading, travelling, eating out, cinema and music (Western). Divorcees (w/o children) very welcome. Midlands based. Photo. Phone appreciated.

Practising Muslim, 6 ft, 24 years old, graduate, respectable family background, executive professional, seeks practising Muslim girl for marriage. To settle down and lead a simple Islamic life together. Age, background, education, no barrier, but must have strong attachment to Islam. Replies/enquiries from individuals or parents welcome.

Calling Mr Right! I'm Jat Sikh female, 5 ft 8, fun loving, westernised, loves socialising, from West Midlands. Seeking someone who is Jat Sikh, 30 years old, young looking, 6 ft tall, handsome. You must be adventurous. Midland based.

Eastern Eye, 19 December 1997.

2.16   Unhappy ethnic marriages

Many ethnic marriages take place by the importation of wives for husbands already resident in Britain. While such unions often work out, in other cases they do not, descending, in some instances, to a cycle of beatings, as one woman recalled of her husband.

One night Nirmal got into one of his rages and for the first time he threatened me with a knife. I was so frightened I escaped and ran for help. Eventually two policemen arrived and questioned Nirmal and me, and I was able to tell them about the knife and show it too. They took Nirmal away, and this time it was a more serious offence. He appeared in court, and I think he might have been sent to prison, but Anuz and Nimmo persuaded me to ring up and withdraw what I had said, because of the disgrace it would bring on the family, on me and the two children. They also said that the children and I would starve, and I believed this, as I thought it was only Nirmal who could draw social security.

Otherwise I would have been very happy to have him in prison, to feel safe and free. I used to wonder what would happen to me and if I would even live to see my little boys grow up. I could hardly remember that I had once been proud of my pretty looks; I was so thin and wretched-looking and Nirmal told me that I was finished as a woman, as I had no bosom. I wondered if I would keep my teeth, as he hit me in the mouth so often, and my front teeth, which were very white and regular, had become loose. Although he did not practise the Sikh religion he wore a steel bracelet, which is a useful weapon. Once when he hit me in the face the bracelet caught my upper lip and split it, so that it bled and bled. I held a cloth to it and hurried to the hospital where it was stitched but it hurt for a long time afterwards. I never told anyone what really happened as Nirmal said he would hurt me much more if I did. There was indeed no escaping from Nirmal's cruelty. He made himself a special leather belt with metal studs in it to beat me with, and I was always covered with marks and bruises.

The Scarlet Thread: An Indian Woman Speaks, London, 1987.

2.17   Ethnic percentage of the British population

In 1995 immigrants and their descendants counted about 3.2 million people, or 5.7 per cent of the total. Nevertheless, the figures in the accompanying table exclude the Irish.

Population by age and ethnicity, 1991 (000)

	Under 16	16–24	25–34	35–44	45–54	55–64	65 and over	All ages
Black Caribbean	109	74	112	51	63	61	28	500
Black African	62	35	60	29	16	7	3	212
Other black	90	34	33	10	6	3	2	178
Indian	248	128	154	137	84	56	34	840
Pakistani	203	83	68	55	34	840		
Bangladeshi	77	29	19	14	13	9	2	163
Chinese	37	28	36	28	14	9	5	157
Other Asian	48	29	43	43	21	9	5	198
Other ethnic minorities	121	44	52	33	18	12	9	290
White	10,027	6,509	7,783	7,264	6,104	5,473	8,714	51,874

Source Office for National Statistics, *Social Focus on Ethnic Minorities*, London, 1996, p. 10.

2.18   Training on the buses

Upon their first arrival in Britain many immigrants found themselves working in new employment, which needed some adjustment. London Transport provided little training, as Handley Best, recruited as a bus conductor from Barbados, recalls.

Chiswick was a big institution then, Chiswick Training Centre. And we just still look back and marvel at the way it was done. They had to physically build a classroom, a type of mock-up bus in the classroom, and give us money to play with. Because in Barbados was dollars and cents and the transition from dollars and cents to pounds, shillings and pence at that time was difficult. You knew that if anybody gave you a pound then and they wanted a shilling fare that you had to give them back nineteen shillings. But to find nineteen shillings physically that you've never seen before took a lot of getting used to, so we had to practise that in the classroom before we were kind of let loose on the public . . .

81

I think we were at Chiswick for two weeks, and then from there we went to the garage and done two weeks on the bus with a conductor instructor, then you went back to Chiswick for a day, where you had like an exam, and after you've passed that, then your conductor's badge was issued and then you went back to the garage and you was on your own then. . . .

My first journey was a nightmare. I was on the 134s, which ran from Potter's Bar to Pimlico, and I can remember I stood for so long fumbling with the change I didn't have a chance to go upstairs many times. I remember somebody asking me, is upstairs a free ride? I didn't have a clue where I was, where the bus was going. That is what made it difficult, because if somebody asks you don't have a clue where they got on, you don't have a clue where they're going. So in relation to the fare chart you didn't know where to look, so that caused you problems to start with, and that slowed you down . . . I found people thought they was doing themself a good turn and they just took advantage of your ignorance. Where people would normally get on the bus and knew that the fare was a shilling and ask for a shilling they took time out to ask you for their destination, knowing full well that you don't have a clue where it is, you don't know where they've got on, and things like that. But other than that it wasn't a problem.

Museum of London, Oral History Archive, 93/131, Interview with Handley Best.

2.19 The worst work of all

The majority of immigrants in Britain found themselves in manual work. Women home workers, particularly Asians and Cypriots, faced some of the worst conditions of all.

If the earnings of the husband are not enough to cope with day-to-day expenses, many wives take up some sort of employment. However, there are quite a few wives who do not like, and perhaps are unable, to work outside their homes for various reasons, such as small children. In the case of some Asian wives their family traditions also create an obstacle. They are not used to work in a factory or office where there are also men.

In Britain there are many employers who provide work at home to such women. If the woman is educated she may get a job of envelope addressing. Those who know typing can get typing work at home. Some women do packing, some knitting and sewing.

The work which is done at home by women can be accomplished in their own time, and since there is no one to supervise them it does not fall heavy on them. They can do the work and at the same time carry on their domestic chores. Since the work is delivered and collected from the home they save the bother and expense of travelling. It is not necessary to even go out and collect their wages, as this also is delivered.

But all that glitters is not gold!

Apparently this all looks very good, but only a few know that the employer does not pay them the right money for the work done. If you give a little serious thought to it you realise this. While a woman is working at home she must have a part of the house set aside in which she is able to carry on this outside work. It must be lit and properly heated, which means that the bills for this light and heating will be bigger. If someone is doing sewing work and the sewing machine is run by electricity, she will have to bear the cost of the extra electricity used.

In addition, when a woman works at home, she is treated as self-employed, which means that she is responsible for advising the authorities (such as the Inland Revenue) about her work. Since she is self-employed this means that the person or persons supplying her with work do not have to pay their share of the National Insurance contribution, with the result that when she is sick she cannot get sickness benefit, similarly she is not entitled to any holiday pay. This puts the home worker at a disadvantage, whilst at the same time it is of great advantage to the employer. It is always the attempt of the employer that this particular employee, who he has made self-employed, remains ignorant of her rights and duties.

Saltley News, issue 17, October 1976, pp. 3–4.

2.20   Early unemployment

By the end of the 1950s immigrants had begun to face unemployment problems, as the example of Pakistanis indicates.

Pakistanis who have come to Britain to seek work have, until recently, mostly been successful but the heavy demand for labour has eased in recent months and there is no doubt that prospective immigrants will find that it is much more difficult to obtain work in Britain.

At the present time about four thousand immigrants from Pakistan are unemployed. For example, there are unemployed Pakistanis in many parts of London for whom it is very difficult to find jobs. Unfortunately, in this city, there are also thousands of immigrants from other parts of the Commonwealth who are unemployed.

In the North Midlands, in towns such as Nottingham, Derby, Scunthorpe, Chesterfield and Leicester, which formerly offered good employment prospects, the position has changed and very few of the recent arrivals from Pakistan have found employment. Moreover, there is little prospect of finding other jobs for those who lose their present ones.

Bradford, the centre of the woollen industry, has always attracted Pakistanis, but since early this year the industry has been facing trade difficulties with the result that employers have had to discharge a large proportion of their unskilled workers. This has meant unemployment for over a thousand Pakistanis. In fact, very many of those Pakistanis who have arrived since the beginning of 1958 have not been able to find any job at all. At present about-one-quarter of the Pakistanis living in Bradford are unemployed. A similar position exists in the Sheffield and Attercliffe areas where iron and steel is the chief industry and where until this year there was a need for unskilled workers. There is no longer a need for additional labour in this industry and, as in Bradford, Pakistanis arriving this year have found that there are no jobs for them.

A great majority of Pakistanis living in Manchester, Oldham and Burnley are unemployed and the prospects for newcomers are very poor indeed. It is now difficult for any unskilled person to find employment in the North West.

In general, the position is that there is no shortage of unskilled labour in Britain and there is much competition for the unskilled jobs which are available.

PRO DO 35 9501, 'Employment of Pakistanis in the United Kingdom, 16 May 1958'.

2.21   The possible consequences of unemployment

In at least one case, that of Aaron Donane, the bitterness and feeling of rejection which unemployment caused led to suicide.

For almost ten years, Aaron Donane told his wife that if no job turned up, he would kill himself. The talk of suicide began on his fifty-fifth birthday, almost ten years to the day from his arrival in England from the West Indies. During the period following his residence in London, he worked jobs, then he was unemployed. Then more jobs then more unemployment. By the time he was fifty, he and his brother Prince were almost always out of work. Both had become angry and depressed. They needed one another badly in these times, but their conversations together invariably ended in bitter quarrelling. Each, apparently, reminded the other of his own sadness, frustration and sense of total failure. Yet they deeply cared for one another and had no one closer, not even their wives and children. For those who knew them or heard them fighting, especially when they had drunk too much, it almost seemed better that both were out of work. If one had been able to find a job and not the other, there was no telling what this might have done to their friendship. Their wives argued this point, however. Both insisted that a job for either one would have been far better than no jobs. Competition, the women agreed, may well lead to death. But unemployment practically guarantees it!

Thomas J. Cottle, *Black Testimony: The Voices of Britain's West Indians*, London, 1978, p. 89.

2.22   Ethnic minority unemployment rates

Economic activity status of males, spring 1995 (%)

Ethnic category	Working full time	Working part time	Unemployed	Inactive	All males aged 16–64 (= 100%) (000)
Black	49	8	21	22	273
Indian	65	7	10	18	306
Pakistani/Bangledeshi	41	8	18	33	216
Other ethnic minorities	51	8	12	29	224
White	62	5	8	15	16,993

Source Office for National Statistics, *Social Focus on Ethnic Minorities*, London, 1996, p. 40.

Into the 1990s both male and female unemployment rates amongts all ethnic minorities remained higher than those for whites, mainly a consequence of continued racial discrimination. The figures are shown in the accompanying table.

2.23 Ethnic minority youth unemployment

The children of immigrants suffered a double blow as unemployment rose during the 1970s and 1980s because they faced racial discrimination and were entering a contracting labour market.

Ethnic minorities are disproportionately represented amongst the unemployed. Young people are also disproportionately affected by increasing unemployment. Young people from ethnic minorities, therefore, suffer in particular. Although they share the experience of the increasing youth unemployment with their white peers, they also suffer additional disadvantage. This is directly related to their ethnic origin and how this affects their place in British society today.

Such disadvantage can derive from low educational achievement, often as a result of disrupted education or teachers' low expectations. However, local surveys have found that lack of effort in the job search and comparatively lower qualifications are often not the most significant factors in the lower success rate by young blacks in finding employment. Yet local studies show that they try as hard as white school-leavers to find jobs, but find it at least three times as difficult. Those who manage to find work are successful as a result of expending three times the application and effort of their white counterparts. It is virtually impossible to escape the conclusion that discrimination, whether intentional or unintentional, is a major factor in accounting for difficulties faced by black youth in their search for work. It is important to recognise that discrimination does not necessarily take the direct form of a refusal to employ someone on the grounds of their race or colour. Nor need it be intentional. Indirect discrimination – applying a condition or requirement which may be described as equal in a formal sense as between different racial groups but discriminating in its effects on particular racial groups – can be equally detrimental.

Disproportionate representation increases during recession. Between November 1973 and November 1977, while national unemployment figures doubled, unemployment figures among ethnic minorities quadrupled . . . This trend is continuing. According to DE statistics, from February 1979 to February 1980, ethnic minority unemployment has risen four times as fast as overall unemployment . . .

The overall change among the unemployed aged 18 in Britain for the twelve months to January 1980 was a *reduction* of 2.4 per cent; the *increase* among ethnic minorities was 7.3 per cent. The disproportionate effect on the older, 19–24 year old, age group is at least as marked when compared on a regional basis . . .

So as the general unemployment situation in Britain worsens, the problem for ethnic minority youth is growing more acute. They are more likely to be concentrated amongst the unskilled and long-term unemployed. A local survey in Bristol in 1978 indicated that one-third of blacks registered as unemployed were in their twenties, over one-third had been out of work for more than twelve months and 90 per cent were either unskilled or semi-skilled.

Such statistics cannot be seen as peculiar and idiosyncratic nor the events in Bristol as isolated and unrelated to circumstances elsewhere. Acute levels of unemployment among blacks are located in 'pockets' throughout the country. These include areas as varied as those immediately identified with higher ethnic minority populations, such as Bradford – suffering drastically from a decline in the textile industry which has been a traditional source of local black employment, as well as more unexpected locations, such as Bristol. Such variety only serves to demonstrate the serious nature of the situation, and the alienation stemming from it.

Commission for Racial Equality, *Ethnic Minority Youth Unemployment*, London, 1980, pp. 6–7.

2.24   Persistent discrimination in employment

Many of the newcomers who moved to Britain found that, despite the possession of qualifications from their homeland, they had to work in menial jobs because of the racial discrimination which they faced, as Pushpa Rani, born in Pakistan, recalled.

I was educated and qualified but couldn't get an office job because

I didn't wear the English dress, so I was working in the factories. I used to make biscuit tins in the factory, I also worked in a laundry and at London Airport. My first job was at the airport, catering. There were both Asian and English people working there. The work didn't suit my qualifications at all! All the time they want experience in this country. I had a very hard time finding an office job, so I had to work in the factories. After that I used to wear English dress, because there was the condition that if I wear English dress they could give me a job. After that I got a job with British Rail as an office typist and later I got a good job at the Civil Service.

I faced a lot of discrimination at the Civil Service. My boss told me to leave because she had a list of 100 English girls who wanted to do it. She was very colour prejudiced. I said, 'Why should I resign? I have fourteen years' service, I can't get a job outside, not even part-time. At my age I won't be able to find a job anywhere.' I didn't resign and it became very difficult. They gave me a very bad time, all the time. They were after me. I used to cry. 'Why should I leave? I have four children to support.' After that I was ill and I got a retirement pension on grounds of ill health.

Ethnic Communities Oral History Project, *Asian Voices: Life Stories from the Indian Sub-continent*, London, 1993, p. 21.

2.25 Racism from trade unions

Not only did immigrants face prejudice from employers, they also experienced it from trade unions.

At the D[artmouth] A[uto]-C[astings] No. 2 works there is a labour force of 370–500 black and 70 white. 100 of the workers there are members of the T[ransport] & G[eneral] W[orkers'] U[nion]. In January 1968 Mr Gill, the shop steward in the foundry section, was sacked. All the black members came out on strike but the Branch secretary, T. Aggar, kept the white members in. The issue over which Mr Gill had been sacked was one of wages.

The day after the sacking, Smith, an A[malgamated] E[ngineering] F[ederation] official, visited the firm and Aggar agreed to the sacking of Gill. Smith told the workers on the picket line that they should go back to work and that an investigation would be held. The workers asked him why the white workers were still in the factory. Smith's reply was both racialist and offensive. He said, 'The whites understand realities – you do not.' He proposed that Gill should be sent to No. 1 DAC works and that the strikers should return to work. The strikers refused to betray their fellow worker and said that their demand was Gill's reinstatement. Gill was in fact reinstated after two weeks' struggle in opposition to the union.

It was following this incident that the Indian workers who felt that the behaviour of the AEF was racialist began to join the T&GWU. Up to this time the T&GWU had no members in this factory.

A further incident at this factory underlined the fact that the AEF have allowed racially discriminatory practices to continue under their nose. There were four truck drivers at the DAC No. 2 works, three black and one white. The white worker got the semi-skilled rate for the job and the black workers got the labouring rates. Over a period of three years, 1965–68, four black drivers gave in their union membership cards to Smith and told him that he had done nothing to obtain them equal wages. One truck driver got so fed up that he took his union card and moved away.

Another matter which drove Indian workers away from the AEF was a wage issue. Pieceworkers in the Dressing Shop got £18 for forty hours. They made a claim for more wages but Smith refused to back them. These Indian workers were forced by the lack of co-operation of the AEF officials to join the T&GWU in order to obtain equal wages with those of the white workers.

In 1967 the speed of the conveyor at the foundry was increased. Whereas previously 260 plates had been produced in fifty minutes and 520 in 100 minutes, it was speeded up so that 780 had to be done in 105 minutes. As a result production was increased and short-time working was introduced.

At the same time casting production was doubled in one box. The white core layers, including the union branch secretary, were given a rise in wages but the Indian workers were not. When the twenty-six Indian workers approached Smith and asked for his help he snubbed them.

Following the constant betrayal by the AEF of the Indian workers in DAC No. 2 works, 100 of them joined the T&GWU...

Having created this situation, the AEF then had the audacity to bring eighty-nine of its claimed 200 membership out on strike –

the issue supposedly being the non-union membership of twenty-six Indian workers. The strike was made official by the AEF in order to get rid of other workers, not fight against the management.

Indians Workers' Association, 'Indian Workers, British Industry and the Trade Unions', undated typescript in British Library of Political and Economic Science, pp. 6–7.

2.26   Racism in high places

Racial discrimination in employment has affected all walks of life, including the Universities, the apparent bastions of tolerant, liberal ideas.

Majid v. London Guildhall University

Dr Majid was a lecturer in law at the university. In 1991, he settled a racial discrimination complaint against the university on the understanding that the university would make changes in its recruitment and selection process for future principal lecturer posts, and that the case would have no adverse effect on his prospects for promotion.

He subsequently brought a further case against the university, claiming victimisation on six grounds including his failure to be appointed to two principal lecturer posts, performance related pay and appraisal reports.

The tribunal upheld his claim on two grounds: it found improprieties in the interview procedures for two principal lecturer posts that Mr Majid had applied for; and found the university's justification for placing Mr Majid on the list of nominations for bonus pay as 'totally lacking in credibility'. Mr Majid was offered £15,000 in settlement plus a two-year sabbatical.

Commission for Racial Equality, *Annual Report, 1995*, London, 1996, p. 22.

2.27   Ethnic businesses in Leicestershire

Whilst ethnic minorities may have significant concentrations amongst the unemployed and lower social groups, by the 1980s they had also begun to open businesses on a significant scale, most conspicuously in the restaurant trade. The follow-

ing alphabetical list gives an indication of the number of Asian
and West Indian eating establishments in Leicestershire.

Ajay's Sweet Mart
111 Narborough Road
Leicester LE5 0PA
Tel. 0533 554112
N. Patel
Manager
Indian sweet mart
1–25 employees

Amber Tandoori Restaurant
5A High Street
Loughborough
Leics LE11 2PY
Tel. 0509 215754
Mr A. Uddin
Director
Restaurant and take-away
1-25 employees

Ambica Sweet Mart
147 Belgrave Road
Leicester
Tel. 0533 662451
Mr Ramesh N. Joshi
Retailers of Asian
  confectionery
1–25 employees

Balmoral
190 Belgrave Road
Leicester LE4 5AU
Tel. 0533 661961
Mr R. M. Patel and Mr N. S. Patel
Public house
1–25 employees

Bilals Fish & Chips
275 St Saviours Road
Leicester
Tel. 0533 736823
Mr Hanif Galaria
Owner
Fish-and-chip Shop
1–25 employees

Blue Peter Club
3–5 Law Street
Leicester LE4 5QR
Tel. 0533 665219
Mr Singh and Partners
Social club
1–25 employees

Bobbys Restaurant
154–156 Belgrave Road
Leicester LE4 5AT
Tel. 0533 660106/662448
Mr D. Lakhani
Manager
Gujurati vegetarian
  restaurant
1–25 employees

Bombay Palace
203 Uppingham Road
Leicester LE5 4BQ
Tel. 0533 766860
Mr F. K. Chowdhuri
Owner
Restaurant
1–25 employees

Leicester Record Office, 'Leicestershire Directory of Asian and Afro-Caribbean Businesses', 1990, p. 70.

2.28 The benefits of Indian businesses

As many Asian businesses have opened in locations with a con-centration of immigrants, usually in the inner city, this has helped to transform previously derelict areas.

Wilmslow Road area in Rusholme is the Southall of the North West. It is within ten minutes of the city centre and a stone's throw from the academic heart of the city where the University of Manchester, University of Manchester Institute of Science and Technology and Manchester Polytechnic create a bustling cos-mopolitan environment.

Before 1970 Rusholme reminded one of a bombsite with its derelict or half-demolished properties. The one-time prosperous residents of Victoria Park had abandoned the area and new immi-grants from the Indian subcontinent were taking over the large neglected Victorian properties. Crummy little shops sold everything from Indian sweets and halal meat to shoe polish and paint brushes. Property was changing hands at throw-away prices.

The early 1970s saw an influx of East African Asians who brought with them some money and a more sophisticated approach to business. They saw a potential gap in the market with the growing number of Asians and an increase in everything Asian in the local population. They bought up the cheap properties and set out to transform the area with their hard work.

The first to change visibly were the grocery stores. The bulky serving counters were replaced with rows of modern self-service shelves packed with masalas and daals as well as baked beans and cornflakes. The outside of the shops bulged with exotic fresh veg-etables and fruit like mangoes, doodhi and karela.

The sweet shops, forced to change by the more vigilant health inspectors, now boasted modern refrigerated glass-covered display cabinets. The old-fashioned curry houses with red and gold flocked wallpaper and canteen-like tables began to vanish. They were replaced by posh restaurants with well-designed interiors. Cooking karahis and tandoors were exhibition items in the shop windows. New signboards went up. Smiths and Rushtons were replaced by Shezan and Shere Khan. Restaurants are in fact the one major factor which has made a significant contribution to the rejuvenation of Rusholme. Every shop premise that has come on to the market in recent years has been bought by a restaurant owner. It has made Rusholme into an eating paradise for the whole of the North West.

Anoo Gupta, 'Rusholme: Realm of Restaurants', in *Asian Enterprise and the Regeneration of Britain*, London, 1989, pp. 17–19.

2.29   Black sportsmen

> While black people have not achieved the sort of economic success characteristic of many Asians, some have become national celebrities as a result of sporting achievement. This may be partly due to the perception in mainstream society that they can succeed in this area. But in order to reach the top they have to overcome constant setbacks. Many of them also faced difficult childhoods. The early years of the footballer Ian Wright illustrate some of these problems.

There were four of us: my eldest brother, Nicky, who is three years older than me; Morris, who's a year or so older; then me; and finally my baby sister Dionne. Our real family name is Maclean, but my dad, Herbert, left us when I was about four, so we took our mum, Nesta's, maiden name. I don't blame my dad for walking out, and I can't say that I really missed him. He would come round now and again and we'd get on, just like I get on with him now when I see him, so I don't have any big hang-ups about him not being around. My step-dad, Winston, was always on the scene, so I didn't miss that father-figure presence.

But it was my mum who was the driving force behind our family. I don't know how she did it at times, but there was always food on the table and we always had decent clothes, which wasn't always the case with families in our part of south London.

I was born in the Woolwich Military hospital on 3 November 1963, and from the moment I was born it seemed that we were always moving house. Deptford, Brockley, Peckham, Crofton Park: you name a part of south-east London and I guarantee I've lived there at some time or another. And it wasn't just the four of us under one roof with mum. When I was ten, my three girl cousins, Margaret, Pamela and Paulette, came to live with us until they emigrated to America. With seven kids in the house, it must have driven my mum crazy . . .

My mum seemed to deal with it and take it all in her stride, except when I would come home with my best shoes smashed to bits through playing football. My trainers would last about two minutes before being busted up from kicking about in the street or school playground. So I'd wear my best shoes, and my mum would just go mad that they were ruined . . .

My first organised game was when I was eight and at Gordon Brock Junior School. I can still remember it because the teacher, Mr King, had to lend me a pair of boots and they were too big. They were the old George Best ones with the little white flash and I thought I was the business. We lost 3–2 to Fairlawn, but I scored and I suppose you can say that's where it all started.

It was also the start of my disciplinary problems. Even at that age I would go mental if we were losing or things weren't going right for me . . . I can still remember one five-a-side competition that my side won, where I was swearing at the referee, at my team-mates, at the opposition and even the people watching. I even cried and raved on the pitch when the other team scored . . .

It wasn't until I started my secondary school, Samuel Pepys in Brockley, that a couple of teachers got hold of me and started to straighten me out a bit. Mr Melborn used to show me that I couldn't go around swearing and slaughtering people or getting into tantrums because things weren't going right. He told me I thought I was God's gift to football and that I ought to come down to earth, and he made sure that happened. He'd disallow a perfectly good goal for offside, and if I dared say anything, that would be it, straight off. If I ever sulked, you could guarantee I wouldn't last long on the pitch, and slowly I began to control my emotions. Mr McCarthy also used to keep me in check. He would never shout at me or really tell me off, but I was a bit scared of him and I respected him, so he could just say something quietly and put the fear of God into me. Between those two, they put me on the right path.

But if my football was beginning to get straightened out, I was still a nightmare in the classroom . . .

I would get caned for swearing at the teachers, smoking in the toilets and playing truant, everything like that . . .

My reports always said the same: Ian could do well, but he just doesn't seem to want to try, and they were right. I was intelligent, in all the top classes throughout my secondary school, but all I wanted to do was muck around and be the clown who everybody liked and laughed with. The teachers always told me I'd regret it, regret not taking care of my education, and even now that I've done all right out of football, I still wish I'd worked harder at school.

Thankfully, I think the teachers liked me, because they never gave up on me. At Samuel Pepys I was suspended for overstepping the mark just once too often, and when I came back they put me in a special class called 'The Unit' where the disruptive kids were lumped together. That was where I finally got my act together because I knew that I had reached the end of the road, and if I went out of line again, I was in deep, deep trouble.

Football was the one thing that was keeping me going in school. If I hadn't had that, then I would have been out of there, big time, and on the street.

Ian Wright, *Mr Wright: The Explosive Autobiography of Ian Wright*, London, 1996, pp. 33–7.

3

Ethnicity

Because of the trauma which they face and the often hostile, and certainly indifferent, surroundings in which they find themselves, immigrants and refugees have attempted to recreate, in a distorted way, the organisations which gave them comfort in their homeland. These have revolved around three areas in particular. The first consists of religion, so that, in the long run, all the major influxes into post-war Britain have established their own places of worship, as well as welfare organisations connected with them. Those who fled for political reasons often re-established their parties in Britain, while many immigrants also became involved in trade union and political campaigning. Finally, all groups of any substantial size in post-war Britain have established a rich social and cultural life, revolving around café society, sport, music and high culture.

3.1 The development of Sikh ethnicity in Gravesend

The evolution of an ethnic community in a particular town takes place in stages over a period of time, as Gurnam Singh Khera recalls of Gravesend.

I was only a few years old when my uncle Kartar Singh Randhawa left India and came to England . . . When I started school I had this dream that when I grow up I shall go to England. That dream came true when, along with my three uncles, I started for England, very excited and enthusiastic. Coming to England was something really great . . .

My uncle's friend Bhagat Singh Aujla used to live in Gravesend. He was the only foreigner in this town and used to work at an oil refinery on the Isle of Grain. They needed some work force and so he came to London and brought us down here. All four of us

96

cramped in the same house he used to live in and we went to work at the same place he used to work. We were young and single, knew nobody here, so worked all the hours we could lay our hands on. The money was good . . . We spent very little because we did not have time to spend it. Our uncle brought us a house in Peppercroft Street. Then within six to seven months, we managed to save enough to buy a large four-storey house in Pier Road (1954) and all of us moved there . . . There were no bathrooms in the house, we used to go to public baths once a week, had our hair cut to save washing it and to mingle with the community. Everybody became clean-shaven.

Back home in India word spread so people started pouring in. Whoever landed at Tilbury came to us first; I used to do the paper-work for them. As we saved some more we started buying individual houses; we needed them. The families started coming, new people who came needed accommodation, we rented out all the rooms, nobody was turned away, we supported each other, the rent was helping us towards the rising expenses of the family and they used to be able to save some to buy their own houses . . .

There were no Indian grocery shops here, we used to get some stuff from London. Things were rationed in those days, we could not get enough butter which we Indians used to think was the most healthy part of our diet, and we were working very, very hard so in order to stay fit and healthy we adapted to an English diet, started eating meat. Meat does not go alone so beers and drinks followed, we became proper Anglo-Indian gentlemen. The wives adapted to the diet but not the dressing-up. It was they who really stuck to the identity. After work and wash the men used to go to the pub. Apart from having a good time there, we used to make friends, meet new people, talk about our problems, solve them and find each other jobs, houses and arrange marriages too.

By 1954 Charan Singh from Jandialy came to Gravesend and he brought our holy book in 1955 and set up a room in his house for it. We used to go there on weekends to say our prayers. By 1957 we gathered enough funds and bought a house in Edwin Street for setting up a Sikh Temple for the community. The community grew bigger and bigger and soon we needed a proper place to meet the needs. So, in 1968, we bought a church building in Clarence Place which is now our Temple, known as *Guru Nanak Darbar*. It seemed too big that time, but is not enough now to cater for the community needs. So the community have bought another two buildings; military barracks in Trinity Road and one building in the Grove to meet the religious, social and educational needs.

As the community started settling, we started thinking of meeting their other needs. For religious functions we now had the Temple, for our own intellectual gratification we formed parties. Some joined the Labour Party, others Indian Workers Associations. So we started to celebrate our religious festival, *Vaisakhi*, as well as our National Day on August 15th, the Independence Day. We used to invite prominent members of the host community and Lord and Lady Murray were our chief guests on these occasions. We entertained sportsmen and other leading figures from India. The Chairman of the Hockey Team, who brought the Indian team to attend the Olympics in Helsinki, enjoyed our hospitality.

Saheli Writers (ed.), *Nobody Sleeps on the Rooftops Now: Memories of other Countries and new Lives in England*, Gravesend, 1994, pp. 3–6.

3.2   The subtlety of Italian difference

Many members of the second generation, especially those with European backgrounds, can assimilate relatively easily, but choose, however, to emphasise their difference, focusing upon a variety of issues, as one social-work student found in Bedford in 1979.

In my interviews with second-generation Italians, I have sought to obtain their views concerning the way in which they have felt able to fit into British society. All have stated that it has been a trouble-free process; I was given no examples of social injustice and most definitely they intend to remain in Bedford. They wish to continue along the same road which brought their parents to England, and thus achieve a stable and successful future in life. The advice of parents may not always be heeded but I was led to believe that it is always listened to. These young people readily mix with other ethnic minorities (unlike their parents) and are quite in favour of the idea of marrying into other groups, although nearly all said, 'But colour matters a lot, Polish or English, yes, but not blacks.' It came across very strongly (as expected) that young men have near total freedom in which to conduct their social lives compared with the girls. Returning to the question of marriage, about 80 per cent of the boys thought that they would prefer to settle down with an Italian wife. Like their parents, they seem to be intent on saving as much of their earnings as possible. One lad commented, 'You English go out all the time and spend your wage packets, but we think before we spend and prefer to put money away for the future.' Seldom, it would appear, do young Italian working boys and girls contribute to the expense of their board and lodging while living under the roof of their parents. 'Our parents want us to be able to have a good start in life and be able to buy our own house when we get married, so they expect us to save as much a we can,' was the common view. Time and again it was pointed out to me that family possessions are 'shared', and the very concept of an individual family member considering something belonged to him alone seemed to be absent. A young man who had commenced employment as an apprentice car mechanic illustrated this by saying, 'If Dad buys a car, it isn't his car, it's our car; I will expect to use it just the same as him when I pass my test.'

Quoted in Open University, *Bedford: Portrait of a Multi-ethnic Town*, Milton Keynes, 1982, p. 31.

3.3   Jamaican worship

Many Jamaicans who attended church services in England found them completely different from the rhythmic, musical ones to which they had become accustomed on their island. Clifford S. Hill, who had a parish in west London, realised this and introduced services for the newcomers.

Although we were having quite a good number of West Indians at our Sunday services, I realised that there was something lacking in the worship for them. I therefore determined to give them the sort of service that they liked. Here I made the mistake of thinking that all Jamaicans are alike in temperament. It was perhaps my intimate acquaintance with a Christian from one of the American sects known as 'the Church of God in Christ' that led me to experiment with a different type of service. I had already arranged, with some success, for a number of Jamaicans to take our evening service one Sunday in July 1953. Two of our West Indians were Lay Preachers;

one of them took the service and the other preached, while about twenty coloured choristers formed the choir. They also sang an 'Anthem', but as our organist would have been quite unable to produce the required rhythm, they were accompanied on the piano by one of their own people. The service was greatly enjoyed by both English and coloured worshippers . . .

In the autumn of that year I arranged for one of my Jamaican friends from the Church of God to conduct a service in the hall one Sunday evening, after our service in the church . . . The service was led by a woman evangelist from the Church of God, and we had a banjo and a tambourine to provide the music. After the choruses one of the men led the Testimony part of the service, and the woman evangelist also preached quite a good exegetical sermon; but only about ten per cent of the congregation joined actively in the worship, while the remainder were mere spectators. The service was thus not a success and perhaps the reason for this could be summed up in the attitude of one of the coloured worshippers, who in answer to my query as to how he had enjoyed the service, replied that it was all right for those who liked that kind of worship, but for himself he preferred the type of service we normally have in our Free Churches. I, therefore, for the time being, dropped the idea of a special Jamaican service and once again concentrated on getting them in to the ordinary services of the Church . . .

The following summer I began again, this time with a more highly organised service, having gathered a number of West Indians who were willing to take responsibility for various parts of the service, so that I myself would not have to lead the worship every week . . . This, from the start, proved much more successful and numbers began to grow as interest in the meeting heightened . . . One of the most interesting developments was in the musical side of the services. Gradually we built up within the meeting a small orchestra, as one by one our Jamaicans either purchased an instrument of their own, or brought along friends who played an instrument. Our guitars, tambourines and trumpet could be heard all down the street . . . Our normal pattern of worship would follow a regular line, although the time allowed for each item in the liturgy would vary according to the number of worshippers and the way in which the spirit moved. We generally started with a hymn from *Redemption Songs*, which is the hymn book we normally used. This would be followed by a period of free prayer, in which all the worshippers would kneel and say their own prayers aloud until one by one they fell into silent meditation. The prayer time would then culminate in a petition offered by the leader, and finally the repetition of the Lord's Prayer. After this we would have another hymn and then Testimony. Between each testimony, or possibly two or three testimonies, we would have choruses led by the chorus leader and each one being quickly picked up by the various instruments comprising our orchestra.

Clifford S. Hill, *Black and White in Harmony: The Drama of West Indians in the Big City, from a London Minister's Notebook*, London, 1958, pp. 58–63.

3.4   The Greek Orthodox Church in Britain

The Greek Orthodox Church represents the main focal point of ethnicity for many Greek Cypriots and their children in Britain. Although services have continued in Greek, literature given out at services also has English translations, owing to the lack of command of Greek of many of the second generation. This English literature includes the sermons issued by the archdiocese, the following from 28 December 1997.

In the wake of the great blessing of the birth of the Incarnate Lord of God, we are confronted almost immediately with a terrible and cruel reaction. For us, as human beings, the premature death, and especially through violent means, of innocent children seems to be the ultimate injustice. Their needless slaughter, at the behest of a bestial and loathsome tyrant, seems to be the ultimate iniquity. How, we ask ourselves, can the Birth of Christ, who comes to bring joy into the world, be reconciled with such a ghastly reaction of such unspeakable cruelty?

Does it help us to accept this tragedy, the fact that, like the birth of the Saviour of the world, this appalling episode was also seen by the prophet Jeremias? Jesus' life was spared because God's angel appeared to Joseph in a dream and told him to take the child and his mother to Egypt for safety, a symbolic act of great mystical significance. Of course, Jesus is destined to undergo an 'unjust' death, being scourged and nailed to a Cross for our salvation.

The truth is that the Son of God, who came into our world by being born of the most pure Virgin, not just in humble, but in humiliating circumstances, was from the very beginning rejected and made an outcast, as an undesirable intruder into the vainglorious plans of human self-aggrandisement. The all-pervasive power of evil threatened to dominate the world, because of a radical misuse and abuse of human liberty. The abominable act which was perpetrated by the orders of a vicious and petty tyrant was also a deliberate one, a free choice of the human will, albeit impervious already to Divine illumination and utterly warped by fear and insecurity. It is a fearsome indication of how the human jealousy, which first appeared in Cain, has become a part of our nature, where hatred demands bloody revenge and darkness seeks to extinguish the Light, though in vain (cf. John 1, 5).

However abominable an expression the almost uncontrollable power of evil may take – and God never directly intervenes to prevent or limit its destructive effects – God's mercy and love, the ultimate and unconquerable power of good, cannot be deflected or quenched. The good will always triumph in the end, because God is Love.

All that we can see around us, by God's loving providence, speaks of mortality and temporality. The souls of innocent victims of any form of outrage against Divine authority are spared further tribulations and are called to dwell in the eternal peace and light of their Creator and Heavenly Father.

We should not despair, for this would be the ultimate, self-inflicted cruelty, playing only into the hands of our adversary. Mourning our very real tragic loss, we must realise that our priorities too have been tested. Our intimacy with our fellow human beings, even those closest to us in our family, our dearest relatives and friends, should not blind us to the very real fact, that there is an infinitely greater intimacy, which God shares with us.

This intimacy, precisely, has been sealed for the very Birth of Christ, Emmanuel, 'God with us'.

Archdiocese of Thyateira and Great Britain, 'Sermon: Sunday after the Nativity of Christ, 28 December 1997, Matthew, 2, 13–23', London, 1997.

3.5 The growth of mosques

Muslim immigrants began establishing mosques wherever they settled in a variety of buildings from their first arrival in Britain. By 1990 the number of mosques had reached 600.

Regardless of its design, a new mosque impresses. Unlike secular buildings or most new churches, it is the unequivocal creation of a shared faith. The use of traditional arches and domes, although often crude and superficial, is free from the polemical, stylistic baggage that encumbers modern classicism. The relationship of the finished building to the beliefs of its makers and users is direct.

'Community' is an overworked and often meaningless word, but mosques in Britain are genuinely the work of their communities. They are places not only of worship, but of the care of the elderly and the education of children. Built by local initiative, they are paid for by donations from their congregations, assisted by gifts from Islamic governments abroad, sometimes of carpets or chandeliers.

For this reason British mosques tend to be built slowly: the Central Mosque in Birmingham took from 1962 to 1975, with work on the minaret starting in 1981. A day centre for old people was added in 1985, and an Islamic school is planned.

At the East London Mosque in Whitechapel, between 200 and 400 people attend each of the five daily prayers, with 4,000 at the midday service on Friday. The secretary of the Birmingham Central Mosque says it attracts 20,000 on days of celebration . . .

The vast majority of Britain's 600 mosques are conversions, usually of houses, but about thirty are purpose-built – enough for a 'British Islamic style' to be identified. It draws on Mogul and Ottoman architecture and on Mohamed's mosque at Medina, directly imitating motifs or abstracting them into arches and faceted, angular shapes. They are generally designed by non-Muslim architects and their Britishness comes from the use of standard British building techniques and climatic suitability: there is not much point in building fountains and courtyards.

British Muslims are motivated by the need to build as much as possible with limited funds and by the wish to give their community an identity. Birmingham Central Mosque asks for funds for its latest complex 'to vindicate the honour, integrity and credibility of the Muslim community'. That Birmingham's dome and minaret are seen as three-dimensional advertisements for Islam is borne out by a large plastic sign fixed to the minaret: 'Read the Qu'ran.'

Independent, 17 October 1990.

3.6   The largest Hindu temple outside India

Like Muslims, Hindu immigrants have established their own
places of worship since their arrival, most spectacularly in
Neasden.

The largest traditional Hindu temple outside India opened in
London yesterday, bringing to fruition the work of hundreds of
volunteer workers and endowing the suburban skyline of Neasden
with domes and pinnacles.

The three-year, multi-million-pound project was funded entirely
from the pockets and fund-raising efforts of Britain's Hindu
community.

A work force of more than 2,000, half of them unpaid, toiled
day and night to complete the Eastern monument, with seven pinnacles and six domes.

Fashioned from almost 3,000 tons of Bulgarian limestone and
2,000 tons of Italian marble – which was shipped to India to be
hand-carved by village craftsmen before making the journey to
London – the temple will accommodate up to 2,000 worshippers.

The 70 ft high, 195 ft long holy temple, or *mandir*, is surrounded
by a moat and has been built to ancient Hindu designs. It contains
no steel – the pieces are slotted together like a jigsaw, structurally
supported by a framework of English oak.

There are concessions, however, to the climate and needs of
modern British society, such as a lift to provide access for disabled
people, under-floor heating, concealed lighting and parking for 550
cars.

The project was conceived by Pujya Pramuk Swami Maharaj,
spiritual leader of the Swaminarayan Hindu Mission, which has
some 20,000 followers and twenty-six centres in Britain.

In 1992 the mission's members embarked on an ambitious fund-
raising campaign, mounting door-to-door collections, sponsored
activities and an aluminium can recycling scheme – seven million
tins were collected in total. Much of the money also came from
individual subscriptions and donations.

The mission hopes the temple will become the spiritual and cultural focal point for Britain's 1.3 million Hindus and is also keen
to encourage tourists to make the trip to Neasden.

Daily Telegraph, 19 August 1995.

3.7   Ethnic education within Britain

Most of the ethnic minorities of any size which have settled in Britain have catered for the educational needs of the first and second generation. For instance, the Bangladeshis established a group called the Bangladeshis' Educational Needs in Tower Hamlets (BENTH). This organisation had a large number of aims.

(a) To identify and advance educational needs of Bangladeshis either living or working in the London Borough of Tower Hamlets (LBTH).

(b) To identify in advance the cultural and historical education of Bangladeshis living or working in LBTH.

(c) To promote religious education of Bangladeshis living or working in LBTH.

(d) To encourage and promote educational courses and projects for the benefit of Bangladeshis, which are not being already provided by any educational or other bodies.

(e) To encourage and promote training courses, including work experience for Bangladeshis, leading to proper employment/further training.

(f) To give individual careers counselling/guidance to work out individual interests, capabilities, aspirations of Bangladeshis living/ working in the LBTH.

(g) To encourage existing educational bodies to facilitate and encourage Bangladeshis to enrol on to existing courses run by them. To encourage educational bodies to modify and alter their curricula to cater for the special needs of Bangladeshis in LBTH.

(h) To encourage educational bodies to employ more Bangladeshi staff.

(i) To encourage policy-making bodies of educational institutions to create more and more appropriate courses for Bangladeshis in LBTH. To ensure Bangladeshi participation in all stages of creating such courses.

(j) To involve local Bangladeshis in all educational/careers/training conferences, seminars and meetings.

(k) To encourage Bangladeshis in LBTH to enrol for educational/training courses through personal contacts, media and existing bodies, such as the Careers Office.

(l) To ensure that all appropriate courses are properly advertised and reach all members of the community in detail. To liaise and contact families and parents of prospective students to inform them of the types of courses available and encourage participation of the students.

(m) To generally work towards equal rights and opportunities for Bangladeshis of LBTH in the field of education.

(n) To ensure Bangladeshi participation in the decision-making process of the Inner London Education Authority (ILEA).

(o) To campaign for and ensure implementation of the recommendations that may be arrived at, through consultation between education authorities, teachers, other professional bodies and the Bangladeshi community.

(p) To liaise with professional bodies associated with educational and cultural affairs in order to initiate both long and short term projects to meet the pressing needs of the Bangladeshi community.

(q) To represent the educational and cultural interests and demands of Bangladeshis living and working in LBTH at all levels.

(r) To initiate research into the types of educational and cultural programmes according to the needs of the Bangladeshi community in Tower Hamlets.

(s) To publish regular bi-lingual news bulletins and books in the field of education, culture and other issues concerning the Bangladeshis in Tower Hamlets. To circulate such publications to Bangladeshis and other communities, educational establishments and other professional bodies in Tower Hamlets as well as within the ILEA boundary.

(t) To encourage non-educational bodies to formulate educational and training courses for the benefit of Bangladeshis in LBTH.

(u) To encourage all educational establishments to implement the multi-racial educational policies. To monitor such establishments to ensure there is no discrimination against both students and Bengali staff (if any).

BENTH Bulletin, June 1983.

3.8   Ethnic newspapers

Every minority of any size has established its own newspapers. *Parikiaki* has run longer than most of the other Greek Cypriot journals and, like many other ethnic newspapers, carries stories about both England and the homeland. Most of *Parikiaki* appears in Greek but it also has an English section. As well as longer stories the latter carries a brief round-up of news from Cyprus.

Greek Cypriot children with cancer and their families, a group of 183 people, travelled to Apostolos Andreas monastery in the occupied north of the island. The children passed into the area with no identity checks and then travelled to the monastery on four Turkish Cypriot bases.

Christakis Constantinou, 27, was remanded in custody at Larnaca District Court after being accused of attacking police officers at the airport. He had tried to get his Bulgarian girlfriend into Cyprus but the Immigration Department ruled that she did not meet legal requirements. Constantinou objected and a scuffle ensued. He apologised to the court.

The British captain of a Panamanian-flagged ship has flown home after being rescued by Cyprus marine police last Tuesday after its mostly Syrian crew staged a mutiny. Police spokesman Glafcos Xenos stated that the police were informed that the Syrian crew had taken over the ship.

The waterworld park in Ayia Napa won two awards recently in the international Waterparks Convention in San Antonio, Texas. It came away with the best award for a radio commercial, against competition from worldwide and the best brochure award.

Thirty-seven scholarships worth around £200,000 were presented to top Cypriot students who could not afford to study by the Loukas Hadjioannou foundation. The foundation emerged after Hadjioannou's vision to create a university in Pedhoulas failed to materialise due to a number problems, and the first scholarships were given this year.

The Cyprus Estate Agents Association reacted to the Friends of Akamas protests with a statement asking the government to give greater importance to the affected communities rather than the environmentalists, who, it claimed, for the most part behave like 'self-appointed sheriffs'.

Parikiaki, 30 December 1997.

3.9   Political isolation in London

Many immigrants who have made their way to England have attempted to obtain information about their homeland. This proved more difficult in some cases than others. People who had moved from the Baltic States did not have an easy time attempting to obtain information from the Soviet Union. Ilmars Petersen, who moved to Britain as a displaced person from Latvia in 1945, was asked about how he found out about the Baltic States before Gorbachev.

Most likely from Western newspapers. Because our contacts from beginning was very limited. We were not able to disclose our feelings or what you thinking about our relatives over there. They're very cautious what they are writing. Very cautious of the letters could be opened. They could be listened. They can be endangered . . . Sometimes the contacts were, er, they were very worried about writing at all. May get in trouble for writing. And now that this year or last year many discover their brothers and parents have even discovered somebody have recently discovered that he had a daughter in Latvia. Only now they've discovered. They've searched, now they've discovered. But all the time they were completely isolated. Silenced. Frightened to write. And not knowing even where their relations are. Are they in America or in Canada or in England. They've got no . . . idea. So they put adverts in papers like searching. And so it happens. In the last few years so many united families. Many people have discovered their relations in Latvia. I had a contact all time but with my parents but again I couldn't say all the truth or more likely they couldn't tell all the truth about it. And sometimes even they couldn't send parcels directly like presents. It has to go some roundabout way. Or me, I couldn't send directly. I sent to somebody else. So it was all sort of done some sort of semi-secret way of dealing with him. And, er, many was not writing because they were again frightened. If they had contact in West, if brother is in West, he may lose his work. He may get demoted or he may get in even, um, fired because he's got contacts in the West. So even a brother was not writing to brother and, er, and sisters because he's got contacts in the West. So even a brother was not writing to brother and, er, and sisters too to other sister because they were simply scared. Of course it is thank goodness it is all over and the Iron Curtain is at last, is broke in pieces. But before, er, before, er, Gorbachev, let's say, before Gorbachev it was still very secretive, very worrying . . . And it was such, and visits were very rare. Very rare indeed.

Museum of London, Oral History Archive, 93/46, Interview with Ilmars Petersen.

3.10   Seeking out fellow exiles

Immigrants and refugees tend to seek out their own people, as Patricia Pons, a Chilean exile, who moved to London with her husband, Pedro, recalls.

I think we used to go to everything that was organised by different groups or parties, because we came after a few years, after a lot of people. They were already organised groups that – they did social events or fund-raising events for different causes, I suppose to send money to Chile to help the political parties to help people. So as Pedro had a lot of friends here we went into a friend's group and knowing one person, getting to know another, we were involved with the Latin American community and all the classes that were held. Most of the people were also Latin American, so it was courses prepared especially for the people who were coming, so we ended up in a community, really, we weren't very isolated. And London had the most of the people, I suppose, because that was really the first stop. After a while they sent people to the different cities – Manchester, Birmingham, er, Glasgow, Scotland – I don't know: wherever they were supposed to go to study, you see. So we just stayed in London. Well, that was in 1971 we came. By 1981 I got involved with a folk group called Mallabe and they used to da – well, they'd dance and sing for a political objective and it was so – anything that was organised against Pinochet or whatever Mallabe was there. Er, we used to perform in a lot of solidarities. Um, the group was formed in 1976, so by the time we got into the group it was already running and very organised.

Museum of London, Oral History Archive, 95/53, Interview with Patricia Pons.

3.11   Black women

With the passage of time immigrants in Britain have established numerous groups involved in a wide variety of broadly 'political' activities, as the example of the Black Women's Group in south London illustrates.

The Black Women's Group was introduced six years ago to enable young women to express themselves freely with other women in the vicinity. This was done through political and social education, workshops and activities which were planned and organised by the women themselves. For example in 1992 the women felt an assertiveness training course was needed. This course took place in the earlier part of the year, whereby eighteen women attended once a week for a period of six weeks.

This course proved to be highly successful because it gave many women the motivation to look for work or go to college to further their careers. It also gave them confidence to approach people in authority and cope better in their own domestic and social situations.

Other activities that took place throughout the year included speakers coming into talk about drugs and sickle-cell anaemia. A short computer course also took place. Sewing, cooking, visits and hair plaiting were also included.

We also gave assistance in counselling, advice and information, filling out jobs application forms and C.V.'s.

Women were encouraged to use the project for various other activities.

The group aims for 1993 to visit Egypt to learn about Egyptian history and culture. We plan to take eight women and two workers who are fund-raising for this event. The women have already fund-raised by doing jumble sales, hair plaiting and most recently 'Guess the weight of the cake' which was made by a group member. The group have opened an account in which to deposit the fund-raising money.

Black Cultural Archives, ROO7, Reports of Organisations, File II, 'Platform One', Annual Report, 1991/92.

3.12   The Association of Ukrainians in Great Britain

Most of the European refugee groups which entered the country at the end of the 1940s established their own national organisations, as the example of Ukrainians illustrates.

The Association of Ukrainians in Great Britain was formed on the 19th January 1946. It was incorporated under the Companies Act as a Non-profit-making Company on the 20th December 1947, and remains the only Ukrainian Welfare Organisation in the United Kingdom.

Active membership has grown from less than 150 to 18,720. Most members' wives and other dependants, among them 2,369 registered children under sixteen, are not included in this figure, but are within the scope of the Association's activities. Advice and assistance are moreover given to any other Ukrainian in need of help, irrespective of membership.

The objects of the Association are:

(a) to provide for the material and moral welfare of Ukrainians, and to give them whatever support and material assistance they require.

(b) in particular, to assist sick, aged and distressed Ukrainians, and to provide for the needs of mothers and children.

(c) to facilitate the resettlement of Ukrainians as useful and happy members of the British community,

(d) to work in close co-operation with the British authorities and with the appropriate organisations, institutions and private persons,

(e) to foster Ukrainian traditions, folk arts and crafts and to encourage and assist their practice,

(f) to provide its members with every facility for a happy social life and to acquire suitable premises as Clubs and Welfare Centres,

(g) to complement the education of Ukrainian children and to assist Ukrainian students at British and foreign universities in their studies,

(h) to assist Ukrainians abroad to rejoin or visit their families or friends in the United Kingdom, and others in Great Britain who wish to re-emigrate overseas.

Central Co-ordinating Committee of Refugees Welfare Organizations Bulletin, vol. 1, 1954, p. 28.

3.13   West Indian Standing Conference

One of the leading West Indian organisations in Britain is the West Indian Standing Conference (WISC).

The WISC inception in 1959, as an umbrella organisation, was itself, a direct reaction to particular problems which the new arriving people from the Caribbean came up against. Its existence is owed in part to the then Prime Minister of Jamaica, who in 1958 visited the UK to consult with West Indian community representatives following the outbreak of racial violence in parts of Britain, including Notting Hill. WISC has operated continuously, taking forward issues which affect the community. It is by all accounts, the longest serving body of Black people to have been formed in the UK.

WISC *aims and objectives*

To represent the interests of Caribbean people in the UK and thereby to make recommendations as deemed necessary to Governments and institutions inside and outside the UK.

To address the problems of racism, racial discrimination, the lack of promotion of Equality of Opportunity in employment, housing, education, business, political and economical decision making, and to promote the ideal of justice and fair play through equal opportunities policies as a means of combating racism and racial discrimination as experienced by Black people.

These very early problems continue to dwarf our community's progress, four decades on, and still occupy much of the energy of officers, staff and members, in combating them.

Membership

Group, individual, and associate membership is offered. Individual affiliation is for people with specialised skills who can be used to enhance the work of the Organisation. These could be in the various professions as lawyers, doctors, nurses teachers, accountants, ministers of religion, practitioners, such as social workers, probation officers etc.

Black Cultural Archives, ROO8, Reports of Organisations, File III, 'West Indian Standing Conference Information Booklet'.

3.14   The Irish in Britain Representation Group

As a result of the IRA hunger strikes and the existence of anti-Irish racism, the Irish in Britain Representation Group came into existence in 1981.

All of the processes at work in the Irish community in the late seventies were accelerated during the period of the hunger strikes of 1980 and 1981. The shock and trauma of it drew the community together in a way that nothing else had done for many years. Consciousness of being Irish was heightened and many more people were motivated to become involved in Irish community affairs. The patronisingly racist attitude of most of the British media was infuriating to Irish people. The frustration at the lack of any organised political voice of the Irish in Britain, the sense of helplessness in the face of the British government's arrogant intransigence, determined many Irish people to do something to give expression to the Irish as a community in Britain. The experience of the period was to act as a forcing house for many of the Irish groups which were established in the wake of the hunger strikes.

A landmark in this process was the founding of the Irish in Britain Representation Group in October 1981. It was started because there was no effective voice representing the interests of the Irish in Britain in social and political matters. By concentrating on the needs and issues affecting the Irish as a community in Britain the IBRG hoped to become a permanent voice representing the Irish in Britain as an autonomous community and to preserve the Irish way of life in Britain.

The organisation was started by a mixture of first and second generation people and now has about twenty branches around the country. Many of the Irish-born founders felt that their Irishness was being sacrificed in settling in this country and it was not being passed on to their children very well. As one member has said about his son's embarrassment at being called Irish, 'My son is seventeen and he finds that his father and mother are being depicted as fools and his nation as stupid. He is asking us, "When are you people going to stand up for your rights?"'

One of the first priorities taken on by the IBRG was to defend the community against the anti-Irish racism and 'jokes' so prevalent in the British media. The stereotype of the thick Paddy had become so widespread that even the word Irish had become a synonym for stupidity. Over the years members of the IBRG have brought many instances of racism in the media to the Press Council with varying degrees of success.

Hearts and Minds: The Cultural Life of London's Irish Community, London, 1987, pp. 17–19.

3.15   The Irish Youth Group

As well as umbrella organisations for the Irish in Britain, others have developed which revolve around specific issues on a local scale.

Who are we?

The Irish Youth Group was formed over two years ago to help deal with the issues affecting young Irish people living in Birmingham. The Group is run by young Irish people who want to help other young Irish people get the best out of life here in Birmingham. It aims to be a voice for us through the links we have established with many organisations in the city.

The group is run by volunteers and encourages others to join and get involved. The work we do is very rewarding and, as a member, you can do something positive for yourself and others. The group is open to all young people living in Birmingham between the ages of eleven and twenty-five.

What we have achieved so far

Welfare work. Most of the work which the group has done so far has been to address welfare issues for Irish students at the College of Food. The Irish community has had links with the College for many years, mainly thanks to the work of the Irish Welfare and Information Centre.

More recently the Youth Group has also given a positive contribution to the College with the preparation of an Information pack for new arrivals from Ireland, running an 'Open' afternoon for Irish students (which enabled the revival of the Irish Students' Society), negotiating better terms for Irish students with Irish banks and regularly meeting with the college management. The latter has led to the establishment of the Irish Students' Welfare Forum which meets four times a year.

Activities. The Group ran a storytelling workshop for the Irish festival in March 1995 which was a great success. We have been involved with the Council Youth Service and, in particular, their review of it, which took place in late 1995 and early 1996.

The Group has spent a lot of its time trying to raise sufficient funds to appoint an Irish Youth Worker to develop and organise activities, events and support for young Irish people. To date we have not been successful.

114

Birmingham Irish Community Forum, *Annual Report, 1995–96.*

3.16 The Islamic Party of Britain

By 1989 Muslim discontent with the traditional political
parties had led to the launch of the Islamic Party of Britain.

The Islamic Party of Britain was launched on September 13 at
Regent's Park Mosque, London to 'present a viable political, economic and social alternative to the British people'. The party will
lobby for political support from the political parties and governments for the needs of both Muslim and non-Muslim people and
field candidates in next May's local government elections.

The party's structure is divided into the Policy Guidance Council,
which consists of the founding members; the Council elects its
Leader and the Executive Body. General membership is open to
every Muslim, male or female. However, at the press conference,
the Leader of the Party, Daud Musa Pidcock stated that the general
membership is open both to Muslims and non-Muslims.

The party, as its manifesto says, wishes to provide 'effective, adequate representation of Islamic principles in the UK' and present
the public with 'the benefit of solutions to the numerous problems
in the political, economic and social spheres of life'.

Muslim News, 22 September 1989.

3.17 Direct action

By the early 1980s, following the first effects of Thatcherite
draconian economic policy, resulting in soaring levels of unemployment, inner-city youth became discontented and took
direct action, resulting in some of the most widespread rioting
in twentieth-century British history. As second-generation
immigrants were concentrated in the inner city and faced a
dual problem of racism and economic deprivation, as well as
lacking a political voice, they played a large role in the rioting,
which affected most of the major English cities.

For the first time in mainland Britain CS gas was used to quell mobs
of rioters rampaging in the Toxteth district of Liverpool as police
lost the struggle to halt looting, burning and widespread destruction.

During the second successive night of violence in the area, at least half-a-dozen canisters were fired by the police, who later confirmed that it was tear gas . . .

Children as young as four and five years old joined looters in Lodge Lane, a local councillor said. 'I have seen them running up and down the road with wire shopping trollies full of groceries and clambering over broken glass to get into the Trustees Savings Bank,' Mr Christopher Davies said.

'Every shop, from supermarkets to small community corner shops, have been smashed and looted,' he said . . .

The National Westminster bank in Upper Parliament Street was set alight and virtually destroyed, and rioters also set fire to Swainbanks furniture store across the road.

The fighting centred on Upper Parliament Street, the scene of the first outbreak on Saturday, spreading through surrounding streets. In Lodge Lane, near by, where shops and a public house burnt, desperate firemen searched for anyone in the buildings, unprotected by the police . . .

The violence appeared to have been premeditated and arose from a volatile mix of hooliganism, unemployment, frustration, alleged over-intensive policing and the claim that black people had been provoked by the police. It was not a race riot in the context of Brixton or Southall but was more the sudden fusing of elements common to black and white youths.

The weekend eruption began on Friday when a black youth was chased by police and fell off a motorcycle when they caught him. He disappeared after being pulled from the police by a crowd of forty black youths, and two hours of sporadic violence followed, in which five officers were hurt.

After the incident the police received an anonymous tip about a 'bloodbath' in Toxteth and a force of men equipped with riot equipment stood by. The police say they were kept from public view.

The Times, 6 July 1981.

3.18   The Rushdie affair

The publication of Salman Rushdie's blasphemous *Satanic Verses* galvanised Muslims in Britain to the extent that they launched demonstrations throughout the country. Bradford represented the centre of the opposition, where demonstrations included burning the book.

More than 1,000 angry Muslims rallied in Bradford city centre today to protest about a novel which they claim attacks their faith.

They cheered and chanted as a copy of the book, *The Satanic Verses*, by Salman Rushdie, was burned outside police headquarters in the Tyrls.

Bradford councillor Mohammad Ajeeb told the crowd: 'This gathering today is an indication of the extreme anger which the Muslim community feels about the book.

'I am pleased that this demonstration is taking place in a peaceful manner because Islam is peace.'

He said he would try to persuade his fellow councillors to ban the book from Bradford libraries.

Many of the crowd waved banners and placards proclaiming 'Ban Satanic Verses', 'Rushdie – Eat Your Words' and 'Rushdie Stinks'.

More than twenty police were present, but the meeting was marshalled by dozens of Muslim officials.

Sher Azam, president of the Bradford Council of Mosques, said they object to the book because it abuses Islam and is based on distorted facts about their faith.

He said: 'There are 65,000 Muslims in Bradford and they are angry and upset about the book. There is no doubt in our minds that it should be banned.'

The book, which has already been banned by fifty-six countries including India, won the 1988 Whitbread Award and almost won a Booker Prize.

Muslims claim Rushdie, an Indian author educated in Britain, challenges the authenticity of their holy book, the Koran.

The publishers have said on behalf of Rushdie that there is no chance of them banning it.

Bradford Telegraph and Argus, 14 January 1989.

3.19   Inter-ethnic conflict

In December 1992, following the destruction of the Ayodha Mosque in India by Hindu extremists, Asian inter-ethnic conflict broke out in Britain, in which Muslims, Hindus and Sikhs attacked each other's institutions.

Hindu temples, cultural centres and business premises were targeted in a third night of arson attacks in Britain, following the destruction of the Ayodha mosque in India on Sunday, but a Sikh temple in Luton also suffered extensive damage.

So far, Sikhs have not been involved in the conflict between Muslims and Hindus in India, and some Muslims in this country were quick yesterday to point to the Luton incident as evidence that Muslims were not responsible for the wave of arson attacks.

Scotland Yard said yesterday that 'a man of Asian appearance' was being questioned in connection with damage to a Hindu temple in Forest Gate, east London. West Midlands Police have said that two white youths were seen in the vicinity of an attack on a Hindu temple in Coventry on Monday night, but elsewhere police have little or no evidence as to who might be responsible . . .

In Huddersfield, West Yorkshire, a fire caused substantial damage to the Indian Workers' Association community centre, which is used by all ethnic groups in the town. Mohinder Singh Chatrik, manager of the centre, said: 'All our members are lost to understand the logic behind the attack because the association has no religious inclination at all.'

In Bradford, the office of a Hindu estate agent and a Hindu shop have been damaged by fire, in addition to five attacks on Hindu temples and Hindu cultural centres there since the weekend. Other attacks on Hindu temples and property have taken place in Wembley, West Bromwich, Birmingham, Bolton, Oldham and Derby, and leaders of Hindhu and Muslim communities have repeatedly appealed for calm.

Independent, 10 December 1992.

3.20   Ethnic minority mayors

By the 1980s and into the 1990s many members of ethnic minorities had made it to the top jobs in local government, standing for both major political parties, usually, but not always, in areas with concentrations of immigrants.

118

Demetris Demetriou, the Cypriot Conservative Councillor for Epping and owner of the Thatched House Hotel in the same area, was inaugurated as the borough's Mayor on Tuesday.

This achievement makes Mr Demetriou the second Cypriot mayor to be elected, following in the footsteps of Mr Andreas Mikkides, who was Mayor of Haringey.

Present at Tuesday's ceremony were Liz Webster, Mayoress of Waltham Abbey, as well as Don Spinks, Vice Chair of Epping District Council, and other officials. A rich reception followed, attended by many friends, relatives and well-wishers.

Demetris, 42, who came to Britain as a refugee from the village of Lapanthos in 1974, has been a councillor since 1988 and opened his hotel in the centre of Epping in 1989. He is married with three children.

Parikiaki, 14 May 1992.

3.21   St Patrick's Day

> Since the nineteenth century the celebration of St Patrick's Day has represented a major event for the Irish diaspora, through-out the world, including England, as one reporter for the *Independent* reveals.

On St Patrick's Day we'll all have tay,
We'll Kick Ian Paisley out of they way!

So sings an old fiddle player in the Irish pubs of Cricklewood. St Patrick's Day was 17 March; at this time of year we should all give thanks for the cheerful presence of the Irish in England, Ulster's troubles notwithstanding.

Last week I was in Liverpool, where the Irish Centre is housed in the magnificent neoclassical Assembly Rooms. Where once the sons and daughters of slave trade profiteers had waltzed, now lively schoolgirls in green smocks were performing Irish dances. Proud mothers compared notes on the hand-sewn scarlet and gold patterns on the tunics, all traditional Celtic themes. Fathers were drinking peacefully in the bar, mothers sat and gossiped in the cafe, and children raced up and down. Later in the evening, a band called Napper Tandy took the stage, and the ballroom slowly filled with couples waltzing to the strains of country guitars and Irish ballads.

Few babysitters are needed when Irish families go out to enjoy themselves, as the children come too, cosiness and domesticity thriving among cigarette ash and beer mats. In Liverpool, many of the Irish are several generations from Eire, yet have preserved intact the innocent merriment of Irish family life . . .

On St Patrick's night, I set out for 'The Thatch', a smart Irish club at Highbury Corner, eager to see how the popular saint would be honoured. I was welcomed by Mr Murphy, the organiser, a big man with a gently humorous disposition, a bright green tie and a sprig of shamrock in his buttonhole. Sophisticated young ladies streamed in, together with young men in suits, all clutching tickets for their reserved seats. No small children came along on this occasion, for dancing would not end till two in the morning. 'The Thatch' out-salooned a saloon bar, with carpets, rows of shiny wooden tables and Mock Tudor beams criss-crossing the ceiling. Such plushness discouraged rowdy behaviour. On the stage, a stout woman played an accordion while a heavily built man with glasses and a goatee beard, like a doctor in Victorian Dublin, sang of old Ireland free. Couples old and young called out to one another cheerfully. Then they sat down to heavy meals, elbow to elbow, making spirited inroads on enormous heaps of mashed potato. All the paper napkins were green. Loud conversation filled the air.

Independent, 21 March 1988.

3.22   Diwali

For Hindus Diwali, the festival of light, represents the most important religious event of the year, resulting in celebrations in the areas with heavy Hindu concentrations, including Leicester.

Dance and music night at *Belgrave Neighbourhood Centre* on *Sunday 7 November* starting at 6:30 p.m.

Featuring *Lohana Majahan Raas Garba Group*, the *Raja Yoga Centre* and mimes from *Rushey Mead School*.

Plus Rangoli Competition 1982 and Belgrave Baheno Cookery Competition prize-givings and finishing with food and hot & cold drinks.

On *Sunday 14 November Raja Yoga* centre will celebrate Diwali with a programme of events to be held at *Belgrave Neighbourhood Centre* from 5:00–7:30 p.m.

All are welcome to this free programme which will seek to reveal the true meaning of *Diwali – the Festival of Light*. It will include a lecture and dialogue, songs, music and dance.

Details about the activities of the Raja Yoga Centre can be obtained from the Centre at 13 Herbert Ave., Leicester, Tel. 62023.

Admission to the programme is free and it will be conducted in both Gujurati and English.

On *Saturday 6 November Belgrave Library Club for Children* will be making Diwali decorations for the library from *2:00–4:00 p.m.* There will also be storytelling. All children welcome . . .

Belgrave playhouse, 132 Harrison Rd, will be having special craft/painting sessions to decorate the building for Diwali during the week from *1–5 November*.

On *Monday 8 November* at 5:00 p.m. there will be a party for children with food, Mendi and games . . .

Rushey Mead Language Centre, Harrison Rd, will be the location for a varied programme of activities covering Indian culture.

On *Thursday 11 November* starting at *2:00 p.m.* there will be displays about teaching resources, cookery, Mendi, a book exhibition as well as a video and films.

In the evening starting at *7:00 p.m.* there will be a *party* – bring a little food and join the fun.

Further details about these events and the work of the *English Language Scheme* can be obtained from *Jean Brown*, Tel. 657919.

On *Thursday 4 November* there will be an *Asian Fashion Show* at the *Belgrave Library Club for Senior Citizens* as part of the afternoon programme from *2:00–4:00 p.m.* Ladies from the *Rushey Mead Language Centre* will demonstrate various styles of Asian dress. Come along and learn how to wear a saree! Everybody welcome!

Leicester Record Office, L301.451, 'Diwali in Belgrave', 1982.

3.23 The Notting Hill Carnival

Perhaps the most visible sign of the African-Caribbean presence in Britain consists of the Notting Hill Carnival.

The Britain that Caribbean migrants settled in after World War II was not a place where people danced on the streets. For most Britons, summer was a fortnight at the beach, paddling in cold water, painfully treading across stony beaches. But now there is also dancing on the streets in the form of Carnival. Most British cities with a Caribbean population stage a carnival. But the Notting Hill Carnival is by far the largest and most spectacular. It began twenty-four years ago as a local event. Within a decade it was attracting a quarter of a million revellers. This year's event is expected to attract two million people over the two days.

The main inspiration for the Carnival comes from the Trinidadian settlers who made Ladbroke Grove in particular, and west London in general, their home. Once it had started, though, carnival appealed to other islanders, especially those from the eastern Caribbean region – St Lucians, Dominicans, Grenadians, and so on. Later the Jamaicans added a whole new dimension to Carnival. Back in Trinidad, Carnival is an island-wide event that breaks down social and racial divisions. It is an exuberant celebration of the island's diverse peoples – Europeans, East Indians, Chinese and Africans.

The Trinidad carnival is an expression of the diverse cultures which make up the Caribbean's most cosmopolitan island. Although no one group can claim to have originated Carnival, there is a strong Roman Catholic influence in the idea of the event. Throughout the New World, the two days before Lent – a period of abstinence – are give over to celebrations. The term 'carnival' is itself derived from the Latin phrase 'Carne Vale', meaning farewell to meat. The most famous of these pre-Lent festivals are the Rio Carnival of Brazil, and the Mardi Gras of New Orleans, and, of course, the Trinidad carnival.

The Notting Hill Carnival departs from these pre-Lent festivals in that it is held in August rather than mid-February. London at that time of year is far too cold. While the occasion for Carnival is rooted in Europe, the contents of the event are drawn from a variety of sources.

Black Cultural Archives, COO4, Carnival, Winston Norman, 'Celebration in Diversity', *Notting Hill Carnival, Official Souvenir Magazine*, 1989.

3.24   Indian dance

With the arrival of Asians in Britain came Indian dance, an
activity which took off in Leicester in the 1970s, as one Asian
resident of the city recalls.

When it came to dance events I remember going with my Gujurati
friends to dance events at De Montfort Hall which were huge,
which were big, and they were, you know, explicitly multicultural,
they were sort of taster sessions for everybody to get to know a
little bit about different forms of dance and different forms of cultures in the same way. So there was a sort of performing group
there that did this dance but then . . . there was this interplay of a
little performance and then public participation. This involved, as
far as I can remember, stick dancing . . . Bhangra . . . Scottish dance,
Irish dance, Polish dance, I remember. It must have been '72, '73,
and possibly again '75, '76.

I do remember that there were Raas and Garba competitions –
Gujurati folk dance competitions.

It is word of mouth but it is also institutionalised community
links – you know, the Patels are doing this and the Sonis are doing
that. Certainly when it comes to those Raas and Garba Competitions that was very much community against community, it was
warfare, you know, in a different media. Very clearly, you know.
It's still like that, of course – yes, it's so different now.

I think at that early stage there was very little formal training, it
was folk dance, it was sort of passed on from mother to daughter,
from friend to friend, word of mouth in a sense again, not formal
structured training as it is now. Now there is much more emphasis
on classical dance, which wasn't there at that time. Before it was
folk, it was mixed things . . . it was film dance a lot because people
watched all these films and you had all these things going on there
that people sort of recreated on stage.

Living History Unit, *Parampara: Continuing the Tradition: Thirty Years of
Indian Dance and Music in Leicester*, Leicester, 1996, pp. 9–11.

3.25   Irish sports in Britain

In the post-war period, sport has become ever more popular
among all sections of society, including immigrants. While

most newcomers have tended to play international sports, notably cricket and football, the Irish have participated in their own peculiar recreational activities.

It is generally accepted that the Gaelic Athletic Association and Irish culture go hand in hand . . .

While London, with clubs based in such outlying areas as Dagenham, Langley, Hayes and Enfield, has dominated the scene for quite a number of years it is gratifying to know that Gaelic fervour also abounds in Warwickshire, Lancashire, Yorkshire, Gloucestershire and Hertfordshire.

The North London GAA Board with its vast potential compares favourably with any in Ireland and despite its indebtedness to the Bank, as a result of purchasing the modern ground at Ruislip, the overall assets are more than quadruple its indebtedness.

The foresight of former officers in purchasing the ground at New Eltham some years back has paid off handsomely, and even at today's depressed market value the fourteen-acre site is worth a quarter of a million pounds. This site has been converted into three pitches with no fewer than nine weekly games played during the summer.

The acquisition of the Ruislip ground and club rooms has proved a wise investment as not only has the Board secured permanent headquarters but the revenue derived from functions and bar takings should ensure that the debt is cleared even ahead of schedule . . .

Despite the gradual decrease in the number of incoming players from Ireland there has been no big reduction in the number of affiliated clubs which now stands at forty-five, representing some 3,000 registered members.

The winning of the championship titles is the ultimate goal of all clubs, a fact which is amply demonstrated by the extra-high standard of play in these particular competitions. In hurling, Brian Boru lead the field with no fewer than twenty-four senior championship titles to their credit and although they relinquished their crown to St Gabriels last season their avowed determination to regain the crown could well be realised.

Irish Observer, 15 May 1982.

3.26   Ethnic radio

By the 1990s ethnic radio stations had sprung up all over London and could, by that time, obtain licences under the Broadcasting Act 1990, having previously run illegally. Such stations existed in areas of ethnic concentration and covered a wide range of issues, as Ravi Jain, the chair of Sunrise Radio, explained.

Sunrise Radio operates in west London. There may be people who do not know that part of London, which is Hounslow, Southall and Brent, and which also has one of largest Asian communities concentrated in a small area of something like a ten-mile radius – we're talking about something like a quarter of a million people – so, apart from the Midlands, there you will find the community is more widely dispersed than the area in which we are operating which is fairly concentrated. So it puts us in a certain advantageous position in the sense that it makes us a financially viable radio station as well. The communities are reasonably prosperous, and they advertise quite heavily on the station, and that has become our mainstay . . .

It is a most interesting area where, like Belfast, political sensitivity and sensibility becomes very important; we have to deal with, among the Sikh community, the whole issue of Khalistan; how do we present that view? Recently, the Kashmir issue; how do you present it? We put on a live interview with the leader of the Kashmir Liberation Front, that didn't please the Indian High Commission, but that wasn't the issue, the issue is that we must put forward views which will help communities formulate their own opinion *as they see*, rather than how it is reported or sanitised by other media. I'm not implying that they do, but it does not provide that 'interaction' and that is the key word which we have picked up in radio, the only way that we can service the community when the community and the audience can respond to it very quickly, and that is the success.

The station, apart from music and phone-ins, has requests for records to be played, but it is interwoven with current affairs, and current affairs is the key around which we build our programming . . .

I'm not trying to imply that we are spending time on politics because we constantly see, at least in summer, a large number of artistes from the Asian subcontinent.

Commission for Racial Equality, *Radio for Ethnic and Linguistic Minorities: Prospects in the 1990s*, London, 1990, pp. 50–2.

3.27 African-Caribbean poetry in England

The culture of immigrant groups has reached a high plane, with the production of plays, literature and poetry, often reflecting the immigrant experience in England, as the work of Linton Kwesi Johnson, Jamaican-born in 1952 and entering England in 1963, indicates.

Inglan is a Bitch.

w'en mi jus come to Landan toun
mi use to work pan di Andahgroun
but workin' pan di Andahgroun
y'u don't get fi know your away aroun'

Inglan is a bitch
dere's no escapin' it
Inglan is a bitch
dere's no runin' whey fram it

mi get a lickle jab in a big 'otel
an' awftah a while, mi woz doin' quite well
dem staat mi aaf as a dish-washah
but w'en mi tek a stack, mi noh tun clack-watchah!

Inglan is a bitch
dere's no escapin it
Inglan is a bitch
noh baddah try fi hide fram it

w'en dem gi you di lickle wage packit
fus dem rab it wid dem big tax rackit
y'u haffi struggle fi mek en's meet
an' w'en y'u goh a y'u bed y'u jus' can't sleep

Inglan is a bitch
dere's no escapin' it
Inglan is a bitch fi true
a noh lie mi a tell, a true

mi use to work dig ditch w'en it cowl no bitch
mi did strang like a mule, but, bwoy, mi did fool

den awftah a while mi jus' stap dhu ovahtime
den awftah a while mi jus' phu dung mi tool

Inglan is a bitch
dere's no escapin it
Inglan is a bitch
y'u haffi know how fi suvvive in it

well mi dhu day an' mi dhu nite wok
mi dhu clean wok an' mi dhu dutty wok
dem seh dat black man is very lazy
but if y'u si how mi wok y'u woulda sey mi crazy

Inglan is a bitch
dere's no escapin it
Inglan is a bitch
y'u bettah face up to it

dem have a lickle fact'ry up inna Brackly
inna disya facktri all dem dhu is pack crackry
fi di laas fifteen years dem get mi laybah
now awftah fifteen years mi fall out of fayvah

Inglan is a bitch
dere's no escapin it
Inglan is a bitch
dere's no runnin whey fram it

mi know dem have work, work in abundant
yet still, dem mek mi redundant
now, at fifty-five mi gettin' quite ol'
yet still, dem sen' mi foh draw dole

Inglan is a bitch
dere's no escapin it
Inglan is a bitch
is whey wi a goh dhu 'bout it

Linton Kwesi Johnson, *Inglan is a Bitch*, second edition, London, 1981, pp. 26–7.

3.28 Chinese classical music

In 1982 Liverpool, with one of the oldest Chinese communities in Britain, became a centre of Chinese classical music.

Deep in the mean streets of Liverpool's urban crisis an orchestra is rehearsing the ageless, authentic sounds of traditional Chinese music. Their tutor is Mr Li Kui Hsiung, a 43-year-old musician who has been specially imported from the People's Republic via Hong Kong to coach Europe's first traditional Chinese orchestra.

He's here for a year, initially, financed by a £4,000 grant from the Calouste Gulbenkian Foundation and a £2,000 bursary from the Arts Council. His base is the Pagoda, a Chinese social and cultural centre opened by Prince Charles in April this year. The centre is run by the Tai-Shen Chinese Play Association, set up in 1976 (helped by an article in the *Guardian*) by Mr Brian Wang to promote Chinese art and culture and increase understanding between Liverpool's self-contained Chinese community and the sceptical Scousers.

The Pagoda already had its own little orchestra of five – three Chinese and two English – studying traditional Chinese music. Now there are more than twenty people taking lessons. 'In the past we have always had to use recorded classical music,' Mr Wang says. 'We want Mr Li to give technical help so that we can promote our own live musical accompaniment – not only accompaniment but a complete Chinese orchestra.'

The first results of Mr Li's appointment will be seen – or heard – next Thursday when the orchestra will provide the music for a performance of *Havoc in Heaven* for the International Women's Guild at the Pagoda. It tells, Mr Wang says, 'how in Chinese legend a monkey causes havoc in heaven by trying to take over from the gods – it's about the contradiction between authority and mischief'.

Guardian, 22 October 1982.

4

Racism

All newcomers who have made their way to post-war Britain have experienced prejudice to varying degrees from both the state and English natives. At the most basic level immigrants and refugees have endured English coldness and refusal to enter into social and economic discourse. Such actions are supported by state functionaries in the form of judges, policemen and immigration officials, whose decisions have been influenced by the ethnicity of a defendant. The media have played the central role in the perpetuation of racism, by their stereotyping and by focusing upon particular issues at particular times. Overtly racist organisations have existed throughout post-war British history, reaching a peak of support with the National Front in the 1970s. Finally, countless individuals have faced violence because of their ethnicity. Individual attacks have taken place throughout the post-war period, while anti-immigrant riots took place in the early decades after 1945.

4.1   The Irish joke

Anti-Irish jokes have circulated in Britain for hundreds of years. When immigrants arrived after the war, many natives already had preconceived views of the Irish, although the presence of Irish people in Britain further fuelled the growth of the Irish joke. The following, relatively tame, but typical, selection gives an indication of the racist nature of such humour, in which the predominant stereotype is of Irish people as 'thick'.

Mercy
Irish judge (to prisoner aged sixty): 'The sentence is twenty years' penal servitude.'

Prisoner (tearfully): 'My lord, I shall not live long enough to serve the sentence.'

Irish judge (benevolently): 'Don't worry. Do what you can.'

One hundred per cent

An Irishman on landing in the United States was accosted by two Americans who were bent on testing his mental abilities.

'How many people live here, Pat?' they asked.

'One hundred,' answered Pat, with a twinkle in his eye. 'I'm the one, and you're the two noughts.'

Taking a chair

A gentleman called at the home of Mrs Murphy and inquired for her. Her husband answered the bell, and calling up to Mrs Murphy informed her that there was a gentleman to see her.

'Tell him to take a chair,' replied Mrs Murphy. 'I'll be right down.'

'Begorra,' yelled Mr Murphy, 'he's taking all the furniture; he's the instalment collector!'

Steam

Here is Mr Patrick Murphy's definition of steam: 'Wather that's gone crazy wid the heat.'

Middle-sex

An Irish theatre recently advertised for 'an organist and pianist, either a lady or a gentleman.'

One of the replies read: 'Dear Sir, – I noticed you have a vacancy for a pianist and organist, either lady or gentleman. Having been both for a number of years I would like to apply for the position.'

The test

Mrs M'Ginty: 'Your twins are so very much alike, Mrs Murphy, that I wonder you can tell them apart?'

Mrs Murphy: 'That's aisy. I sticks me finger in Paddy's mouth an' if he bites I know it's Mike.'

Have you Heard this One? Best Scottish, Irish, Jewish and Irish Jokes: A Picked Collection of Really Funny Stories about these Delightful Folk, London, 1953, pp. 75–7.

4.2 Political incorrectness

Part of the problem with adult racists lies in the fact that they pick up their ideas in childhood, through their parents, the media and children's books. One of the most politically incorrect of children's books, *The Story of Little Black Sambo*, first appeared in 1899 but came out in a new edition in 1996, having gone through dozens of reprintings since 1945. The book begins in the following way.

Once upon a time there was a little black boy, and his name was Little Black Sambo.

And his Mother was called Black Mumbo.

And his Father was called Black Jumbo.

And Black Mumbo made him a beautiful little Red Coat, and a pair of beautiful little Blue Trousers.

And Black Jumbo went to the Bazaar, and bought him a beautiful Green Umbrella, and a lovely Pair of Purple Shoes with Crimson Soles and Crimson Linings.

And then wasn't little Black Sambo grand.

Helen Bannerman, *The Story of Little Black Sambo*, Andover, 1996, pp. 7–19.

4.3   Restaurant racism

The everyday experience of racism in Britain in the early post-war years included social snubs for people with dark skins, irrespective of their social status.

I feel I must bring to your personal attention a very regrettable incident of colour in a restaurant, which has been reported to the Colonial Office.

I think you may know already that we have in this country His Highness the Kabaka of Buganda, Mutesa II, a sovereign ruler of a large territory in Uganda, who is an undergraduate at Magdalen[e] College, Cambridge. The Kabaka was recently the guest of Captain Oliver Messel, the well-known artist who, together with a friend, Mr Reis-Hansen, was taking the Kabaka out to dinner. They went to the Restaurant Le Cerf, 151 Fulham Road, SW5, where the Maître d'Hôtel refused them service on the grounds that they were in the company of a coloured person . . .

I am sure that you will appreciate the political implications involved here, and I think I should say that in the Colonial Office everything possible is being done to see that the Kabaka is well treated over here and returns to his own country with a good impression of England and English life. He has in fact done very well at Cambridge and it would be politically disastrous if shocking incidents of this sort were to spoil all our efforts. Naturally I take the strongest exception to this most blatant example of colour prejudice to which he has been subjected. The fact that this incident has involved the Kabaka is, of course, the more embarrassing because of his position, but I am sure you will agree that it is the principle of the matter which should be raised, because there are large numbers of coloured Colonial people in this country and this kind of thing might spread, unless it is checked in the early stages.

PRO CO 537 2110, 'Letter of Arthur Creech Jones, Colonial Secretary, to John Strachey, Minister of Food, 7 August 1947', in Ronald Hyam (ed.), *The Labour Government and the End of Empire, 1945–1951*, IV, *Race Relations and the Commonwealth*, London, 1992, pp. 19–20

4.4   Early police brutality

Complaints against the police

Name	Territory	Address	Date of offence	Nature of complaint
Mr and Mrs S. C. Farquharson	Jamaica	176 Manningham Lane, Bradford 8	25/10/58	Forceful entry without a warrant, damage to property and unlawful arrest (Bradford Police Station)
Mr Dudley Gordon (Carpenter)	Jamaica	32 Craven Park, Harlesden, NW10	14/2/59	Wrongful arrest.
Mr Henry Seaforth	British Guiana	33 Eldbrooks Road	–	Unlawful detention, assault with brutality (Harrow Road Police Station)
Mr Sidney White Ex-RAF and licensed Street Trader	Jamaica	4 Algar Buildings, Webber Row, London, SE1.	28/2/59	Assault, wrongful arrest and brutality

Source PRO CO 1031 2541.

From their first arrival in Britain immigrants, especially West Indians, have faced victimisation from an overwhelmingly white police force. Examples are detailed in the accompanying table.

4.5   Racism from the white Church

West Indians experienced hostility in the most unexpected of places, as one newcomer, 'Frank', recalled.

I remember, one beautiful Sunday evening, I was spending that weekend in London. I decided I would go to Evensong at the church, and I did go. And I didn't see another person like myself there. Nevertheless, I didn't feel any way uncomfortable because it was a church like . . . I was use to in the Caribbean. Anyhow, the last hymn was sung, I began to follow the people out, and I was walking behind a lady. The lady spoke to him [the priest] . . . he wished her good night. And I looked directly at him, held my hand out to shake his hand . . . and he made no move. So I said, 'Good night to you,' and I put my hand out again, thinking he might not have noticed. But he stared me in the face and, deliberately, withdrew his arm. I made my way to the door and went off.

I thought about it for a long time after, how strange it was that a parish priest, instead of welcoming someone who he'd seen for the first time come to his church, . . . making the person feel, well, you are welcome to come back again. But to behave like that was quite a shock to me. I talked to many other people since then, and they told me, yes, they did actually [go], not only to that church but the other churches – Methodists, Pentecostal and other churches – and they were 'cold-shouldered'. And this really worried me a great deal, because I never thought it would happen in Britain. This is the sort of thing I would have expected to happen in South Africa, in the United States – but not in Britain.

Black Cultural Archives, MOO6, Migration, 'Birmingham Black Oral History Project'.

4.6   The Union Movement

Since the end of the Second World War a series of small, extreme right-wing political parties have focused a large amount of their attention upon Commonwealth immigrants. One of the first of these consisted of the Union Movement, which had a stronghold in North Kensington, a constituency which included Notting Hill. Its leader, Oswald Mosley, stood as a candidate there at the 1959 general election and later put forward his position in his autobiography.

I stood on the general policy of the party covering British, European and world issues which was summarised in more detail than is usual in an election address, but our attitude on the question of coloured immigration was made clear beyond a shadow of a doubt. This was not a racialist policy, for I held to my principles . . . of opposing any form of racialism in a multi-racial Empire. Our Empire was gone before 1959, and it was already clear to me that much of the new Commonwealth would not last long and that the future of Britain now lay in Europe. Nevertheless, hostility to other peoples or the domination for any purpose of one people by another – in my reiterated definition the sole reason on which a charge of 'racialism' can rest – remained as alien as ever to my beliefs and policy.

The principles of racialism had nothing whatever to do with the issue in North Kensington. The injury to our people in suddenly importing to already disgracefully overcrowded areas a large population with an altogether different standard and way of life would have been as grave if it had been Eskimos or angels instead of Negroes. For nearly two generations the repeated pledge to rebuild the slums and to house our people properly had been broken . . .

British people and Jamaican immigrants were equally the victims of these conditions. The Jamaicans had already been hard hit by British government policy in their own country through the breach of binding undertakings to buy their sugar, which had resulted in widespread unemployment and mass hunger. These poor people were driven to Britain by the lash of starvation, and their arrival created inevitably a still more acute housing shortage, coupled with the threat of unemployment to British people if the competition for jobs became more acute in an industrial crisis. A situation which was bound to make trouble was created by the deliberate policy of the British government, and has resulted in a series of new laws ineffectively attempting to remedy or mitigate the error.

Much damage had already been done, but not nearly so much as was to follow from continuing and increasing immigration. My proposal was simply to repatriate immigrants to their homeland with fares paid and to fulfil the Government's pledge to buy sugar from Jamaica by long-term and large-scale contracts, which, together with other measures, such as bauxite production, would have restored that island to prosperity.

Sir Oswald Mosley, *My Life*, London, 1968, pp. 448–9.

4.7   The Notting Hill riots

Oswald Mosley's campaigning, combined with the social and economic conditions in the area, helped to lead to the outbreak of the worst anti-immigrant riots in post-war Britain, which occurred in Notting Hill in September 1958. Colin Eales, a local journalist, described the events of 1 September.

On Monday evening at 7.30 outside Ladbroke Grove station, all was quiet and it was nigh-on impossible to think that this was the same area where, less than twenty-four hours earlier, police had arrested seventeen people in street fights and beatings. West Indians had been savagely assaulted and petrol bombs had been thrown by the mobs into the homes of coloured people. But this was the main road and it was only 7.30.

Mob of 700

Walking down Lancaster Road, people looked unconcerned and oblivious to the seething pot that was Notting Dale. Further down the street towards Bramley Road, groups began to form and head for Latimer Road station. Shouting was coming from a few blocks away. As I turned into Bramley Road I saw a mob of over 700 men, women and children stretching 200 yards along the road. Young children of ten were treating the whole affair as a great joke and shouting: 'Come on, let's get the blacks' and '. . . the coppers, let's get on with it!'

'Kill the niggers'

In the middle of the mob of screaming, jeering youths and adults, a speaker from the Union Movement was urging his excited audience to 'get rid of them' (the coloured people). Groups of policemen stood at strategic points carefully watching the 'meeting', while police cars and Black Marias waited round the corner. Suddenly hundreds of leaflets were thrown over the crowd, a fierce cry rent the air and the mob rushed off in the direction of Latimer Road shouting, 'Kill the niggers!' Women grabbed their small children and chased after their menfolk. Dogs ran in among the crowds barking. Everywhere there was riotous confusion. Police cars and vans wheeled out to cut off the mob.

Meanwhile other police cars and vans in the area stood by to deal with the impending wave of violence.

Women laughed

Within half an hour the mob which had by now swelled to uncontrollable numbers had broken scores of windows and set upon two negroes who were lucky to escape with cuts and bruises. Women from top-floor windows laughed as they called down to the thousand-strong crowd 'Go on, boys, get yourselves some blacks.'

As the crowd swung around into Blenheim Crescent milk bottles rained down from tenement roofs where coloured men were sheltering. Accompanied by a dozen bottles, down came a petrol bomb in the middle of the mob. One eighteen-year-old youth was led away with blood streaming from a head wound. Unable to get at their attackers the inflamed rioters moved off to vent their wrath on other coloured men.

Whilst a mob was active in another street, a young boy of five was dragged off his bicycle in Westbourne Park Road, and beaten up by coloured men. The news spread like wildfire through the streets until it reached the ears of the rioters. Screaming for revenge they broke off from their widow smashing.

The mob was now moving towards Ladbroke Grove. Cars and lorries were halted as the inflamed rioters poured across the main road into Westbourne Park Road. One youth at the head of the mob ran straight into a passing car in his enthusiasm for window smashing and blood. He was taken to hospital with a suspected broken leg.

Broken glass and bricks

Once in Westbourne Park Road the rioters, hundreds strong, swore and shouted at a house where West Indians lived. Scores of milk bottles were hurled through the air, smashing the windows where coloured men had appeared. Broken glass and bricks were strewn across the road.

'Alright, boys, we're here'

The rioters left to continue their rampage through the street. Apart from the mob itself, smaller groups of fifteen to twenty were moving round the district independently. All through the evening, gangs of hooligans from all over London came to join in. They came on foot, by train, bus, motor bike, car and lorry, shouting, 'Alright, boys, we're here.' Those on motor bikes and in cars toured the district looking for coloured people. When they found them they went back to tell their friends. In this way I saw many coloured people pounced on.

In St Mark's Road a group of fourteen youths picked up bottles and bricks from a piece of waste ground. For a while they urged the coloured owner of a hairdresser's shop to come out. When their patience was exhausted they smashed two windows of the upstairs flat and the plate-glass shop front . . .

Flying milk bottles

Further up Talbot Grove a group of youths leaned against a wall watching the windows of a house. A coloured man was peeping from behind the curtains. The next thing I saw was a dozen milk bottles sweeping through the air towards the house. There was a crash and the tinkling of glass. The house was minus three windows. Within seconds a police van was on the scene and police were all over the street. The window smashers? The birds had flown.

Kensington News, 5 September 1958.

4.8   The aftermath of the Notting Hill riots

One year after the Notting Hill riots, relations between West Indians, the local police and the native population in the area remained tense.

The reports about conditions at Nottinghill continue to be the cause of great concern.

The Commission has received continuously reports of a persistent feeling on the part of West Indians that the Police are not impartial (for instance moving on a group of West Indians and leaving a group of others across the street), and have by indifference failed to make arrests or have shown partiality in making arrests where West Indians have been involved ...

Another source of growing concern are reports of increased activity in vice of some West Indians and yet others who have house parties of a disturbing character. Here we are concerned only for those who become the victims of the circumstances of poor housing conditions and the absence of proper meeting places to satisfy the normal impulses to meet each other in healthy social intercourse. These impulses tend to drive decent citizens towards and into these undesirable clubs, cafés and practices.

The situation is further aggravated by the unrelated activities of movements like Mosley's which are reported to distribute their propaganda sheets from door to door and incessantly stimulate ill feeling against the West Indian. The legislation contemplated for the preservation of law and order against issues of this kind cannot be too speedily enacted.

PRO CO 1028 50, 'Letter from the Commission in the United Kingdom for the West Indies, British Guiana and British Honduras to the Secretary of State for the Colonies, 1 September 1959'.

4.9   Middlesbrough, 1961

In August 1961 another race riot broke out, this time in Middlesbrough, where the major victims consisted of Pakistanis.

Street disturbances which broke out in a Middlesbrough coloured district on Saturday night continued yesterday afternoon. A cafe was wrecked in incidents involving several hundred people.

Strong police patrols were moved into the area and last night the Chief Constable, Mr Ralph Davison, said that twelve people had been arrested during Saturday's disturbances and five more yesterday. They would appear in court this morning.

All leave was stopped for Middlesbrough police, six of whom had to receive hospital treatment for injuries suffered from flying stones and bottles. Three police vehicles were also damaged.

The Chief Constable appealed to the public to keep away from the area of the disturbances, and said he did not think that it was a racial dispute in the sense that Middlesbrough people were hostile to coloured people.

The trouble began after a large and hostile crowd had assembled near a café in Cannon Street, Middlesbrough, on Saturday night. The cafe is close to the spot where an eighteen-year-old Middlesbrough youth was fatally stabbed on Friday night. An Arab was later charged with murder.

Police were sent to the cafe, the Taj Mahal, after a crowd of several hundred started throwing stones. As the police tried to control the crowds, a small fire started in the cafe and some of the crowd managed to enter the premises.

More police reinforcements were called in and after several arrests had been made, the crowd gradually dispersed and the police restored order.

Middlesbrough Fire Brigade were called to the fire, which involved a table, but it had been put out by the police before they arrived.

The café, owned by Mr and Mrs Meah, was considerably damaged, but none of the occupants was injured.

It is understood that no coloured people were involved in the incidents.

The policemen were injured when the angry crowd started throwing stones and bottles . . .

A second disturbance flared up in the Cannon Street area of the town yesterday afternoon. Shortly after the public houses closed, crowds gathered in Cannon Street and Boundary Road – where part of Middlesbrough's coloured population live – and stones began crashing through the windows of houses and shops and ugly scenes began to develop.

The police were on the spot and at times bricks were hurled out of the crowd at them.

This time no police were injured although police cars and vans arriving back at headquarters showed signs of damage from the incidents. One car had a cracked windscreen and a dent on its side caused by bricks.

More arrests were made and it later appeared that other cafés run by coloured people in the town were becoming targets for stone throwers.

The main troublemakers, who were hustled off in police vans, appeared to be youths. Many of these who made up the crowd of over 500 took no active part in the disturbances. At all times the police showed great restraint and handled the crowds well.

The Chief Constable and senior police officers toured Cannon Street and the numerous side streets running off it to assess the situation.

After about two hours the streets were comparatively quiet again although police were patrolling in two's.

Yesterday, considerable numbers of coloured residents, particularly in the Cannon Street area, were seen to be leaving in cars and taxis. They were going, they explained, to stay with relatives and friends in West Hartlepool, Darlington and other North-east towns until the trouble blows over.

Northern Echo, 21 August 1961.

4.10   The Birmingham Immigration Control Association

In Birmingham the hostility towards immigrants manifested itself most clearly in the formation of the Birmingham Immigration Control Association in 1960. Its chairman, John Sanders, published a leaflet in 1965, in which he made blunt remarks about the consequences of immigration into Britain.

The margin of error in the conduct of human affairs is appallingly great, and history is largely a lamentable record of its tragic consequences. But where in our history can we find a more damaging instance of it than in the persistent refusal of our politicians to close the door against the unexpected, massive inrush of Afro-Asian immigrants that has occurred over the past decade?

Resulting from this visibly senseless deviation from our long established policy of careful restriction of immigration, we are now confronted with the enormous economic and social problems which were bound to be created by the sudden addition to our population of more than a million unassimilable people, for whom we must import food and provide with houses and the expensive amenities of a highly sophisticated society.

This huge addition to our population, consisting of multi-racial, largely unskilled, illiterate immigrants, who for the most part have not our language, was never contemplated, much less planned or called for: it was just allowed to happen, as if it were a chastisement which we *had* to suffer.

No one really knows how many of these resented and resentful people are already in our midst, but the evidence indicates that there can be no less than a *million*. And no one can say what the total would be now but for the belated and largely ineffectual Commonwealth Immigrants Act, which was introduced in June 1962, after great pressure from the electorate, and against bitter opposition from the Socialist and Liberal politicians. Official figures published, however, indicate that the total would be no less than twice as great.

Be that as it may, it has been estimated that the numbers of those now actually here will be increased to more than three millions in the next fifteen years, by natural growth, and at the present rate of entry . . .

The vast economic burdens on our overstrained economy are only now beginning to be perceived, for, like the iceberg, they are only three-tenths visible to the ordinary citizen. But, unlike the iceberg, they will not melt away. They will trouble us for generations.

And the ineradicable social problems created by the introduction of this huge alien population into our midst are only beginning to develop. But already the day is gone when a Briton returned from a foreign land can walk our streets feeling that he is again among his 'ain folk'.

John Sanders, *Immigration: The Incredible Folly*, Birmingham, 1965, pp. 4–5.

4.11   Enoch Powell

Enoch Powell did more than any other individual to cause resentment against immigrants, making blunt statements which led to his expulsion from the Conservative Shadow Cabinet in 1968. On 20 April that year he gave his most infamous speech of all at the Midland Hotel in Birmingham, in which he forecast an apocalyptic future for a multi-racial Britain. He prefaced his soothsaying with statements about the Britain of the 1960s.

A week or two ago I fell into conversation with a constituent, a middle-aged, quite ordinary working man employed in one of our nationalised industries. After a sentence or two about the weather,

141

he suddenly said: 'If I had made the money, I wouldn't stay in this country.' I made some deprecatory reply, to the effect that even this government wouldn't last for ever; but he took no notice, and continued: 'I have children, all of them been through grammar school and two of them married now, with family. I shan't be satisfied till I have seen them all settled overseas. In this country in fifteen or twenty years' time the black man will have the whip-hand over the white man.'

I can already hear the chorus of execration. How dare I say such a horrible thing? How dare I stir up trouble and inflame feelings by repeating such a conversation? The answer is that I do not have the right not to do so. Here is a decent, ordinary fellow Englishman, who in broad daylight in my town says to me, his Member of Parliament, that this country will not be worth living in for his children. I simply do not have the right to shrug my shoulders and think about something else. What he is saying, thousands and hundreds of thousands are saying and thinking – not throughout Great Britain, perhaps, but in the areas that are already undergoing the total transformation to which there is no parallel in a thousand years of English history.

In fifteen or twenty years, on present trends, there will be in this country $3\frac{1}{2}$ million Commonwealth immigrants and their descendants. That is not my figure. That is the official figure given to Parliament by the spokesman of the Registrar General's office. There is no comparable official figure for the year 2000; but it must be in the region of 5–7 million, approximately one-tenth of the whole population, and approaching that of Greater London. Of course, it will not be evenly distributed from Margate to Aberystwyth and from Penzance to Aberdeen. Whole areas, towns and parts of towns across England will be occupied by different sections of the immigrant and immigrant-descended population.

As time goes on, the proportion of this total who are immigrant descendants, those born in England, who arrived here by exactly the same route as the rest of us, will rapidly increase. Already by 1985 the native-born would constitute the majority. It is this fact above all which creates the extreme urgency of action now, of just that kind of action which is hardest for politicians to take, action where the difficulties lie in the present but the evils to be prevented or minimised lie several Parliaments ahead.

Bill Smithies and Peter Fiddick (eds), *Enoch Powell on Immigration: An Analysis*, London, 1969, pp. 35–7.

4.12 Racism in schools

Those children who arrived or were born in Britain during the 1960s found themselves in an Anglocentric system in which racism operated both covertly and overtly, as Sandra Knight, who moved from Trinidad to Shepherds Bush in 1960, remembered.

We went to Flora Gardens School but before we went there my mother tried to get us to go to John Betts, which was a lot nearer to us, but at that particular time there weren't any Black children in the school and I think that was why we didn't get in. So we went to Flora Gardens which was a mixture of children. I was very aware of being Black at that school although they tried to cover up a lot of things. I remember one incident where we were told to draw what people look like in the Caribbean and draw beach scenes and stuff like that. Everybody had to do it, English children did slides and water chutes and that kind of stuff. I just did kids playing on the beach and I remember the teacher coming up to me and saying 'Where's the grass skirts?' and this sort of thing. I couldn't under-stand what she was talking about and she said people have grass skirts and bones through their noses and things like this . . . There was endless sports days and plays, another incident was when they were doing a play about Vikings and I wanted to be a Viking and this teacher said 'Vikings have red hair.' That's when I really started realising what was going on, even when you're that young, seven or eight, you can still feel things . . .

When I was eleven I went to the famous at the time Holland Park School, it was supposed to be very liberal and very open minded and modern. It was nothing of the sort, it was just under a new guise. They had a grading system, there were H-forms and P-forms.

They didn't admit to this but most of the P-forms were Black kids, very, very few Black kids were in the H-forms. The H-forms consisted mainly of privileged kind of people like Wedgie Benn (that's what we used to call him), his son went, all those people were always in there and they came straight out of boarding or public school and into this 'trendy' school. There was definitely a class divide because even if a lot of the children didn't have the ability they were still put in H-forms, it was really obvious. I used to play the piano and when I went to Holland Park I tried for years to get into the music productions at Christmas and the teacher who held all these classes he'd always say 'Waiting list, waiting list.' In the end I just gave up, what I should have done was stick it out and insisted. They use to have really huge productions like the *Mikado* which used to be on the television at Christmas – you know, 'A Holland Park Production' – and it was always the H-forms that were in it.

I had one white friend, we were in the same class. I don't know what happened in the playground, we were just swinging on a bar and something happened, she turned around and called me a wog and ran off. So I chased after her and we ran into the foyer of the school where there was this big dignitary meeting going on and I just laid into her. That was it, I didn't have any white friends after, I just didn't want to know . . .

A lot of Black children were encouraged to do domestic science and sports, high-jump and running and that sort of thing. I rebelled in the end, I just didn't want to know. Everybody was put into a little niche, what they were expected to do. It was very stereotyped, it kept you back, it kept you down. When these H-forms were busy doing their languages, Classical Greek, Latin, etc., a lot of them were exempt from sports so they could have extra lessons in Maths or whatever, everybody else would be running up and down tracks and that sort of thing. It was a class and racist system.

Ethnic Communities Oral History Project, *The Motherland Calls: African Caribbean Experiences*, London, 1992, pp. 21–2.

4.13   Racism in football

During the 1970s and 1980s black players in Britain faced constant racial abuse at all levels, from local to professional, as one member of Highfield Rangers, a predominantly black team from Leicester, recalls.

We seemed to get racial abuse all the time. It's funny because we found it more when we went out to these country teams. I remember one particular incident when there was a little boy, a white family, and we ran out on to this pitch and this little boy's remark was, 'Mum, they haven't got tails!' and the two of us who heard it just looked round at the mother because you couldn't look at the boy. Others, like, say an incident or a tackle, the first thing was it wasn't a bad tackle but straight away, 'God, you black this or black that.' Some of the players started to react to that. It was hard to keep quiet about it, but we loved playing football so much, we took it as sport and that's it. We didn't expect to get all this abuse.

Living History Unit, *Highfield Rangers: An Oral History*, Leicester, 1993, pp. 51–2.

4.14   The National Front

Few organisations have done as much as the National Front to harm the position of immigrants in Britain. It has been the most successful extreme right-wing political party in British history, reaching the high point of its success in the middle of the 1970s. In 1974 it campaigned for repatriation.

Everyone wants to see better race relations in Britain and through-out the world. In this we agree with the other parties.

We differ from them, however, in believing that better relations can best be achieved by separation rather than integration. All experience has shown us that African, Asian and West Indian immigrants cannot be successfully assimilated into the British population. Where they settle in large numbers there is almost invariably community strife and tension. They bring with them living habits which it is not our purpose to criticise but only to say that they are habits strange and alien to the British people. Their settlement in great numbers in British towns has transformed those towns out of all recognition to the native inhabitants. We believe that this transformation has not been for the better . . .

The National Front advocates a total ban on any further non-White immigration into Britain, and the launching of a phased plan of repatriation for all coloured immigrants and their descendants already here. This programme will be put into operation with the greatest possible humanity, but we do not suppose that it can be effected without some hardship to a portion of the people concerned. We simply prefer to risk hardship to one generation of immigrants than ensure hardship for countless future generations of people in this country.

To those who argue that we depend on immigrants for the running of essential services, we reply that at the moment this indeed may be so. However, the British people themselves have run these services before and can do so again. Repatriation of the immigrants will not be completed overnight but will take place at a pace which will allow their jobs to be filled by British people, if necessary at better wages. The change-over of labour may indeed present some initial difficulty, but this is small in relation to the gravity of the problem that we are storing up for ourselves if we opt instead for a permanent multi-racial Britain ...

White Commonwealth immigrants who have come to this country in recent years are a totally different case. They are not present in large enough numbers to create an overcrowding problem, and they are descended from stock the same as our own and are therefore assimilable by our own. These immigrants should be given completely free entry into Britain and full rights of British citizenship.

National Front, *For a New Britain: The Manifesto of the National Front*, London, 1974, pp. 17–19.

4.15   The aftermath of the Birmingham pub bombs

> Some of the worst discrimination faced by the Irish in Britain occurred after the IRA pub bombs in Birmingham in November 1974, manifesting itself most overtly in violence.

Petrol bomb attacks hit Irish targets in Birmingham during the night.

School, pub, social centres and businesses, all with Irish connections, were the targets of what detectives were today treating as 'reprisal raids' after the pub bombings.

Thousands of pounds' worth of damage was caused. But no one was hurt.

In two of the attacks petrol bombs were hurled through windows.

One of these was at the College Arms public house in College Road, Erdington, kept by Irish licensee Mr James McDonnell.

It is the pub at which less than two weeks ago a British soldier was refused service because he was in full uniform – although Mr McDonnell later apologised for his barman's decision.

In the 1 a.m. assault the lounge window was smashed. A bottle filled with petrol and with a rag 'wick' flaming at the neck was pushed through the window.

The bottle broke and rolled under a seat. The fire started caused more than £5,000 worth of damage and put the lounge out of action. Firemen saved the rest of the public house.

Worse damage was prevented because of a prompt call for assistance.

Mr McDonnell was still up when the attack occurred and heard the noise.

Police found another bottle primed for use at the side of [the] pub in Warren Farm Road. It was taken away for expert examination.

An hour earlier at the Irish Community Centre in Digbeth, Birmingham, there was a similar attack.

But it misfired when the alarm system was set off as the fire started.

Police found a window smashed and the carpet beginning to burn inside the lounge. They quickly forced access to the premises so that firemen could prevent any spread of the blaze.

The bottled petrol bomb found – still intact – was taken away to be compared with that found at Erdington.

First of the four attacks during the night was shortly after 11 p.m. at St Gerard's Roman Catholic School in Yatesbury Avenue, Castle Vale.

Many of the staff and families with children attending the school are Irish.

Petrol was sprinkled round the outside of the timber-built junior and infant wing and ignited.

Flames caught the sides of an entrance area and fanned beneath the building which is set on brick piers. An observant passer-by – an Irishman – saw the smoke and raised the alarm.

He, the caretaker and other volunteers grabbed fire extinguishers and attacked the flames as they roared along a section of the outer wall and started to burn through the floor of the building from underneath.

They had the situation under control when firemen arrived within minutes.

Although a number of vandal attacks in the city have involved petrol in the past police and fire officers were not convinced that this was the explanation this time.

The other attack was on £20,000 worth of lorries parked at an open-air depot of the building and demolition firm of J. J. Gallagher and Co. Ltd.

Again a passer-by was in time to prevent a major inferno.

He saw smoke from among the six vehicles parked in the yard in Little Green Lane, Small Heath, and called firemen.

They called police after discovering petrol-soaked rags burning in the cabs. Upholstery and roof linings in the vehicles were damaged, but the fire crews were able to prevent the fire spreading – and in two of the lorries smouldering material had burned itself out.

The intruders are thought to have scaled a high wire mesh fence to enter the yard.

Birmingham Post, 23 November 1974.

4.16   Prevention of Terrorism Act

The Prevention of Terrorism Act, passed in November 1974 in the aftermath of the Birmingham pub bombs of that month, represented one of the most draconian pieces of legislation ever passed by a peacetime Parliament and allowed the arrest and detention of Irish people for up to seven days. The journalist Paddy Prendeville faced arrest during a brief holiday in December 1979.

I spent the first twenty-four hours in a filthy cell, completely naked for the first few hours as all my clothes had been taken off me, but was subjected to no questioning at all . . .

But on the Thursday morning I was led upstairs to an office by two well-dressed members of the Anti-Terrorist Squad (ATS) who proceeded, with chilling efficiency, to administer to me the most terrifying few days of my life. After cursory details of my life and family had been taken they insisted that I had no right to silence . . .

But that night I thought over my position again. I realised that even my innocent 'alibi', which would include references to dozens of individuals and friends I had met in the last few days, most of them concerned in left-wing politics, could inadvertently place question marks over others and even myself. I determined, whatever the consequences, to answer no more questions.

On the Friday morning they became very threatening and interrogator number one told me that I was definitely linked to the 'hair-raising' events of the last few days . . . 'It would make your hair curl, Paddy,' he kept repeating. His number two nodded seriously in agreement. Number one then threw a second bombshell at me: 'We also have evidence to link you with Airey Neave's murder last March!'

I could feel my jaw sag as he started to question me about various political activities in Ireland. The fact that I knew some of those named (as indeed my job requires) appeared to be proof positive in his mind that I was implicated in the two most serious offences of 1979. But more was to come. He leaned over the table into my face and said, 'I told you that you are linked to the two biggest terrorist crimes of the last twelve months; well, I was wrong, you're also involved in a third – the Provo bombs in London last Christmas!' I nearly fainted and he walked over to the door. 'Let's bring him down to his cell,' he said to number two, 'and I hope your hair does not turn white tonight, Paddy. I bet you don't get much sleep', he added . . .

The next morning, Saturday, I tried to appear determined as I announced my intention to remain completely silent. I told them that they had terrified me (which was true) by accusing me of several major crimes. As each innocuous answer I had given only seemed to incriminate me, I was saying nothing until I saw my solicitor.

Number one looked quite angry and repeated that I was in it up to my neck. 'A right hornets' nest,' he added, 'but I'll tell you what I'll do. If you tell us exactly what we want to know' (he paused and waited for the offer of a Queen's pardon for offences which I had not committed) 'at the end of the day I'll see you fine.' Assuring myself that I would not have accepted any offer (no informer me, not even of fiction!), never mind this ridiculous one, I repeated my adamant intention to remain silent.

They suddenly became very concerned. How could they persuade me that they only wanted to help me? I answered, again truthfully, that they could not. Then suddenly they changed course. They assured me that their main concern was to prove my innocence which they were almost convinced of. They had not really accused me of involvement in the incidents mentioned. The number two (a Scot) assured me that he actually had many Irish friends; they were great people, 'nice and decent just like you, Paddy'. I smiled for the first time in four days and number one raised his eyes to the ceiling. He leaned over and told me to seize my self-confidence. 'You're a man, aren't you Paddy? I suppose you would prefer us to beat you; then you could hate us and it would be no problem resisting us.'

I was not at all sure about this but decided to agree with him, adding the black lie that I thought they were very civilised. 'Well then,' he said, 'why not be straight with us?' I tried to look non-committal and number one asked me if I would like some lunch. My stomach heaved at the thought of any food, but anything was better than this game of poker and so I tried to look as if no more appetising suggestion had ever been made to me and we adjourned.

They were back in a couple of hours with more sweetness and kindness. Would I like a change of clothes that my sister had brought in? There was a toothbrush and paste in the same bag. Would I like to use them? They didn't mention that my sister's parcel was handed in forty-eight hours earlier. With a whimper of gratitude I accepted the offers and spent about five minutes furiously brushing my teeth for the first time in four days.

Sitting down to our next session I was swamped with kindly offers of coffee, fruit that my sister had sent in ('Little angel isn't she?' said one) and, absolute luxury, clean underwear. I accepted all the blandishments as gracefully as possible and waited for their next move.

It came in the form of a political diatribe against IRA extremism and an appeal to my moderate sensibilities. I still insisted on remaining silent and there was another long pause. 'OK!' sighed one, 'bring him down to his cell.'

Ten minutes later they returned to the cell and casually asked me if I would like to go. As calmly as possible I walked to the cell door and, after collecting some personal items at the station sergeant's desk, I was ushered to the two ATS members' car. I declined their offer of a pint (had they discovered the best way to make me talk?) and we arrived at my sister's house at approximately 6 p.m.

Catherine Scorer and Patricia Hewitt, *The Prevention of Terrorism Act: The Case for Repeal*, London, 1981, pp. 49–51.

4.17   The Irish experience of everyday prejudice

Irish immigrants in post-war Britain have always faced every-day discrimination, particularly at times of heightened IRA activity, as one resident of Islington recalls.

It's dreadful, really. I've been put out of shops, down the West End, Great Portland Street – had a lady panic, send for her husband. He came downstairs, threw me out of the shop. I could have done something about it, but what's the point? Just one or two incidents. Even mates that I've worked with for years. Eddie from Wales, I've seen him blank me. Mates in the pub, they come out with comments like 'Bloody Irish murderers, they should all be shot'. Even governors, some of them can be well bad culprits.

Mary Hickman and Bronwen Walter, *Discrimination and the Irish Community in Britain*, London, 1997, p. 215.

4.18   Attacks upon individuals

Although large-scale rioting against immigrants had declined by the 1970s, small-scale vicious attacks upon individuals and their families in particular areas of the country had taken off, especially in east London, aggravated by a lack of police action against thugs. The following incidents, typical of countless others, took place in May 1977 against a Bengalee family and their four young children.

The family originally living in one room in Bow applied for GLC accommodation in August 1976. In May 1977 the family moved into Tidey Street, E3, after having been made two unsatisfactory offers of accommodation. The first had been totally vandalised on the family's arrival. The second was occupied by squatters.

The family moved in a sofa and cooker to Tidey Street. On their return they found the entire flat daubed with racist slogans ('NF. Black Bastards, monkeys', etc.) Within three weeks all the windows in the flat had been broken by outsiders. The family car was vandalised and bottles and stones were hurled at the family daily. The father was attacked by gangs of white youths on three to four occasions. The gang also threatened to kill the small children on the one occasion they were allowed out of the flat to play. Police phoned the family many times during this period, but, according to the family, took little action. They are believed to have advised the family to catch the culprits themselves, whereupon the Police would assist them in taking out a private summons.

The family then complained to the local community relations officer who arranged for a senior Police officer to visit them. The officer duly visited the family and undertook to protect its members. The same evening the home was stoned by a gang of youths. The police arrived two hours after being called. Eventually the GLC arranged for the family to be transferred to another flat, in Morris Street, E1.

Bethnal Green and Stepney Trades Council, *Blood on the Streets*, London, 1978, pp. 66–7.

4.19   The view from the mainstream

While mainstream politicians may not make the sort of overt statements characteristic of the extreme right, they have the power to implement their ideas and policies. Margaret Thatcher developed her views on immigration and race during her period in opposition.

Ever since Enoch Powell's Birmingham speech in April 1968 it had been the mark of civilised high-mindedness among right-of-centre politicians to avoid speaking about immigration and race at all, and if that did not prove possible, then to do so in terms borrowed from the left of the political spectrum, relishing the 'multi-cultural', 'multi-racial' nature of modern British society. This whole approach glossed over the real problems that immigration sometimes caused and dismissed the anxieties of those who were directly affected as 'racist'. I had never been prepared to go along with it. It seemed both dishonest and snobbish . . .

At the same time, large-scale New Commonwealth immigration over the years had transformed large areas of Britain in a way which the indigenous population found hard to accept. It is one thing for the well-heeled politician to preach the merits of tolerance on a public platform before returning to a comfortable home in a tranquil road in one of the more respectable suburbs, where house prices ensure him the exclusiveness of apartheid without the stigma.

It is quite another for poorer people, who cannot afford to move, to watch their neighbourhoods changing and the value of their house falling . . .

Policy work on immigration had been proceeding under Willie Whitelaw's direction for some time by January 1978. But it had not progressed very far – certainly not as far as many of our supporters, vocal at Party Conferences, wished. This was only partly because Willie himself was instinctively liberal-minded on Home Office matters. The problem was that it was very difficult to see what scope existed to cut down on present and potential future immigration . . .

Closing loopholes, tightening up administration and some new controls on primary and secondary immigration – all of these offered opportunities to reduce the inflow. But I knew that the single most important contribution we could make to good race relations was to reduce the uncertainties about the future. It was fear of the unknown rather than the awkwardness of the present which threatened danger. Willie Whitelaw shared that basic analysis, which is why he had pledged us at the 1976 Party Conference 'to follow a policy which is clearly designed to work towards the end of immigration as we have seen it in these post-war years'.

Although I had not planned any specific announcement on immigration, I was not surprised when I was asked in an interview on *World in Action* about the subject. I had been giving it a good deal of thought, having indeed expressed myself strongly in other interviews . . .

Before my interview, the opinion polls showed us level-pegging with Labour. Afterwards, they showed the Conservatives with an eleven-point lead. This unintended effect of a spontaneous reply to an interviewer's question had important political consequences. Whatever Willie in his heart of hearts and my other colleagues felt about it, it provided a large and welcome boost at an extremely difficult time. It also sharpened up the discussion within the Shadow Cabinet of our proposals. Within weeks we had a comprehensive and agreed approach which satisfied all but the diehard advocates of repatriation and which would see us through the general election.

Margaret Thatcher, *The Path to Power*, London, 1995, pp. 405–9.

4.20   The death of Ahmed Iqbal Ullah

In some cases racist violence has resulted in murder, and, in a
few, has involved children.

On Monday, 15 September, Darren Coulburn, a thirteen-year-old
white pupil, punched an Asian boy in Ladyburn Park, knocked him
down, split his lip and began to torment and bully him. Ahmed
Iqbal Ullah saw the bullying. He intervened and humiliated Darren
Coulburn, making him look stupid.

The following day, rumours were running around the Lower
School that 'there's going to be a fight in the park after school'.
Ahmed and Darren were to have a showdown. A crowd gathered
in the park, encouraging them. The proceedings began. Darren
punched Ahmed in the face. Ahmed bled, but fought back. Ahmed
was winning and Darren retreated. Ahmed pursued him but older
pupils intervened.

Ahmed had gone home victorious, but with cut lips and bruises.
He told his mother about the fight, and that Darren had threatened
to kill him. His mother was anxious but he laughed it off. The same
evening, Darren said to his friends: 'Let him start again and I'll stab
him.'

On the morning of Wednesday, 17 September, Mrs Ullah did not
want Ahmed to go to school before she had a chance to speak to
his teacher about the fight. However, Ahmed said he was fine. As
Darren walked to school, he took out a knife and boasted that if
Ahmed started on him again, he would stab him.

Darren and Ahmed met in the corner of the playground by the
gap in the railings. A crowd of boys gathered. Darren appeared to
be avoiding the fight. Ahmed was keen. Ahmed pushed Darren.
Darren then bent over – the next instant he stabbed Ahmed in the
stomach. The blade came out covered in blood. Ahmed staggered
away and fell. As he did so, one eye witness heard Darren Coulburn shout: 'Do you want another one, you stupid Paki; there's
plenty more where that came from.' A few minutes later, he was
seen by fourth and fifth year students at the gate of the Upper
School, freaking out, running about and saying: 'I've killed a
Paki.'

Runnymede Trust, *Racism, Anti-racism and Schools: A Survey of the
Burnage Report*, London, 1989, p. 7.

4.21   Black deaths at the hands of the police

One of the most blatant indications of racism in Britain is the number of black people who have died at the hands of the police.

Clinton McCurbin was a twenty-four-year-old black man who had lived in Wolverhampton all of his life. An unemployed welder and member of the Church of God of Prophecy, he has been described as a 'loner by nature, not given to violence and, being of slight build, did not represent a threat to anyone'. On 27 February 1987, McCurbin went shopping in Wolverhampton's Mander Centre, a shopping precinct fitted out with a sophisticated surveillance system. McCurbin was in the Next shop when he came under suspicion of using a stolen credit card. The shop assistants, on instructions from the credit card company, deflected McCurbin's attention and called for the police.

Two police officers, PCs Michael Hobday and Neil Thomas, came into the shop and, when McCurbin resisted arrest, forced him to the ground and, with the help of a white customer in the shop, physically restrained him. PC Hobday, in particular, held McCurbin in an armlock around his neck for several minutes. PC Hobday was later to claim that his hold was on McCurbin's head and chin and not on his neck, although he admitted 'in hindsight' that it may have caused McCurbin to lose consciousness and die. But a shop assistant told the inquest into McCurbin's death that the latter was having difficulty breathing when held by Hobday, and other witnesses said the police officer was 'practically strangling' McCurbin and failed to release him even after he had stopped struggling. Another worker in the shop confirmed that several black customers pleaded with the police to release their hold on McCurbin, and a third officer who arrived at the scene to handcuff McCurbin said that, although McCurbin's arm was totally limp at the time, he thought 'he might have been faking it'. In fact, McCurbin was probably dead by this time.

Immediately after his death, the police denied that McCurbin had ever been handcuffed and issued a statement that his death may have been caused by a heart attack induced by drug abuse. It was also falsely suggested that McCurbin had been a Rastafarian. In fact, separate post-mortems carried out by two pathologists confirmed that no evidence of a heart attack or traces of drugs were found in his body and that his death had been caused by asphyxiation due to the obstruction of his airway.

Institute of Race Relations, *Deadly Silence: Black Death in Custody*, London, 1991, pp. 11–12.

4.22   The nearly all-white criminal justice system

Numerous reports have demonstrated that black people face a greater chance of prosecution than white people. Part of the reason lies in the virtual absence of black people from the judicial bench, as the table demonstrates.

The ethnic composition of the judiciary

	1992		1995	
Judicial posts	*Total*	*Ethnic origin*	*Total*	*Ethnic origin*
High Court judge	82	0	95	0
Circuit judge	480	3	514	5
District judge	257	0	339	2
Recorders	784	7	897	13
Assistant recorders	475	8	341	9
Totals	2,078	18	2,086	29

Source National Association of Probation Officers and the Association of Black Probation Officers, *Race, Discrimination and the Criminal Justice System*, London, 1996, p. 2.

4.23   Social discrimination into the 1980s

Three decades after West Indians first arrived in Britain their children were still facing basic social discrimination, as one youth recalled.

When you go to a nightclub, no matter how you're dressed, if you're wearing a shirt and tie and all that, they say you're not dressed right, and then a white guy comes up in casual clothes and gets straight in.

All the clubs in town have a system where they only let in a handful of blacks, just to cover themselves. One of them even has a black bouncer to turn away black people, so that you can't say they're prejudiced. Even if you're perfectly dressed they'll find some reason to stop you, like no single men, or no groups, or they don't like your hair. I was even told once there weren't enough buttons on my shirt.

Black Birmingham, Birmingham, 1987, p. 49.

4.24 Press racism

Immigrants have faced hostility in the press from their first arrival, a situation which continues unrelented. Since the end of the 1960s much attention has focused upon the apparent threat of illegal immigrants, despite their small numbers.

Britain is being swamped by a tide of illegal immigrants so desperate for a job that they will work for a pittance in our restaurants, cafés and nightclubs.

Immigration officers are being overwhelmed by work. Last year, 2,191 'illegals' were nabbed and sent back home. But there are tens of thousands more, slaving behind bars, cleaning hotel rooms and working in kitchens. And when officers swoop on an establishment, they often find huge numbers of unlawful workers being employed.

Case one. Last month officers raided the Casey Jones burger bar at Waterloo Station in London. Ten staff were carted off.

Case two. In May, 1987, immigration officials swooped on London's swanky Hilton Hotel in Park Lane in a 2 a.m. raid, after a tip that one of the cleaners was working there illegally. They ended up taking away THIRTEEN Nigerians, all employed illegally.

Case three. In Tenby in Dyfed, West Wales, police arrested the chef of the Golden Curry Indian restaurant last May. Unfortunately, they forgot to tell the diners. Customers were still waiting for their meals two hours later.

The battle to hunt down the furtive workforce is carried out by a squad of just 115 immigration officers.

Yesterday *The Sun* revealed exclusively how an illegal immigrant was nabbed in the kitchen of Deals, the restaurant in Chelsea, West London, run by the Queen's nephew, Viscount Linley.

And now the Home Office have announced they are planning to draft in an extra forty men to track down more. Illegals sneak in by:

- *Deceiving* immigration officers when they are quizzed at airports.
- *Disappearing* after their entry visas run out.
- *Forging* work permits and other documents.
- *Running* away from immigration detention centres.

They have little difficulty finding jobs, especially in London, because unscrupulous employers know that they can pay rock-bottom wages.

Sun, 2 February 1989.

4.25   The British National Party

Although racist parties declined in the late 1970s as the National Front lost its influence and Margaret Thatcher rose to power, one group which achieved brief success in the 1990s, when it won a local council seat in Tower Hamlets, was the British National Party. Its 1997 manifesto spoke in overtly racist language.

Whatever the immediate problems and tensions caused by immigration . . . these pale into insignificance compared with the long-term consequences for Britain of continued non-white immigrant influx, the relatively higher ethnic minority birthrate and the inevitable intermingling and intermarriage that will increase as the ethnic minority population increases as a proportion of the whole; there will be a drastic change in the British population, with the eventual result that the British nation will become something wholly different, racially and culturally, to what it has been over the past centuries of magnificent British achievement.

Britain will become less and less a white European country and more and more a Third World country.

It is not too late to stop this happening, but it will be too late if action is not taken at a fairly early stage of the coming century. In the United States, where the process of non-white immigration, a prolific non-white birthrate, widespread inter-racial marriage and the raising of mixed-race children has been going on much longer and on a comparatively greater scale, it is predicted that the white peoples, whose ancestors built the country, will become a minority by around 2050. The same thing will happen to the British people – a bit later, perhaps, but it *will* happen – if we are not determined to stop it.

By the middle of the next century the Americans could lose their country. By the end of it, if not before, we could lose ours!

By 'we', we mean of course the Anglo-Saxon and Celtic peoples whose unique blend of Northern European stocks gave Britain her greatness and her genius. Do we want this to happen? Certainly, powerful and influential people in politics and the mass media want it to happen and are doing their best to speed up the process by a ceaseless onslaught of propaganda in support of multi-racialism. We don't believe, however, that the majority of the British people – deep down in their hearts – want it to happen.

The desire that the future generations of our nation should look like us, think like us and have our aptitudes and qualities is as basic to human nature as the desire that our own children, grandchildren and great-grandchildren should do so.

British National Party, *Britain Reborn: British National Party Election Manifesto, 1997*, Welling, 1997, p. 44.

5

Multiracialism

The issue of whether Britain has become multiracial is complicated and depends, in part, on the meaning of the term. If it refers to Britain in a 'cultural' sense, then dramatic changes have taken place. People dress differently, eat different foods and speak different languages. Britain has also become multiracial because of the willingness of many native whites to go out of their way to assist the immigrants. Finally, the state has put much effort into creating a situation in which the population accepts ethnic difference as normal, as well as assisting immigrants and their children upon arrival.

5.1   What is an English person?

One of the problems with concepts of multiracialism lies in the fact that many sections of society have not accepted black people as British, while black people themselves have doubts about their own nationality, as Mike Phillips, a Guyanese immigrant, explains.

The crucial issue in this country for both black and white people is what does it mean to be an English person? Am I English, having lived here since 1956? I was coming in from France the other day and I had forgotten to fill in a landing card – I still have a Guyanese passport. This girl in her twenties, working as an immigration officer, told me to fill it in. So I did. But it struck me I had been living in this country considerably longer than she had been alive. And that goes for a number of my colleagues, and the kids whom I am teaching. So I feel that they can't tell me what it means to be English. I've been English longer than they have. I feel English, my kind of English. I'm not an English person like Ken Livingstone or

Prince Charles, I'm my own kind, the kind of English person who came here in 1956 and lived in bloody Islington and has lived in London most of his life. With a different history and so on, but that's still what it means to be English too. That is the struggle, that is one of the things *we* have to begin to understand. In the United States a black population like ours would be saying, 'We are Caribbean-Americans.' If we worked by the same logic here we would be saying, 'We are black English people, this is the kind of English people we are; as such we are part of this state and this state should reform its identity to allow for that.' In fact, what we do is this business of adopting or re-adopting Caribbean manners and dialects and music and so forth. Which seems to me a sort of cop-out, this never having had the confidence to make a claim on the identity of this nation.

Jonathan Green, *Them: Voices from the Immigrant Community in Contemporary Britain*, London, 1990, p. 277.

5.2   The club scene

Since the Second World War black popular music and dance have fundamentally changed popular culture throughout the world, playing a leading role in the birth of 'pop music'. This has largely occurred as a result of international record companies, which have sold black American music. In Britain the presence of West Indian immigrants and their children has facilitated this process, evident in the formation of black British pop groups and in the growth of clubs, many of them playing music sung or influenced by black people.

- *The Raw Club*
112a Great Russell Street, WC1 (Tel. Marie on 0171 436 1510).
   There's much happening at the Capital's 'deepest down' venue including these . . . 'I HAVE A DREAM' every Friday attracts a more appreciative and trendy crowd with Maura Miller, Lloyd Life, Boogie Boy Lloyd and Keith Lawrence in the Soul R&B Room. Plus Gary and Mackie, Adrian Pitch, Markey Sparks plus House 4 rent in the Uplifting Room.
   'KINGSIZE' every Saturday has just moved in and dez rez Sean McLuskey brings a blend of criminally eclectic grooves to the West End. He says his move to the Raw is 'to start the fight against the

corporate moralisation of the epicentre of style, because we all know how real style has no morals!' Fair enough . . . See Sean and loadsa guests in the coming weeks.

Times: 8 p.m.–2 a.m. Tax £5/Ladies FREE.

• *Broadway Boulevard*

1–10 High Street, Ealing, W5 (Club Tel. 0181 840 1616).

West London's busiest venue provides plenty of action for weekend hedonists within reach . . .

'DELICIOUS' every Friday boom house and garage with DJ's on rotation: Roy the Roach, Darren Pearce, Jon Da Silva, Nicky Holloway, Graham Gold, Dave Lambert, Tall Paul and many more! It's strictly over 18's and NO trainers.

Times: 10 p.m. to 4 a.m. Tax: £5 b4 11 p.m./£7 after.

'DECADENCE' every Saturday is the recently launched night club that has three rooms for those wanting to get, er, decadent. Room 1 gets fully loaded upfront dance, room 2 has that 'livin' it uplifting house & room 3 plays host to the cooler, deep & soulful. DJ's include Messrs. Pearce, Lambert, Holloway, Normski and plenty more.

Times: 10 p.m.–4 a.m. Tax £6 b4 11 p.m./£7 after.

'WIDE LOAD' plays house music all night long every Sunday in the venue's Rock Café. It's full of lunatic wide loaders such as Larner and Hardy, Branston Blob, Bloated Joe and special guest Rod Hull & Emu (*that's what it says on the flyer!*)

Times: 8 p.m.–2 a.m. Tax: £5 all night.

'BUMPIN' SUNDAY' meanwhile carry on in the main area with Dave Morrison with the able assistance of Ras Kwame plus guests. Both pack 'em in for this cream Sunday night swing and rap jam. More info? Then contact the club or Dave on 01895 637580.

Times: 8 p.m.–2 a.m. Tax: free b4 10 p.m./£2 for ladiez & £5 for fellaz thereafter / ladiez free with flyer b4 midnight also . . .

• RULIN' @ The Ministry of Sound

103 Gaunt Street, SE1 (Tel. 0171 378 6258)

Continuin' to rule the area is the Ministry's long runnin' Saturday night spinin' cuttin' edge garage, house and deep beats. 7 December sees those fabulously, gorgeously delectable Puscha people in the house with L. T. J. Bakem offering a house set while Frankie Foncett, K. Klass, Darren Darling and many more helping out proceedings. 'Rulin' warms the cockles through the rest of December so call the club for more details.

Times: 12 midnight–9 a.m. Tax: £10 members/£15 non-members.

Blues and Soul, 26 November 1996.

5.3   Eddy Grant

One of the most famous of black British musicians is Eddy Grant.

Grant came to Britain in 1960, at the age of twelve. His schooling, in Kentish Town, came to a halt when he opted to join the group of musicians who became The Equals. Their name underlined the ideal of inter-racial harmony that bound the group's black and white members. Their string of chart successes ran from the late Sixties to the early Seventies, finishing, fittingly, with 'Black-skinned, Blue-eyed Boys'. At this point, Grant suffered a heart attack, and decided to leave the group. He intended to produce their records, but the management had other ideas. 'I realised that the only way I would stay in the business was to control the means of production, in the words of Malcolm X,' Grant recalls. The first move was to set up the Coach House recording studio in North London's Stamford Hill. He also established Ice Records, concentrating on selling records to a Third World market, 'with only a slight bow towards England and wherever else I sold records with The Equals. These were the places that were saying, "You're finished, you can't make music any more."

'I knew then that they had it wrong,' he continues, 'and it was just a question of time, and being able to sustain one's existence, before you could prove them to be wrong. A very good friend had said that it could take me ten years, and I laughed at him. He said: "You'll be surprised how cruel people can be in the music business."

'At that time, the general consensus among business people was that artists were scum. The other thing was that black artists were aggravation. A black artist was all right if he had a manager and managers were always white so there was a degree of control. In my case, suddenly having to deal with an artist who was black, managing himself – this was too much!'

As much businessman as musician, Grant spent nearly the whole decade out of the public eye. Then, in 1979, came 'Living on the

Frontline'. Although contemporary in sound, it continued to integrate black and white styles of music in the way that had given The Equals their trademark sound. Grant departed for a warmer climate from where he was able to observe the chart progress of his second string of successful records; songs like 'Electric Avenue', and 'I Don't Wonna Dance'.

Independent, 12 January 1988.

5.4   A diploma in black dance

At the end of the twentieth century black dance has become
an academic subject in Britain.

Knees bent, elbows arched and back flat, Paulette Ryan, a professional dancer, holds the Kumina movement for a few seconds then, flat-footed, inches forward. Her hips rotate to the strong beat of the Caribbean drums. The musicians pound out the traditional sounds. The Kumina dance, which originates from the Congo, East Africa, is a demanding style . . .

Guiding Paulette's movements is choreographer Jackie Guy . . . As course co-ordinator on the country's first diploma in African and Caribbean dance, he knows what he's doing.

IRIE! Dance Theatre, one of Britain's leading black dance companies, based in south-east London, is behind the drive for accreditation for African and Caribbean dance. Artistic director Beverley Glean has been with IRIE! since it started in 1985. She says the idea for a diploma emerged from the struggle to find performers trained in African-Caribbean dance.

'Rehearsals for the Theatre and other black companies have become increasingly difficult,' she says. 'Most of the dancers we use in our company have no formal training in the dance styles rooted in the African-Caribbean tradition. Since IRIE! started, we've had to use our rehearsal period as a training ground for black dancers in this country. Instead of concentrating on the art form, we spend time explaining why it's necessary to do certain techniques.'

Four years ago, Glean began developing the diploma. Last year the scheme was awarded a £238,000 lottery grant and given accreditation by Birkbeck College, University of London. There are eighteen places on the year-long course, which will use the studio and study space at Greenwich Dance Agency and City and Islington College.

Guardian Education, 31 March 1998.

5.5   Asian v. English food

When Asian children went to school they had to endure English school dinners. Apart from their lack of taste, they also often consisted of forbidden meat, as a group of Asian girls explained to Laxmi Jamdagni. Naseem and Akhtar are Pakistani Muslims while Gurendra and Surinder are Indian Sikhs.

Gurendra. We had an English dinner yesterday – it was sickening.
Naseem. I'd rather prefer the Asian ones.
Me. Do you all have school dinners here?
All. Yeah.
Me. It's always English, is it?
Surinder. We were talking the other day about having Asian meals. [*laughs.*] When the dinner didn't arrive, we thought they'd probably send us some Asian food!
Naseem. That'd be great if they did.
Surinder. You get bored of English food every day.
Akhtar. I don't think we get very much choice. For the English, they have meat and beef.
Naseem. We only get a bit of salad and something else.
Gurendra. The salad isn't much.
Me. Are you vegetarian?
All. No.
Akhtar. They have the same thing we can have, and meat as well. So they have a choice of three things, we have a choice of two.
Surinder. We can eat meat but you [*to Akhtar*] don't eat it 'cos it's from an English butcher.
Akhtar. Yeah, but . . .
Surinder. A dinner lady can't exactly say, 'You're not having that meat . . .'
Me. *You* can eat what meat you want to eat.
Surinder. Yeah.
Gurendra. But if you don't have chicken pie or whatever it was, right, you can't have mashed potato what they give it you in an ice-

cream thing [scoop], and you can't have beans, 'cos you haven't had the pie – then all you're left with is the cob and the bit of salad and the pudding afterwards . . . yeah, we get a small cob, a knob of butter, one tomato, load of carrots if you want any [*laughs*], cheese and this tastes horrible.

Naseem. Very rarely do we get fish.

Gurendra. Sometimes you can get a boiled egg.

Surinder. Yes, but the trouble is that most Indian girls won't eat hot dinners because they're bought from English butchers' shops. And they won't eat pork, I agree with the pork.

Naseem. But you wouldn't eat that beef.

Surinder. No, I goes to her, 'Is that beef?' She says, 'Yes.' I says, 'Well, I don't want it.'

Me. Did you tell her why?

Surinder. No.

Gurendra. No, what I said is that if you want potatoes and things you can't 'cos you haven't had the meat.

Akhtar. Yesterday they had Spam and egg, and I says to the dinner lady, 'Can I have just the egg?' and she says 'No.' We're not allowed to have Spam 'cos it's made out of – I won't say the word, p – i – g [*spelt out*].

Leicester Record Office, L362.7, 'Hamari Rangily Zindagi: Our Colourful Lives. Report by Laxmi Jamdagni of her Work with Asian Girls in the Midlands', 1980, pp. 65–6.

5.6   The growth of 'Indian' restaurants

One of the most visible impacts of immigrants in post-war Britain lies in the way in which they have affected English food through the opening of restaurants. This process was well under way by the 1960s, when 'Indian' restaurants were being opened by people who came from all over the subcontinent.

The Pakistani business community here is, generally speaking, a thriving one, encompassing most phases of commercial activity. Consider for example the restaurants alone. Among the 300 restaurants dotted all over the country, 150 are situated in London, and their number is increasing rapidly. In almost every case these establishments are given the names of well-known places or people associated with their homeland. There is for example the Lahore restaurant, the Dacca, the Karachi, the Chitaggong, the Kashmir, the Rawalpindi and so on – names that mean much to the Pakistanis far from home. Some of their restaurants are named after their country itself. The majority of these restaurants are profitable concerns, many with a goodwill estimated as being worth thousands of pounds. It is, of course, a romance in itself how these people first arrived here with little more than the clothes they stood in, and how in time they acquired their present wealth and prosperity. These restaurants are usually operated by 100 per cent Pakistani staff, who in turn purchase their provisions from the Pakistani grocery stores – which again are numerically considerable.

But the clientele of these restaurants strangely enough are predominantly British or other Europeans. For the Western demand for exotic Eastern foods is growing steadily. Not the least surprising is the terrific impact these Pakistanis have made on the conservative way of life of the British. Slowly a liking for 'curry and rice' and 'chapati' has infiltrated into even the humblest of homes, where once the pre-eminent savoury dish was 'fish and chips'. The seeker after unusual foods is enabled now to purchase pre-cooked Eastern dishes in flavour-seal containers.

This partiality for the dishes of Pakistan has encouraged the British manufacturers, for there are few grocer shops that do not now stock Eastern spices. Selfrdige's, Whiteley's, Harrod's, some of the largest stores in London, have departments for the sale of spices, curries and representative foods from the East. The smallest grocer shops sell curried chicken, curried beans, curried prawn/veal and even just tins of sauce made of curry and other spices in which you are able to cook raw meat or chicken or fish, etc., without the tedious job of preparing a complete curry yourself. Thus the direct result of this friendly incursion is completely altering the eating habits of the nation.

Kathleen Hunter, *History of Pakistanis in Britain*, Norwich, 1962.

5.7   The spread of Indian food

The spread of Asian cuisine led to the establishment of firms producing exotic foods.

'New' and 'authentic' were the watchwords when Raj Foods went into business five years ago with four varieties of frozen curry, and the idea was a winner: today this Park Royal based family firm produce no less than twenty different frozen dishes including full meals with rice and nineteen types of snack foods.

Raj Foods, a leader in their field, specialise in authentic pre-cooked Indian frozen foods such as chicken and lamb curry, vegetable curry, samosas, vegetable spring rolls, onion bhajias and tandoori chicken, as well as crunchy, spicy savouries like Bombay and Gujurat Mix, spiced peanuts and Ghathia.

All these tempting dishes and snacks are made from traditional recipes perfected by Raj Radia and wife Shobhna – the 'most important half behind the business', according to her husband. They achieve quality and authenticity by using fresh products and spices. There are no compromises on flavours and no artificial preservatives are used. The frozen foods are ideal for that special curry at home or as a convenience food for those in a hurry!

They are packed in vacuum sealed 'boil-in-the-bag' pouches in colourful sturdy packages. The snacks are available in attractive transparent packs – all designed by the Radias . . .

Shobhna has a diploma in domestic science which was helpful as the couple made a detailed survey of the market then set out to devise products to meet – and create – the need. And the need, they found, was for 'authentic curries'. Those available on the market almost always contained apples and sultanas and that is hardly authentic.

Raj Foods operate from modern purpose-built premises in Park Royal, London, which are specially fitted out with the latest equipment and machinery, and have their own distribution covering greater London in a twenty-five-mile radius.

Asian Business, 28 October 1988.

5.8   Curry as the national dish

By the end of the century every high street in Britain has its own Indian restaurants and take-aways, meaning that most people living in England eat curries on a regular basis. The following extracts from a menu represent the standard dishes which most restaurants serve.

Indian Cottage
Indian & Balti Express
Take Away
Halal
Authentic Indian Cuisine
79 The Parade,
Oadby, Leicester LE2 5BB

STARTERS

Onion Bhaji.. £1.50
Deep fried onions with specially prepared batter

Samosa £1.50
*Wafer thin pastry stuffed with meat or vegetables deep
fried*

Sheek Kebab £1.50
Spicy lamb meat

Shami Kebab...................................... £1.50
Spicy lamb meat

Chicken Tikka.................................... £1.90
Tender pieces of marinated chicken, tandoori baked

Lamb Tikka....................................... £1.90
Pieces of marinated lamb, tandoori baked

Chicken Shaslicks £2.50
*Chicken tikka with onions, fresh tomatoes and green
peppers*

Prawn Cocktail £1.70
Prawns served with seafood mayonnaise

Tandoori Chicken £1.80
Chicken on the bone marinated, tandoori baked

Tandoori King Prawns £3.10
Marinated and baked in a tandoori oven

King Prawn Butterfly.............................. £3.10
Covered with batter and deep fried

Prawn on Puri £2.25
Cooked with spices and herbs served over crisp bread

Kashmiri Prawns £2.25
Cooked with spices and fruits

Kashmiri Prawns on Puri £2.75
Cooked with spices and herbs served over crispy bread . . .

MASSALA DISHES
This is a very popular dish cooked with fresh cream
which gives it a rich sauce.

TANDOORI DISHES
Tandoori dishes are marinated and cooked in a charcoal
tandoori (clay oven). Served with green salad.

CURRY DISHES
Curries are available in different strengths
Curry – Medium (price as below)
Madras – Medium Hot (25p extra) Vindaloo – Hot (30p extra)

BHUNA DISHES
Traditionally a dry but spicy dish
cooked with onions and capsicum.

ROGAN JOSH
This dish is specially prepared with onions and tomatoes.
Spicy to taste available in different strength of spice.

DHANSAK
This dish is served medium in strength,
slightly sweet taste cooked with lentils

DOPIAZA
Prepared with Indian herbs and extra onions, tomatoes cooked
together with small amount of garam massala.

SAGG DISHES
These dishes are prepared with spinach, onions and spices

MILD DISHES KORMA
Korma is a mild sweet curry prepared with cream

KASHMIRI DISHES
Prepared with mixed fruit, cream and almonds

BALTI SELECTION

This type of cuisine is the latest phenomenon in Britain. Each delicious dish is cooked in the Balti of cast iron or a stainless steel wok. It is a small saucepan with a handle on either side. Handed down from the tribesmen of the Khyber Pass, who cooked their food this way upon an open fire. Each dish ordered is individually cooked in its own Balti, which enhances the flavour and aroma of this type of cuisine. Spices and green herbs such as coriander, combine to make a different and special alternative to any other style of Oriental cooking.

PATHIA DISHES
This dish is mainly served as sweet and sour.

PASSANDA DISHES
Prepared with almonds and cream.
This is a very popular mild curry.

BIRYANI DISHES
Biryanies are cooked with rice and have a medium spicy taste.
Served with vegetable curry sauce.

VEGETARIAN DISHES, NANS, RICE

Menu in possession of the author.

5.9 Cypriot drinks for sale

Members of all immigrant minorities have opened ethnic food shops. Some members of the Greek Cypriot community also established off-licences, importing spirits, sherries and wines from Cyprus, as well as selling British products. The following advert reveals the range of products for sale from one such establishment.

Trodos Wines the Falkland Stores
71 Falkland Rd. Lon. NW5.
Tel: 01-485 8106 & 01-485-3507
CASH AND CARRY Prices Only

SMALL CANS PER CASE

Carling Black Label	£2.45
Skol Lager	£2.50
Carlsberg	£2.60
Long Life	£2.75
Harp Lager	£2.70
Heineken	£2.90
Skol Special Straight	£3.15
Stella Artois (Bottles)	£4.30
Double Diamond	£2.76
Light Ale	£2.45
Mackeson	£3.00
Guinness	£3.50
Guinness (Bottles)	£2.90

WHISKY *Per Bottle*

Johnnie Walker	£3.37
Teachers	£3.49
Bell's	£3.59
Grant's Stand Fast	£3.59
Haig	£3.45
Vat 69	£3.55
White Horse	£3.55
Mackinlay	£3.30
J & B Rare	£3.50

SODAP WINES *Per Bottle*

Kolossi Red/White	£0.95
Arsinoe	£0.95
Afames	£0.95

TRODOS WINES *Per Bottle*

Red/White Dry	£0.84
Red/White Sweet	£0.95

TRODOS SHERRIES *Per Bottle*

Cream Sherry	£0.89

COMMANDARIA

Trodos Commandaria	£0.95
Keo Commandaria	£0.99
St John Commandaria	£0.99
St Varnavas Commandaria	£1.05

LARGE CANS PER CASE

Skol Lager	£3.85
Long Life	£4.10
Double Diamond	£4.25
Carlsberg	£4.10
Skol Special Strength	£4.75

KEO BEER

Bottles 24 small in case	£4.25
Bottles 12 large in case	£3.85

CYPRUS BRANDY

KE0***	£2.90
KEO VO	£3.45
KEO Five Kings	£4.60
Keo Alpha	£3.15
SODAP VO	£3.00
Haggipavlou***	£2.75
Haggipavlou Agglias	£3.15

CYPRUS WINES (KEO) *Per Bottle*

Othello	£0.99
Aphrodite	£0.99
St. Pateleimon	£0.99
Hock	£0.99
Bellapais	£1.25

CYPRUS SHERRIES *Per Bottle*

Mosaic Cream	£0.95
Mosaic Medium	£0.95
Mosaic Dry	£0.95

Cream Medium	£0.89	GREEK WINES *Per Bottle*	
Cream Dry	£0.89	Corinth Red Dry	£0.90
Emva Cream	£0.95	Corinth White Dry	£0.90
Emva Medium	£0.95	Corinth Rose Wine	£0.90
Emva Dry	£0.95	Corinth Retsina	£0.90
		Domestica Red	£1.03
PURE CYPRUS DRAUGHT WINE		Domestica White	£1.03
Red Dry Per Gallon	£4.25	Metaxa Retsina	£0.95
Red Sweet Per Gallon	£4.75		
Medium White Sweet		OUZO	
Per Gallon	£4.75	KEO Ouzo	£3.29
Medium White Dry		SODAP Ouzo	£3.19
Per Gallon	£4.25	Haggipavlou	£3.25
		Achaia Clauss	£3.29

Vema, 22 December 1975.

5.10   The embarrassment of traditional dress

Many Asian groups continued to wear their traditional dress upon first arriving in Britain. However, when they forced their children to dress in the same way it often caused resentment.

In the early years before hordes of Punjabis arrived, my mother dressed us like the English. My brother and I associated with English friends. As our parents did not want to be different in any way, they assured our learning the language properly. When our relatives came, everything changed drastically. The women would come to our house and say, 'Don't you think Nimi's hair should be braided now that she is ten?' or 'Nimi should not go to school with bare legs, otherwise she will grow up to be immodest.' Immediately my mother's attitude changed. I was no longer to be like the English, but was to dress and be like the Punjabi villagers, whom I began to abhor.

Quoted in Arthur Wesley Helweg, *Sikhs in England: The Development of a Migrant Community*, Calcutta, 1979, pp. 54–5.

5.11   The turban issue

After the foundation of Sikhism in the fifteenth century, the turban gradually came to symbolise the most important outward symbol of the believers of this faith. The arrival of this group caused hostility among a variety of British institutions, but Sikhs fought doggedly for their right to continue wearing their traditional headdress.

A march by silent Sikhs in Wolverhampton yesterday stretched for more than a mile, with demonstrators seven abreast. There were 4,000 Sikhs and 100 women.

They had answered the call of the two Sikh organisations, the Sikh Brotherhood and the Central Organisation of Sikhs, to demonstrate publicly against the refusal of the Wolverhampton Transport Committee to allow Sikh bus crews to wear beards and turbans on duty.

Though a seven-strong Sikh delegation was received by a representative of the Mayor, the silent marchers were otherwise ignored by members of Wolverhampton Town Council. Not a single councillor was present.

From all over Britain the marchers responded to the call. They came from London, Huddersfield, Slough, Manchester and Bradford. They were headed by a pathetic looking, white bearded Goru Bakiftawar Singh from Walsall, Staffordshire. The marching columns carried banners proclaiming . . . 'Sikhs laid down their lives for Britain in beards and turbans.'

In the middle of the column was a silent covey of European faces. They were Anglican, Congregational and Quaker supporters. One of them, the Reverend Stuart Gibbons, chairman of the Wolverhampton Council of Churches, said: 'We are supporting freedom of religious expression.'

At the head of the column marched Mr Tarsem Singh Sandu, aged twenty-three, the Wolverhampton bus driver who began it all last July when he reported for work in beard and turban and was suspended. He still has taken no job 'because I believe I will get my job back'.

After handing in a protest letter for the Mayor at the Town Hall Mr S. Panchi, Midlands Sikh leader, said: 'If this fails we will organise a Sikh day of protest throughout the whole world.' In the letter the Sikhs emphasise 'only the Wolverhampton Council is out of step'. Other authorities had commendably relaxed their rules to allow beards and turbans to be worn.

Guardian, 5 February 1968.

5.12   The pride of traditional dress

By the 1980s, as second-generation immigrants became more
established and self-confident, they not only took pride in their
dress but also challenged the courts to establish their legal right
to dress as they wished.

Woolworth stores have dropped a rule that female staff must wear
skirts after a sixteen-year-old Muslim schoolgirl complained that
her culture forbade wearing clothes which revealed her legs.

The Commission for Racial Equality said yesterday that when it
took up the case, Woolworth admitted that its uniform ruling was
unlawful under the 1976 Race Relations Act.

All Woolworth managers have now been told that job applicants
who cannot wear skirts because of their custom or culture should
be allowed to wear trousers.

The girl concerned, Miss Shapar Chowdhuri, has been offered a
job as a Saturday sales assistant at Woolworth's Northampton
store. Miss Chowdhuri, a Bangladeshi Muslim, was originally told
that she could not have the job unless she wore a skirt.

'I was tormented by the decision as I wanted the job but I was an-
guished at the prospect of breaking my tradition,' she said. 'In the end
I decided I could not forgo my culture and went in wearing trousers.'

She was turned away by the store and went for help to the
Commission for Racial Equality.

Its regional complaints officer, Mr Barjinder Sahota, said: 'It was
somewhat surprising that a large store such as this was not aware
of the unlawful implications of an insistence on skirt-wearing for
such a job as this.

However, I am encouraged that Woolworth's has taken steps to
change this rule in future.'

Guardian, 7 April 1984.

5.13   The use of native language

All communities in post-war Britain continued to use their
native language, as a Polish priest in Bradford recalled.

The problem of communication is this, that the Polish people here,
with few exceptions, didn't see any need in learning the English lan-

guage in the very beginning. Maybe they didn't have the opportunity, because if you're a miner or if you work in textiles, in dusty and noisy conditions, who do you talk to? To nobody, you know, you talk to yourself. Then when you come home to your Polish wife, or to your Polish husband for that matter, then you converse in the language which is the easiest for you. Then I think it is also true that some Poles lived with the hope that one day, sooner or later, the Polish question would be resolved and everybody would kind of return, so what's the point?

Bradford Heritage Recording Unit, *Destination Bradford: A Century of Immigration*, Bradford, 1987, p. 48.

5.14   Early days at English school

Many children from immigrant communities had difficult early days at school because of their lack of English, as Argiri Shiokkas, born in Fulham, of Greek Cypriot parents, recalls.

My first language when I went to school was Greek. I think I only knew 'Hello' in English. I was very quiet at school. I didn't understand a word they said, I just sat there. I'll never forget my first day, I remember it was playtime and I thought it was home time. Then the bell went and we had to go in again, and it seemed like ages. Then it was lunch time and I thought, 'It must be home time now'. No, we were back in again. By the third playtime, I thought it 'definitely must be home time by now'. I found a friend of mine and I said, 'When are they letting us go home?' And he said, 'I don't know,' in Greek and then I thought it must be a boarding school or something, and that we were never going to see our parents again. It was really frightening. I just burst out crying. It was like I would never see the end of the day.

After that I don't remember much about my infant education, but I do remember singing 'Six currant buns in a baker's shop' and 'Wee Willie Winkie' and listening to 'Snow White and the Seven Dwarfs' on the radio. I loved playing with Plasticine and doing jigsaw puzzles. But, because I didn't know English then, I found reading and writing a bit difficult; but maths I thought was fantastic, because we just used the same numbers, so I became really good at maths and really good at art, I still don't like writing, but I did learn to read and write in the end. [Laughs.]

I never thought I was on the same level as English kids. I always used to think I was worse than them, but now I'm a teacher and I see a lot more people, I couldn't have been that bad because my spelling's very good, and some of the English people can't spell. I don't know why that is, but I managed to get there in the end.

Ethnic Communities Oral History Project, *Xeni: Greek Cypriots in London*, London, 1990, pp. 27–8.

5.15   West Indian English

While West Indians speak English, their dialect is quite different, which led to problems of understanding for newly arrived pupils in English schools.

West Indian children are suffering from difficulties of *hearing*, in the sense that their framework of reference for the sounds which strike their ears is one of perception according to Creole and not according to English English. They are suffering from difficulties of *understanding*, because even if they hear the words correctly those words and the grammatical constructions in which they are being used may have slightly or even grossly different meanings for them. They are suffering from difficulties of *expressing* themselves, since teachers do not easily understand the mode of speech in which the children are uninhibited, that is, their Creole dialect, and if they are attempting to use the teacher's dialect there is a certain degree of inhibition which would tend to make them dry up and keep silent. And they suffer these disabilities within a psychological situation which makes it important to them that they already speak good English.

The psychological and psycho-linguistic problems are of two kinds but both derive from the fact that the West Indian family has been conditioned by the past *mores* of a colonial society in which a white skin, an English accent and a top job all went together and in which the person who wished to get on in the world had to acquire an education through the medium of the model language, which was supposed to be English English . . .

But now there is the additional frustration that the command of English so painfully acquired in the West Indies is itself found to be of less value than had been imagined, since even educated West

Indian English is conservative in comparison with English English and a number of the phonological, grammatical and of course most of the semantic difficulties of the Creole remain in the educated variety.

P. C. C. Evans and R. B. Le Page, *The Education of West Indian Immigrant Children*, London, 1967, pp. 19–20.

5.16   Children's stories for a multiracial society

Some of the children's books which worked using racial stereotypes have begun to disappear, to be replaced by publications written by authors in a Britain in which people of colour have become the norm. One of these writers, Errol Lloyd, describes the process of putting together such a book.

As an author and illustrator whose main task is to create children's books which cater for a multi-cultural society, I have for the moment accepted the restriction that the books I create will have a human element and that the main characters will be black.

This I think serves two functions. Firstly it puts the black character in a central role, taking decisions and having a specific character which expresses individuality. This has the result of creating what is generally acknowledged as 'positive images' which the black child is often starved of in contemporary children's literature. Secondly, it also means that the black child does not have a 'token' presence as can often be the case when black characters are included in stories simply to give the publication a 'multi-cultural' dimension.

The lack of a black presence in children's literature of the past is not the only source of problems, however, as we quite often find that, when black children have been the central character of books created by white authors, the result has been patronising and the main character little more than a caricature. A good example of this is 'Little Black Sambo' which, in spite of the affection that many who were brought up on these stories may feel for him, can cause offence to black people. There is therefore a legacy of negative images that the present day author/illustrator of children's books, black or white, comes up against and is consequently under greater pressure to create books which help to challenge this legacy.

When all is said and done, however, the primary task which any creator of children's books faces is to create a story and pictures which appeal to children. There are bad books of all sorts including 'multi-cultural books' and if children don't relate to them, then the whole point of the book is lost.

Judith Elkin and Pat Trigges (eds), *Children's Books for a Multi-cultural Society*, 0–7, London, 1986, p. 34.

5.17 Trade union support for immigrants

Although at the local level trade unions often committed acts of overt discrimination during the 1950s, the leadership of the TUC and many of its leading components spoke out against such actions, as well as against the race riots which broke out during the early post-war decades, particularly the disturbances in Notting Hill.

Since our last issue appeared the nation has been shocked by some ugly manifestations of the silliest of all possible enmities, the enmity based on the colour of a person's skin. Such a hatred can only arise in minds that are empty of everything except festering ignorance, and the shock we all felt was caused by the revelation that there is so much ignorance about. To most of us this superstitious ignorance is the real enemy to be overcome, not the pathetic participants in the knife-and-bottle affrays that disfigured our home towns. If our sympathies go to the coloured immigrants it is because they are so overwhelmingly outnumbered (even in their most thickly settled districts). If we feel any anger towards persons, it is levelled against the fascists and Empire Leaguers who have actively encouraged race-hatred.

There is a very real problem in the Harlem towns and suburbs. In these places, settled communities have had their established way of life disturbed by the superficial imposition of alien patterns of behaviour. The significant word is 'alien', not 'black' or 'inferior'. It would have been equally disturbing had it been any strange peoples to whose habits the natives were unaccustomed.

It is simple hypocrisy to pretend that all the coloured immigrants' behaviour is all times free from offence. Many of them are more used to living squalid lives in conditions of squalor than we are.

Their living standards are low – have been deplorably low for more than a century. We have helped to keep those standards low. The white employers of native labour in the colonies have made their profits from labour forces working for low wages, deplorably housed, and with education, sanitation and public health facilities provided on only the most grudging scale. We have been benefiting from the degradation of our fellow citizens all our lives through our supplies of cocoa, fat, bananas, citrus and other commodities at prices only possible under production by slave-labour.

It would be wrong to say that under such conditions moral standards necessarily deteriorate; they never get a chance to attain heights at which deterioration is possible. The only moral code that can exist in such conditions is that generated by the ordinary instincts of decency, common, in greater or lesser degree, to all humanity, black and white.

Negro morals are reputed to be less strict than those of their white neighbours. If this is so, perhaps that is because the white folk are living with their own kin, in their own homes, while the West Indians and Africans are strangers, in a strange land. It is not uncommon for inhibitions to be shed when large groups of men find themselves far away from home – how may careful parents are there who have no qualms whatever about allowing their teenage daughters to go to work every day in a factory or office full of men, but would tighten up security regulations very considerably if a group of very similar men (and equally white) but dressed in the uniform of the army came into camp near by.

But the problem of settlement still remains. It will not be solved while given districts are set aside as 'black'. That system must mean the continuance of separate, mutually irritant if not hostile, communities. These people are our fellow citizens, often our fellow trade unionists. If their standards are lower than ours, we are to blame. We are responsible for them, and for their education up to our standards.

We are also responsible for the bedraggled, vicious kids who make our streets offensive for decent folk, both white and coloured, with their bad manners, foul language and gang-handed aggression. We haven't really given them much of a chance, have we? We have brought them up in a world of speciousness, false values and insecurity. They too are outcasts, of their own choice, from a spirit of bravado. But they too are our brothers.

Coloured newcomers, white panic-gangsters, both need integrating into the established communities, in which they will be accepted; to which they will develop loyalties. Every trade unionist, particularly every active member of his branch, has an inescapable responsibility and a very special opportunity to provide leadership within his own community in this work of social construction.

Transport and General Workers Record, October 1958, pp. 2–4.

5.18   Trade union rules to combat racism

By the 1980s trade unions had taken positive steps to combat racism among their members. The Lambeth branch of NALGO, through its Race Equality Sub-group, issued a handbook on racism.

Lambeth NALGO policy on race

Lambeth NALGO played a most important part in the successful campaign of lobbying and pressure which led to this Council issuing an Equal Opportunities Policy Statement in October 1978 – the following became branch policy at AGMs, 1976 and 1977 respectively:

Racialism. This branch of Lambeth Municipal Officers' Guild deplores the recent rise of racial tension both in this borough and in this country as a whole . . .

Combating Racialism and Fascism. This branch considers that the politics of the National Front are incompatible with the principles of trade unionism, and therefore resolves that:

(i) no member of the National Front or other fascist organisation shall hold office in the Guild;

(ii) no member of the National Front or other fascist organisation shall be a member of the Guild.

Furthermore, as part of this branch's commitment to play an active part in implementing the jointly agreed Equal Opportunities Policy the branch unanimously agreed the following resolutions . . .

Lambeth NALGO and race relations

(a) This branch urges the Council to make the appropriate arrangements to ensure that all its jobs and services are provided without racial discrimination. It is committed to examine monitoring procedures to determine their effectiveness and to participate in the institution and operation of future monitoring procedures.

(b) This branch urges the Council to (i) adopt disciplinary rules which define racially discriminatory practices as 'gross misconduct' and (ii) penalise any member of staff who fails to carry out the Council's race relations policies through unfair treatment on grounds of race and colour of both members of staff and the public during the course of their work.

(c) Furthermore, this branch should set up a separate disciplinary procedure to withdraw or withhold membership from members of staff found guilty of gross misconduct on the grounds of racism . . .

Use of terms 'blacked/blacklisted, etc.'
We find the use of terms such as 'blacked and 'blacklisted' at NALGO to be particularly offensive and an anachronism today . . .

Racial discrimination
The Racial Equality Sub-committee recommends that the branch adopts the following policy:

1. That membership of Lambeth NALGO should be withdrawn from any member found by the Council as a result of disciplinary proceedings to have committed gross misconduct through racial discrimination in carrying out their official duties . . .

2. That members who believe that they have evidence of gross misconduct by racial discrimination should refer this to management with the assistance of a Branch Officer of their choice . . .

3. That members who feel that other members are acting in a racist manner which effectively incites racial hatred, i.e. racist remarks, jokes or sentiments, should refer this to their Directorate Shop Stewards' Committee . . .

4. That members who believe they themselves are the subject of racial discrimination by other members of staff should take this up with management and/or their Directorate Shop Stewards . . .

Establishment of national race equality committee
In view of NALGO's policies against racism and fascism, both at a local and national level, and the fact that the evidence available indicates that local members of racial minorities are not adequately reflected in employment in NALGO's services, this branch requests

that Annual Conference set up a National Race Equality Committee to pursue the following activities:

a. The promotion of equality of employment and training
opportunities in NALGO's services for people from racial
minorities.

b. The issues of racial discrimination with NALGO.

c. The promotion of membership and activity within NALGO
by workers from racial minorities.

d. Negotiations with employers of an equal opportunities clause
in appropriate conditions of service.

e. The pursuance with employers of the incorporation of a race
dimension in training courses.

f. To report on these matters with recommendations to the NEC
and Annual Conference.

Race Equality Sub-group of Lambeth NALGO, *Racism: A Handbook for
NALGO Members*, London, 1981, pp. 17–20.

5.19   Local multiracial initiatives

While most immigrant groupings may have faced racial hostility, some local communities made efforts to foster good race
relations. The Handsworth Good Neighbours Committee
issued a leaflet in 1961, containing advice to both natives and
immigrants.

Your West Indian neighbour

may be planning a spring-clean.

All over Handsworth, coloured people have been painting their
houses this summer.

More and more West Indians have been tidying their gardens,
mending their fences. The average number of West Indians living
in each Birmingham house is falling steadily.

Local police will tell you the coloured man is no more likely to
be a thief or a criminal than your white neighbour.

There are some black sheep among them of course . . . coloured
folk who are noisy, dirty and ignorant of English life (there are
noisy, dirty and inconsiderate white people, too).

But most immigrants only want a job, a home, a family and
friends, the same as any English man.

If a coloured man moves into the house next door, our advice is 'don't panic, don't rush to sell up and move out. Sit tight and treat them in the same way you would treat new English neighbours'.

MOST PROBLEMS BETWEEN ENGLISH AND WEST INDIAN NEIGH-BOURS CAN BE WORKED OUT BY FRANKNESS AND COMMON SENSE. IF THESE FAIL, WE ARE AT YOUR SERVICE. OUR ADDRESS IS BELOW ... PLEASE WRITE.

Your White neighbour

may be suspicious of you.

He has heard stories about West Indians who are dirty and noisy, who throw garbage in the gutters and gardens, who are terrible neighbours.

You know very well most West Indians don't do these things.

But there are people who are letting the coloured folk down. There are West Indians who spit in the street and throw garbage anywhere (just as there are white folk who really believe in the colour bar).

Your neighbour will be asking – which sort of a West Indian are you? It's the coloured folk who are bad neighbours that most often complain of a 'colour bar'.

If your white neighbour doesn't seem friendly, don't assume he doesn't like the colour of your skin. Give the man a chance to get to know you.

Remember – English people are hard to know. English neighbours sometimes don't speak to each other for months or years. Somebody once said, 'An Englishman's home is his castle,' and at times you can almost see the defences.

SHOW AN ENGLISHMAN THE STORIES HE HEARS ARE NOT TRUE ABOUT YOU, AND YOU SHOULDN'T HAVE BAD NEIGHBOUR TROUBLE.

BUT IF YOU ARE WORRIED – WELL, THERE ARE PLENTY OF WEST INDIANS ON OUR COMMITTEE. DROP US A CARD.

Birmingham Christian News Series, mid-September, 1961.

5.20 The Anti-Nazi League

Of the various organisations which developed to combat racism at the national level, the Anti-Nazi League (ANL) became one of the best known. Connected with the Socialist Workers' Party, it directed much energy to opposing National

Front marches, even if the result was violence against marchers
and the police who protected them. On 21 April 1979 a flare-
up occurred in Leicester.

By early morning the massive police operation employed to protect
the Nazis was plainly visible to anyone who dared to venture into
the centre of Leicester and ignore the Chief Constable's warning to
'stay away'. Over 5,000 police from twenty-one forces, from as far
away as West Yorkshire, Greater Manchester and London, were
deployed in militaristic fashion throughout the city centre. Supported by mounted units, dogs, the brutal Special Patrol Group, a
television-equipped helicopter and riot gear, it was quite evident
that 'trouble' was expected and that no one would be allowed even
near Wyggeston Collegiate School where Nazi leader John Tyndall
was to make antisemitic references to 'hook-nose dwarfs' at the NF
'public' meeting held there later that afternoon. Coaches bringing
ANL supporters on the motorway were stopped, searched and
diverted.

By midday, six hundred or so NF supporters had assembled at
the recreation ground, on the other side of the city, waiting for their
march to begin at 1.00 p.m. Meanwhile, several thousand anti-
Nazis, in militant mood, occupied the Front's planned route
through the city centre. In Belvoir Street, packed with banner-
waving demonstrators, the police gave the first indication of their
aggressive attitude to the anti-racists; Transit vans were driven
through the crowds at high speed and police 'wedges' attempted to
force a passage through – an impossible, pointless, highly dangerous and provocative exercise.

In view of this opposition, the Front were re-routed through side
streets to their meeting at the school, but even this did not prevent
their continual harassment by groups of enraged anti-fascists, and
several times the march was fragmented following missile attacks.
It was clear that the Nazis were unwelcome in Leicester and that
the expensive protection operation mounted by the police was
insufficient against such strong opposition.

Having been allowed out of the city centre, the anti-racists,
angered by the actions of the police, marched through side streets
towards the school, continually being challenged and beaten back
by police in full riot gear. From this point on it was clear that there
was a danger of escalating violence between the police and demon-

strators and many arrests were made after police retaliation turned into open aggression.

However, the worst violence was to come at the University. Satisfied that access to the school was impossible, the main contingent returned to Victoria Park and processed through the campus up to the police cordon near the school with the intention of 'verbally demonstrating' their opposition to the NF. In minutes, a savage police charge had panicked and provoked the peacefully assembled demonstration and spontaneous stone-throwing broke out. Police retaliation was swift and vicious, with dogs being unleashed on the frightened demonstrators. It was only when everyone had returned to the park that calm returned.

Leicester Anti-Nazi League, *Support the Leicester eighty-seven! Quash the Convictions! Release the Jailed Anti-racists! Disband the SPG!*, Leicester, 1979, pp. 7–10.

5.21   Let's Kick Racism Out of Football

Another organisation which aimed at combating racism consisted of Let's Kick Racism Out of Football, which had the following aims for the 1996–97 season.

1. *Continue our work in professional football.* Whilst it is clear that the Let's Kick Racism Out of Football campaign has made an impact in tackling most overt forms of racism at football matches, the evidence suggests that many problems remain. We will continue to work with Premier League and Football League clubs, focusing on:

- continuing activities to raise awareness of the campaign's aims;
- action to deal directly with racial abuse at grounds, through the active involvement of important bodies such as the Football Safety Officers Group and the police.

Following last year's successful 'Weekends of Action', high profile campaign activities will be spotlighted on the third Round of the FA Cup Sponsored by Littlewood's at the beginning of 1997.

2. *Grassroots football.* Whilst professional football grabs all of the headlines, more than one million people play the game on a regular basis at different levels. It is clear that problems of racial abuse does exist, whether it is directed by the supporters of non-

professional league clubs against black players or by players against each other at lower levels of the game. We will work with County Football Associations and local authorities to raise awareness of the issue and define methods of counteracting abuse . . .

3. *Europe.* The Let's Kick Racism Out of Football campaign is widely recognised in Europe as leading the way in the fight against abuse and intimidation at football grounds. We aim to work with UEFA (Union of European Football Associations) and FIFPro (Federation of International Footballers Professional) to co-ordinate activities around the Continent with the aim of providing a united approach against racism in Europe.

4. *Schools competition.* A major target of the campaign has been to influence young people, mainly through the distribution of educational materials aimed specifically at 11–16 year olds and the very successful ARC Theatre play *Kicking Out*, which was seen by 130,000 children over the last two years.

Following a very successful competition run in schools in conjunction with the Euro 96 championships, we aim to raise the profile of the campaign through a similar initiative. Through the active involvement of educational and commercial sponsors, the themes of the campaign will be presented to young people in an informative and interesting manner which will encourage them to take an active part in the campaign.

5. *Asians in Football.* Whilst players from African and Caribbean backgrounds have made a great impact in professional football, there are currently no Asian professional players. This is despite the growing popularity of football amongst Asian youngsters. A recent research project 'Asians Can't Play Football' has examined the issue in detail . . .

6. *Kicking Out.* Commissioned by Leyton Orient Football Club, ARC Theatre Ensemble's play, *Kicking Out*, is a unique and extremely powerful piece of theatre. The author, Clifford Oliver's aim was to influence the attitudes and behaviour of 13–16 year olds to racism in football, and to wider issues of prejudice in society.

Northern Asian, vol. 1, No. 2, spring 1996, pp. 34–5.

5.22 School reception arrangements

During the 1960s and into the 1970s British schools in areas of immigrant settlement found themselves with high percentages of children who could not speak English, and therefore had to take measures to ease the problems of these pupils, as a Department of Education and Science report from 1972 revealed.

In most of the areas visited the number of immigrant pupils has continued to rise – but in many cases at a slower rate than previously. One area had the highest percentage of immigrant pupils in the country. Of the 3,197 at the secondary age, 342 were considered by their headteachers to be unable, by reason of language difficulties, to follow a normal school curriculum with profit to themselves . . .

Reception and English language teaching centres operate in only six of the sixteen major areas involved in the survey. In one city in the West Riding, the Education Department receives all immigrant pupils, undertakes some documentation and arranges also a medical examination as well as a simple test in English before allocating them to a centre. Non-English-speaking pupils between 11 and 13 years of age are sent to one of five special schools in junior high schools. Pupils with some English, but still in need of help in English language, join withdrawal groups in the junior high schools or second-phase classes in the 13+ schools.

A centre for all immigrant pupils was established in September 1968 in one of the Greater London boroughs included in the survey. It caters for all newly arrived immigrants of school age who have not previously attended schools in this country, and those entering the area who have previously attended a British school for less than one term. In the school year 1969/70 the centre received 147 immigrant pupils of secondary school age and retained them for periods lasting from four to eight weeks. The centre negotiates all admissions of immigrants to secondary schools in consultation with the authority's schools section and the heads of schools themselves. It keeps pupils' records and hands these on to the receiving schools. The aim of the centre is to equip pupils with enough spoken English to cope with the work of a normal school curriculum. For those who come with no knowledge of the English language to do this during a maximum period of eight weeks hardly seems feasible and a recent appointment of a teacher, part-time at the centre and part-time peripatetic, should make it possible for a little follow-up work to be carried out with some pupils when they transfer to normal school.

In one West Midlands town immigrant pupils attend, if necessary, one of four centres for up to one term and a half and then return part-time for continuing support and reinforcement. Another West Midlands town operating an induction centre also recognises the need for continuing support to former full-time immigrant pupils by arranging for the centre staff to visit secondary schools and keep in touch with them for up to nine months after they have left the centre. Much more of this follow-up and after-care by and from the centre requires to be undertaken if the continuing needs of the pupils are to be satisfactorily catered for.

In some areas secondary school pupils attend English language centres on a full-time basis – in others on a half-time basis. In two areas language teaching centres, which previously catered for pupils of secondary school age, now admit pupils of primary school age only. One West Midlands town had a centre some ten years ago but this was not a success and was closed; since then individual schools have been left to manage for themselves.

Department of Education and Science, *The Continuing Needs of Immigrants*, London, 1972, pp. 5–6.

5.23   Race Relations Act 1976

Despite state acceptance from the 1960s of the existence of racism and the passage of measures attempting to counter it during this decade, the most important anti-discriminatory legislation came in 1976 in the form of the Race Relations Act, which began by defining racial discrimination.

Discrimination to which the Act applies

1. – (1) A person discriminates against another in any circumstances relevant for the purposes of any provision of this Act if –

(a) on racial grounds he treats that other less favourably than he treats or would treat other persons; or

(b) he applies to that other a requirement or condition which he applies or would apply equally to persons not of the same racial group as that other but –
(i)   which is such that the proportion of persons of the same racial group as that other who can comply with it is

considerably smaller than the proportion of persons not of that racial group who can comply with it; and

(ii) which he cannot show to be justifiable irrespective of the colour, race, nationality or ethnic or national rights of the person to whom it is applied; and

(iii) which is to the detriment of that other because he cannot comply with it.

(2) It is hereby enacted that, for the purposes of this Act, segregating a person from other persons on racial grounds is treating him less favourably than they are treated.

2. – (1) A person ('the discriminator') discriminates against another person ('the person victimised') in any circumstances relevant for the purposes of any provision of this Act if he treats the person victimised less favourably than in those circumstances he treats or would treat other persons, and does so by reason that the person victimised has –

(a) brought proceedings against the discriminator or any other person under this Act; or

(b) given evidence or information in connection with proceedings brought by any person against the discriminator or any other person under this Act; or

(c) otherwise done anything under or by reference to this Act in relation to the discriminator or any other person; or

(d) alleged that the discriminator or any other person has committed an act which (whether or not the allegation so states) would amount to a contravention of this Act,

or by reason that the discriminator knows that the person victimised intends to do any of those things, or suspects that the person victimised has done, or intends to do, any of them.

(2) Subsection (1) does not apply to the treatment of a person by reason of any allegation made by him if the allegation was false and not made in good faith.

3. – (1) In this Act, unless the context otherwise requires –

(a) 'racial grounds' means any of the following grounds, namely colour, race, nationality or ethnic or national origins;

(b) 'racial group' means a group of persons defined by reference to colour, race, nationality or ethnic or national origins, and references to a person's racial group refer to any racial group into which he falls.

(2) The fact that a racial group comprises two or more distinct racial groups does not prevent it from constituting a particular racial group for the purposes of this Act.

(3) In this Act –

(a) references to discrimination refer to any discrimination falling within section 1 or 2; and

(b) references to racial discrimination refer to any discrimination falling within section 1,

and related expressions shall be construed accordingly.

(4) A comparison of the case of a person of a particular racial group with that of a person not of that group under section 1(1) must be such that the relevant circumstances in the one case are the same, or not materially different, in the other.

Race Relations Act 1976.

5.24 Equal opportunities in employment

In recent decades many large companies have implemented equal opportunities policies, which have not usually been completely successful, as the example of the AA in Cardiff illustrates.

Equal opportunity policy

In May 1989, the Executive Board of the AA agreed on a number of measures to bring the company into line with recommendations of the *Race Relations Code of Practice in Employment*. These included: the adoption of an equal opportunity statement; a training programme for managers; an Equal Opportunities Committee; a review of selection practices; consultation with [the trade union] APEX; and, most importantly, the introduction of ethnic monitoring of job applicants and employees from April 1990. Both the Commission and the Race Relations Employment Advisory Service have given support for these developments at national level.

At a local level in Cardiff, the supervisors interviewed had not actually seen the company's equal opportunity policy, and one of them had not received written guidance on the subject. No one was aware of any review being carried out, and no positive action had been instituted, although one supervisor had personally encouraged an ethnic minority employee to join a training course.

Ethnic Monitoring

Workforce. A workforce analysis in November 1989 showed that nineteen out of the 955 strong workforce (2.1 per cent) were of Afro-Caribbean, African or Asian origin; three were men and sixteen were women. By September 1990, the figure had risen to thirty (3.1 per cent), but this was still low when compared with the 4–5 per cent ethnic minority population in the travel-to-work area. One should also take into account the fact that, according to the 1981 Census, the Labour Force Survey and our own Cardiff survey, proportionately more ethnic minority women work than white women, and the Cardiff office is located within a mile of Butetown. All ethnic minority employees were at trainee level, or at basic grades 1–3.

Recruitment. No special attempt was made by the AA to advertise vacancies within the local ethnic minority communities; indeed, until the end of 1989 no records were kept of the ethnic origins of applicants. As we have seen, there was also uncertainty among supervisors as to whether they should interview the relatives, friends or neighbours of employees who had heard about internally advertised vacancies.

Commission for Racial Equality, *Employers in Cardiff: Report of a Formal Investigation*, London, 1991, p. 24.

5.25 Attempting to help the Chinese in Glasgow

Under the 1976 Race Relations Act, Strathclyde Community Relations Council came into existence, with a Chinese Officer, Chi Khen Pan, who described efforts made by the city to help his community to the Home Affairs Committee on the Chinese Community in Britain in May 1984.

We welcome you, on behalf of Glasgow, to Glasgow, especially on behalf of the Chinese community. 'Glasgow's Miles Better', but the Chinese community still have special needs. You should have by now plenty of evidence on the needs and problems of the Chinese in the United Kingdom. However, recognising their needs is one thing, and trying to overcome them effectively is another. Naturally, funding is a main factor. The Urban Programme is good, but it cannot substitute Section 11 grants. We can see the effect already on the handful of Chinese workers employed within the very few Urban Programmes in Strathclyde. There are two examples. Firstly, we have two Chinese assistant home visitors employed by the Education Department. Two of them, at the end of last year, applied for another post, to serve more effectively and more closely the Chinese community. In fact, one of them has already left the post, and one still remains because of domestic reasons. For example, on my left is Miss Maggie Sung. She works for the interpreting services. Over the last three years we have changed twice for our Chinese interpreter. They all are good workers, but they look forward to opportunities with security in terms of employment (and I do not blame them). Also our Chinese clients are often confused by our situation and why people are leaving after a short time. The Chinese casework handled by our Council and the interpreting service is ever-increasing day by day. This highlights their needs not being met by the various departments of the local authorities.

Home Affairs Committee, Series 1984–85, *Chinese Community in Britain*, II, *Minutes of Evidence*, London, 1985.

5.26   Strathclyde against racism

During the 1980s and 1990s numerous local authorities have made efforts to combat racism.

Last year, on 17 September 1986, nursery schools, playgroups, parents and community groups released balloons with anti-racist slogans to launch Strathclyde Multi-Racial Action Year.

The campaign has been led by a steering group initiated by Strathclyde Community Relations Council and Strathclyde Regional Council supported financially and morally by Glasgow District Council, Dumbarton, Strathkelvin and a growing number of others.

The focus of the campaign which will end on 30 September 1987 is to raise awareness about racial issues and equal opportunities initiatives throughout Strathclyde.

Many individual playgroups, schools and colleges are planning to hold multi-cultural/anti-racist exhibitions, multi-racial parents' meetings, teaching initiatives on anti-racism and culture or to ensure that their stocks of books and toys reflect the multi-racial nature of Scotland today.

Another Strathclyde Multi-Racial Action Year Initiative is to ensure that all schools receive a copy of our multi-lingual publication *Community Voice*, which is produced monthly. We would welcome any news of anti-racist action in the school or community.

Kelvingrove Art Galleries have run an exhibition for Strathclyde Multi-Racial Action Year about the variety of Glasgow's cultures, called 'Community Connections' – a valuable exhibition for helping to overcome some of the white supremacist ideas about 'backward' cultures.

We are distributing information packs to all schools in Strathclyde and hope that the contents will encourage discussion and action among staff and pupils which will begin to sow the seeds for a multi-cultural anti-racist Strathclyde.

Scottish Council for Racial Equality, *Annual Report, 1986–87.*

5.27 The Scarman report

After the 1981 riots the government decided that it needed to act to prevent further disorder of such a serious nature. The appointment of Lord Scarman by William Whitelaw, the Home Secretary, to head a committee to look into the disorders in Brixton and their causes represented the only step in this direction, as the Thatcher government paid little attention to issues of race relations. Scarman made a series of recommendations.

The evidence which I have reviewed . . . leaves no doubt in my mind that racial disadvantage is a fact of current British life. It was, I am equally sure, a significant factor in the causation of the Brixton disorders. Urgent action is needed if it is not to become an endemic, ineradicable disease threatening the very survival of our society. It would be unfair to criticise Government policy for lack of effort. The real question is whether the effort, which is undoubted, has been properly directed . . . 'Institutional racism' does not exist in Britain: but racial disadvantage, and its nasty associate racial discrimination, have not yet been eliminated. They poison minds and attitudes: they are, and so long as they remain, will continue to be, a potent factor of unrest.

The role of the police has to be considered against this background. As I have said . . . the police do not create social deprivation or racial disadvantage: they are not responsible for the disadvantages of the ethnic minorities. Yet their role is crucial. If their policing is such that it can be seen to be the application to our new society of the traditional principles of British policing, the risk of unrest will diminish and the prospect of approval by all responsible elements in our ethnically diverse society will be greater. If they neglect consultation and co-operation with the local community, unrest is certain and riot becomes probable . . .

The attack on racial disadvantage must be more direct than it has been. It must be co-ordinated by central government, who with local authorities must ensure that the funds made available are directed to specific areas of racial disadvantage. I have in mind particularly education and employment. A policy of direct co-ordinated attack on racial disadvantage inevitably means that the ethnic minorities will enjoy for a time a positive discrimination in their favour. But it is a price worth paying if it accelerates the elimination of the unsettling factor of racial disadvantage from the social fabric of the United Kingdom. I believe this task to be even more urgent than the task of establishing on a permanent basis good relations between minorities and the police. Good policing will be of no avail, unless we also tackle and eliminate basic flaws in our society. And, if we succeed in eliminating racial prejudice from our society, it will not be difficult to achieve good policing.

The Brixton Disorders, 10–12 April 1981: Report of an Inquiry by the Rt Hon. Lord Scarman, OBE, London, 1981, pp. 135–6.

5.28   A multiracial police force?

Sixteen years after the Brixton riots, limited progress had been made towards the creation of a multiracial police force, even though this has very much represented a clear aim of police forces since that time.

There is widespread agreement that the composition of police forces should reflect the society that they serve. The reluctance of members of the ethnic minorities to join the police service has been a cause of concern for many years. At the end of 1994, out of a total of 127,290 police officers in England and Wales, 2,100 were from ethnic minorities, about 1.6 per cent as against 1.5 per cent in 1993. The highest rank held by an ethnic minority officer was that of Chief Superintendent. On the other hand, a much higher proportion of London's Special Constabulary (volunteer police forces who perform police duties as auxiliaries to the regular force) are Black or Asian. The number of people from the ethnic minorities recruited to the police service has been rising in recent years. In 1993 4,885 police officers were recruited, of whom 193 (4 per cent) were from the ethnic minorities, a slightly higher proportion than in 1992. In addition, a number of police forces are taking positive steps to give ethnic minority applicants a more equal chance of selection. A Black Police Association in the Metropolitan Police has been established that will act as a support network for ethnic minority officers and civilian staff.

All police forces in England and Wales have:

- developed and published equal opportunities policies;
- drawn up grievance procedures relating to police and civilian staff;
- developed some form of monitoring scheme; and
- embarked on structural training programmes.

Forces in Scotland have also developed equal opportunities policies and training programmes.

Annual statistics submitted by forces contain detailed information on the ethnicity of police and civilian staff. HM Inspectorate of Constabulary uses this information to encourage forces to look critically at their selection, appraisal, postings and promotion procedures in order to remove artificial barriers to equality of opportunity. Minimum height requirements and upper age limits for candidates have been abolished, widening the range of potential recruits.

In 1992 London's Metropolitan Police Service published a training handbook for all recruits entitled *Focusing on Fair Treatment for All* as part of its equal opportunities training.

Central Office of Information, *Ethnic Minorities*, London, 1997, pp. 78–80.

Guide to further reading

General

Anyone wishing to study the history of immigrants in Britain should start with Colin Holmes, *John Bull's Island: Immigration and British Society, 1871–1971*, London, 1988, which, however, is only partly concerned with the post-war period. The same applies to his *A Tolerant Country? Immigrants, Refugees and Minorities in Britain*, London, 1991, and the collection of essays he edited on *Immigrants and Minorities in British Society*, London 1978. There is also Jim Walvin's *Passage to Britain*, Harmondsworth, 1984, which has a greater concentration on the post-war period. Students should also consult John Solomos, *Race and Racism in Britain*, London, 1993, Dilip Hiro, *Black British, White British*, London, 1971, and E. J. B. Rose *et al.*, *Colour and Citizenship: A Report on British Race Relations*, London, 1969.

Those wishing to consult primary sources can begin with David Goldsworthy (ed.), *The Conservative Government and the End of Empire, 1951–1957* III *Economic and Social Policies*, London, 1994, and Ronald Hyam (ed.), *The Labour Government and the End of Empire, 1945–1951*, IV, *Race Relations and the Commonwealth*, London, 1992, both of which examine official repsonses. Those interested in the experience of immigration from the point of view of the newcomers themselves must start with the publications of the Ethnic Communities Oral History Project, including *Asian Voices: Life Stories form the Indian Sub-continent*, London, 1993, *The Motherland Calls: African Caribbean Experiences*, London, 1992, *Xeni: Greek Cypriots in London*, London, 1990, and *Passport to Exile: The Polish Way to London*, London, 1988.

Numerous books have appeared on individual minorities, only a few of which can be listed here. For African Caribbeans, the best of the early works include Michael Banton, *The Coloured Quarter: Negro Immigrants in a English City*, London, 1955, and Ruth Glass, *Newcomers: The West Indians in London*, London, 1960. More recent publications include Edward Pilkington, *Beyond the Mother Couuntry: West Indians and the Notting Hill White Riots*, London, 1988, which, despite its title, looks at the whole experience of African Caribbeans during the 1950s, and Mike Phillips and Trevor Phillips, *Windrush: The Irresistible Rise of Multi-racial Britain*, London, 1998.

Of Asian immigrants, one of the most important general studies is Vaughan Robinson, *Transients, Settlers and Refugees: Asians in Britain*, Oxford, 1986. Studies on Sikhs include Arthur Wesley Helweg, *Sikhs in England: The Development of a Migrant Community*, Calcutta, 1979. For Pakistanis readers should consult Kathleen Hunter, *History of Pakistanis in Britain*, Norwich, 1962, and Muhammad Anwar, *The Myth of Return: Pakistanis in Britain*, London, 1979. One of the best books about Ugandan Asians is Valerie Marrett's *Immigrants Settling in the City*, Leicester, 1989.

European immigrants have not received the same amount of attention as newcomers from the Commonwealth, but studies have appeared of most of the major groupings. The Irish remain the most understudied group, considering their numbers. Readers can consult J. A. Jackson, *The Irish in Britain*, London, 1963, and Kevin O'Connor, *The Irish in Britain*, Dublin, 1974, which, however, do not concentrate just on the post-war period, and David Owen, *Irish-born People in Great Britain: Settlement Patterns and Socio-economic Circumstances*, Coventry, 1995. Italians are covered in Terri Colpi, *The Italian Factor: The Italian Community in Great Britain*, Edinburgh, 1991, part two of which deals with the period after 1945. The standard work on Greek Cypriots is Floya Anthias, *Ethnicity, Class, Gender and Migration: Greek Cypriots in Britain*, Aldershot, 1992. The two most importat books on European Volunteer Workers are J. A. Tannahill, *European Volunteer Workers in Britain*, Manchester, 1958, and, more recently, Diana Kay and Robert Miles, *Refugees or Migrant Workers? European Volunteer Workers in Britain, 1946–1951*, London, 1992. Studies of Poles include J. Zubrzycki, *Polish Immigrants in Britain: A Study of Adjustment*, The Hague, 1956, and Keith

Sword, Norman Davies and Jan Ciechanowski, *The Formation of the Polish Community in Great Britain*, London, 1989. There is also Geoff Dench, *The Maltese in London: A Case Study of the Erosion of Ethnic Consciousness*, London, 1975. One of the largest of contemporary groups consists of the Germans, for whom see Lothar Kettenacker 'The Germans after 1945', in Panikos Panayi (ed.), *Germans in Britain since 1500*, London, 1996, pp. 187–208.

Studies of smaller minorities from beyond Europe include David Killingray (ed.), *Africans in Britain*, London, 1993, most of which, however, is concerend with the period before 1945, David Parker, 'Chinese People in Britain', in Gregor Benton and Frank N Pieke (eds), *The Chinese in Europe*, London, 1988, and Carol Dalglish, *Refugees from Vietnam*, London, 1989.

Immigration

The best publications on the evolution of immigration policy are Zig Layton-Henry, *The Politics of Immigration: Immigration, 'Race' and 'Race Relations' in Post-war Britain*, 1992, Kathleen Paul, *Whitwashing Britain: Race and Citizenship in the Postwar Era*, London, 1997, and Ian Spencer, *British Immigration Policy since 1939: The Making of Multi-racial Britain*, London, 1997. Paul Foot, *Immigration and Race in British Politics*, Harmondsworth, 1965, Vaughan Bevan, *The Development of British Immigration Law*, London, 1986, and Panikos Panayi, 'The Evolution of British Immigration Policy', in Albrecht Weber (ed.), *Einwanderungsland Bundesrepublik in der Europäischen Union: Gestaltungsauftrag und Regelungsmöglichkeiten*, Osnabrück, 1997, pp. 123–39, all cover more than just the period after 1945.

Publications on the migration process include Margaret Byron, *Post-war Migration to Britain: The Unfinished Cycle*, Aldershot, 1994, R. King, 'Italian Migration to Great Britain', *Geography*, vol. 62, 1977, Robin Oakley, 'Family, Kinship and Patronage: The Cyrpiot Migration to Britain', in Verity Saifullah Khan (ed.), *Minority Families in Britain: Support and Stress*, London, 1979, pp. 13–34, and Pnina Werbner, *The Migration Process: Capital, Gifts and Offerings among British Pakistanis*, Oxford, 1990. Two oustanding oral histories are Mary Chamberlain, *Narratives of Exile and Return*, London, 1997, and Caroline Adams (ed.), *Across*

Seven Seas and Thirteen Rivers: Life Stories of Pioneer Sylhetti Settlers in Britain, London, 1987.

Geography, demography and economics

The geographical patterns of individual immigrant groups have received much attention. For West Indians see, for instance, Sheila Patterson, *Dark Strangers: A Sociological Study of the Absorption of a Recent West Indian Migrant Group in Brixton*, London, 1963, and Ceri Peach, *West Indian Migration to Britain: A Social Geography*, London, 1968. A good essay on the Irish is Judy Chance, 'The Irish in London: An Exploration of Ethnic Boundary Maintenance', in Peter Jackson (ed.), *Race and Racism: Essays in Social Geography*, London, 1987, pp. 142–60. A seminal study of an area which witnessed the influx of several groups is John Rex and Robert Moore, *Race, Community and Conflict: A Study of Sparkbrook*, London, 1967.

The best books on demography include D. A. Coleman (ed.) *Demography of Immigrants and Minority Groups in the United Kingdom*, London, 1982, and Muhammad Anwar, *British Pakistanis: Demographic, Social and Economic Position*, Coventry, 1996.

Much has been written on the economic position of immigrants in post-war Britain. Publications on the unemployed and the underclass include John Rex, *The Ghetto and the Underclass: Essays on Race and Social Policy*, Aldershot, 1988, and Malcolm Cross, 'Ethnic Minority Youth in a Collapsing Labour Market: The UK Experience', in C. Wilpert (ed.), *Entering the Working World: Following the Descendants of Europe's Immigrant Labour Force*, Aldershot, 1988, pp. 56–88. The best studies of working-class immigrants include Sheila Patterson, *Immigrants in Industry*, London, 1968, and Ron Ramdin, *The Making of the Black Working Class in Britain*, Aldershot, 1987, which is mainly concerned with the period since 1945 and also covers Asians. Successful Asians receive attention in N. K. Basi and M. R. D. Johnson, *Asian and White Businessmen in the Retail Sector: A Comparative Analysis of Development Patterns*, Coventry, 1996, while anyone interested in succesful African Caribbeans should read Ernest Cashmore, *Black Sportsmen*, London, 1982, as well as biographies and autobiographies of individual sporstmen.

Ethnicity

One of the most important and thorough books on post-war immigrant ethnicity is James L. Watson (ed.), *Between Two Cultures:
Migrants and Minorities in Britain*, Oxford, 1977. Other gerneral
books include David Mason, *Race and Ethnicity in Modern Britain*,
Oxford, 1991.

The best books for religion include Philip Lewis, *Islamic Britain:
Religion, Politics and Identity among British Muslims*, London,
1994, Danièle Joly, *Britannia's Crescent: Making a Place for
Muslims in British Society*, Aldershot, 1995, and Clifford S. Hill,
*Black and White in Harmony: The Drama of West Indians in the
Big City, from a London Minister's Notebook*, London, 1958.

For political and trade union activity see John DeWitt, *Indian
Workers' Associations in Britain*, London, 1969, and Shamit
Saggar, *Race and Politics in Britain*, London, 1992. The most
important books on the inner-city riots of the early 1980s include
John Benyon (ed.), *Scarman and After*, Oxford, 1984, and John
Benyon and John Solomos (eds), *The Roots of Urban Unrest*,
Oxford, 1987. Students should also consult Lord Scarman, *The
Brixton Disorders, 10–12 April 1981: Report of an Inquiry headed
by the Rt Hon. Lord Scarman, OBE*, London, 1981.

Important publications which focus upon 'cultural' aspects of
ethnicity include Parminder Bhachu, 'Culture, Ethnicity and Class
among Punjabi Sikh Women in 1990s Britain', *New Community*,
vol. 17, 1991, pp. 401–12, and Sasha Josephides, 'Associations
amongst the Greek Cypriot Population in Britain', in John Rex,
Daniele Joly and Czarina Wilpert (eds), *Immigrant Associations in
Europe*, Aldershot, 1987, pp. 42–61.

Racism

Hostility towards immigrants has received an enormous amount of
attention. The best general books include Robin Cohen, *Frontiers
of Identity: The British and the Others*, London, 1994, Paul Gilroy,
'*There ain't no Black in the Union Jack*': *The Cultural Politics of
Race and Nation*, London: Routledge, 1987, Clifford S. Hill, *How
Colour Prejudiced is Britain?*, London, 1967, Charles Husband
(ed.), '*Race' in Britain: Continuity and Change*, second edition,

London, 1987, and Robert Miles and Annie Phizacklea, *White Man's Country: Racism in British Politics*, London, 1984.

Individual aspects of hostility towards immigrants have also received attention. The atttitudes of the police and judiciary are dealth with by Paul Gordon, *White Law: Racism in the Police, Courts and Prisons*, London, 1983. Books which have focused upon the media include T. van Dijk, *Racism and the Press*, London, 1991 and Barry Troyna, *Public Awareness and the Media: A Study of Reporting on Race*, London, 1981. The best surveys of the extreme right in post-war Britain include the relevant sections of Richard Thrulow's *Fascism in Britain: A History, 1918–1985*, Oxford, 1987, as well as Tony Kushner, 'The Fascist as Other? Racism and neo-Nazism in Contemporary Britain', *Patterns of Prejudice*, vol. 28, 1994, pp. 27–45. The most important studies of physical attacks include the relevant essays in Panikos Panayi (ed.), *Racial Violence in Britain in the Nineteenth and Twentieth Centuries*, London, 1996, together with Paul Gordon, *Racial Violence and Harassment*, London, 1986, Keith Tompson, *Under Siege: Racial Violence in Britain Today*, Harmondsworth, 1988, and Bethnal Green and Stepney Trades Council, *Blood on the Streets*, London, 1978.

Multiracialism

Some aspects of multiracialism have received little attention. This particularly applies to the influence of immigrants upon British eating habits. One of the few serious publications in this area is Vina Narayan, 'Eating Cultures: Incorporation, Identity and Indian Food', *Social Identities*, vol. 1, 1995, pp. 63–86. Dress has also received little attention, but see, for instance, the relevant essays in Juliet Ash and Elizabeth Wilson (eds), *Chic Thrills: A Fashion Reader*, Berkeley and Los Angeles, 1992, and Ann Bridgwood, 'Dancing the Jar: Girls' Dress at Turkish Cypriot Weddings', in Joanne B. Eicher (ed.), *Dress and Ethnicity: Change across Space and Time*, Oxford, 1995, pp. 29–51.

The best study of an anti-racist organisation is Benjamin W. Heineman, *The Politics of the Powerless: A Study of the Campaign Against Racial Discrimination*, London, 1972.

For the activities of central government see, for instance, S. Abbot, *The Prevention of Racial Discrimination in England*,

London, 1971, and, more recently, Richard Jenkins and John Solomos (eds), *Racism and Equal Opportunity Policies in the 1980s*, second edition, Cambridge, 1989. Local government is dealt with by Wendy Ball and John Solomos (eds), *Race and Local Politics*, London, 1900. For an introduction to the problems of multiracial education and racism in schools generally see Barry Troyna, *Racism in Education: Research Perspectives*, Buckingham, 1993.

Index

Index